Advance Praise for *When Half Is Whole*

"Murphy-Shigematsu explores our exponentially growing Hapa demographic with personal insight and fearless self-examination. Both rigorous and graceful, this book is smart, readable, and very needed."

—Kip Fulbeck, author of *Part Asian, 100% Hapa*

"What a moving and thought-provoking book! Brilliantly nuanced, searingly honest, and beautifully written, *When Half Is Whole* raises profound, often uncomfortable questions about race, identity, and the search for human connection. I couldn't put it down."

—Amy Chua, Yale Law School Professor
and author of *Battle Hymn of the Tiger Mother and Day of Empire: How Hyperpowers Rise to Global Dominance—and Why They Fall*

"*When Half Is Whole* is a beautiful book, a near-perfect bridge of genres, scholarly in its insights and the knowledge base from which it proceeds, but rich in stories and the voices of mixed-race, complicatedly Asian individuals. Stephen Murphy-Shigematsu tells their stories in prose that is like cool water running down hill. I read the book in one sitting. I will surely read it again when I need its wisdom, or when I just want to enjoy the company of Stephen Murphy-Shigematsu's unique voice."

—Paul Spickard, University of California, Santa Barbara

"Part memoir, part oral history, and part ethnography, this volume transcends distinctions among literary and social science genres much as its subjects' lives transcend racial, sexual, and national boundaries. This is a deeply moving and groundbreaking work."

—Evelyn Nakano Glenn, Professor of Gender and Women's Studies and Director, Center for Race and Gender, University of California, Berkeley

"*When Half Is Whole* is a fascinating, constantly-surprising guided journey through the varied, complex worlds of multiethnic Asian Americans. Murphy-Shigematsu writes with a subtle, engaging style that sometimes verges on poetry."

—Carlos E. Cortés, author of *Rose Hill: An Intermarriage before Its Time*

"In this engaging and powerful book, Stephen Murphy-Shigematsu skillfully uses his own experience as a biracial individual as a springboard to construct incisive and penetrating narratives that describe how biracial Asian Americans compose their lives and deal creatively with the pains and promises of living within and across borders and boundaries. This is a significant, timely, and needed book that will become an essential reference in the field of race and ethnic studies."

—James A. Banks, Kerry and Linda Killinger Endowed Chair in Diversity Studies and Founding Director, Center for Multicultural Education, University of Washington, Seattle

"A fascinating and moving portrait of how individuals reflect upon, navigate, and reconcile multiple, and at times contradictory, social identities based on notions of race, ethnicity, and nationality. The individuals profiled here resist existing categories and boundaries by fashioning their own unique hybrid identities—ones that give meaning and purpose to their lives."

—Michael Omi, University of California, Berkeley

When Half Is Whole

ASIAN AMERICA
A series edited by Gordon H. Chang

The increasing size and diversity of the Asian American population, its growing significance in American society and culture, and the expanded appreciation, both popular and scholarly, of the importance of Asian Americans in the country's present and past—all these developments have converged to stimulate wide interest in scholarly work on topics related to the Asian American experience. The general recognition of the pivotal role that race and ethnicity have played in American life, and in relations between the United States and other countries, has also fostered the heightened attention.

Although Asian Americans were a subject of serious inquiry in the late nineteenth and early twentieth centuries, they were subsequently ignored by the mainstream scholarly community for several decades. In recent years, however, this neglect has ended, with an increasing number of writers examining a good many aspects of Asian American life and culture. Moreover, many students of American society are recognizing that the study of issues related to Asian America speak to, and may be essential for, many current discussions on the part of the informed public and various scholarly communities.

The Stanford series on Asian America seeks to address these interests. The series will include works from the humanities and social sciences, including history, anthropology, political science, American studies, law, literary criticism, sociology, and interdisciplinary and policy studies.

A full list of titles in the Asian America series can be found online at www.sup.org/asianamerica.

When Half Is Whole

MULTIETHNIC
ASIAN AMERICAN IDENTITIES

Stephen Murphy-Shigematsu

STANFORD UNIVERSITY PRESS
STANFORD, CALIFORNIA

Stanford University Press
Stanford, California

Printed in the United States of America on acid-free, archival-
quality paper

Library of Congress Cataloging-in-Publication Data

Murphy-Shigematsu, Stephen, author.
  When half is whole : multiethnic Asian American identities /
Stephen Murphy-Shigematsu.
      pages cm. — (Asian America)
  Includes bibliographical references and index.
  ISBN 978-0-8047-7517-5 (cloth : alk. paper) —
  ISBN 978-0-8047-7518-2 (pbk. : alk. paper)
    1. Asian Americans—Ethnic identity. 2. Racially mixed
people—United States—Ethnic identity. 3. Transnationalism.
I. Title. II. Series: Asian America.
  E184.A75M87 2013
  305.895'073—dc23
                              2012015160

Typeset by Bruce Lundquist in 11/14 Adobe Garamond

Contents

Prologue

My sixteen-year-old son observed me daily for months as I sat in my office writing this book. One day I could feel his presence behind me, watching me intently, but I kept on writing. Finally, he broke the silence: "So, like, what's so great about writing books, anyway?"

I realize that he is trying to understand why his father spends so much time on something as seemingly unexciting as writing and I need to explain to him why I do this. I know that a glib answer is insufficient; they never are with him. So I paused for a moment to ponder the question. What was he asking me? Why bother writing? Why is it so important to me? Who cares? Who will read it? What difference will it make in their lives? Why was I writing this book, anyway?

I turned to face him and said, "Well, I feel it's important for me to pass on what I've experienced, what I've learned in my life, and to use my gifts, my talents. I can write, so I think it's something I should do. I don't know who will read it, but for those who do, I hope it helps them in some way in their lives. It's my way of contributing something to the world. I listen and gather people's stories. Then I write them down in a way that I hope will communicate something to others, so that seeing these stories will give readers something of value. I tell myself that this isn't going to be done unless I do it, just because of who I am. It's a way of making my mark, leaving something behind . . . not that I'm planning on going anywhere right now."

My son seemed to ponder my answer, shrugged his shoulders, and walked away without a word. I went back to writing, with a clearer purpose to my endeavor. My son had forced me to reflect on what I was doing and I had a better understanding of why I was writing this book. Did he understand what I was trying to say? Perhaps not, but maybe someday he will understand why his father spent so much of his precious time writing this book. Given my life circumstances and experiences this was a way to find meaning.

Writing the stories in this book has been a labor of love: leaving my wife in a warm bed in the early morning darkness and chill, petting the dogs, checking the kids, making chai, and sitting down to write, then writing until the rest of the family started to stir and I needed to attend to the daily mundane realities as mindfully as I could. I often questioned what I was doing and when I didn't, people in my life like my son challenged me to be clear about my purpose. I know that good writing connects people to one another and to other living creatures. It enables readers to see the world from a different perspective. My writing is simple—I ask questions, listen, observe, and share what I have learned with others.

As the child of a native Japanese woman and an Irish American father, a salient feature of my life has been this ethnic heritage and the circumstances into which I was born in post–World War II Tokyo. My life, between Japan and the United States, has been marked heavily by my connections to these diverse roots. I have found meaning in my life through learning to accept and appreciate these roots, to balance their influences and blend them into a synergistic whole. While others may see me as "half," I know that I am whole. This whole me is greater than the sum of its parts and connects me to something beyond my self, to communities of others and to a collective self.

I have lived an idealistic life in which making meaning of these life circumstances has been a central focus of my existence. I have been fortunate that my career has included extensive opportunities to do research, reading the work of scholars who have studied about people of mixed heritage in the United States, and to meet and interview mixed ancestry individuals myself. I received institutional support to study in Asia, and subsequent jobs allowed me to pursue these studies as part of my work—to research, counsel, and write. I feel it is my responsibility to give back what I have learned, and here is what I have produced from my study and exploration.

When Half Is Whole tells of my encounters with some amazing people. Over the past thirty years I have sought contact with persons of mixed ancestry in Asia and America, listened to their stories, and read their poems and prose, receiving them as gifts to share. These encounters with others have stimulated encounters with my self, and their stories and my stories have become interwoven. I offer them to you.

I tell stories because I have found that there is nothing more important in life than connecting with others. And one way that we connect with others is through sharing our narratives. We each have stories that are universally human, similar to those of other people, and yet also unique, individual. All stories are capable of touching other human beings, helping them to remember and to tell their own stories in their own way.

These stories have been gathered from individuals whose lives blend Asian and American in their families of origin. Among the people they identify as parents, biological or adoptive, are people with roots in Asia and people with roots in some other part of the world. The themes of the storytellers' lives involve balancing, connecting, and finding meaning in these roots. The stories here show how these individuals have engaged in the process of becoming not "half" this or "half" that but whole.

The stories are ordinary in some ways, extraordinary in others. The people in them have all dedicated their lives to making meaning of their mixed roots. In searching for their roots, they discover connections that bring them into contact with communities. Their journeys have engaged them in healing themselves and healing others, a process of transition toward meaning, balance, wholeness, and connectedness, within individuals and between individuals and their environments. Their personal healing releases healing energy to entire communities. They recover surrendered identities and become spokespersons for identities as found in multiple, flexible, and diverse ways.

The stories begin where I began my life, in Occupied Japan, and end where I now live, between California and Tokyo. They explore the topic of the increasingly transnational and multiethnic nature of identities in a globalized world through the lives of mixed ancestry Asian Americans. The narratives take place on both sides of the Pacific, showing how lives are influenced by legal, political, and social forces and how people assert themselves in ways that overcome victimization, claim agency, and bring cultural change. The stories reveal how identities are constructed beyond existing categories and boundaries of nation, race, and ethnicity.

I present these narratives as a way of combating a pervasive feature of life for many people —being "Othered," seen as different, marginalized, and isolated. I believe that this dehumanizing "us versus them" consciousness can be overcome through the telling and receiving of stories that reveal the fullness and richness of individual lives. Narratives humanize by showing commonalities in universal struggles and uniqueness in particular struggles.

Each chapter is framed around an individual's story, my account of their lives as written from interviews and autobiographical writing. The writing is reflexive, integrating self-reflections; the search is both personal and professional, forcing me to delve into the past, confront harsh realities, and imagine ideal developments. Those whom I encounter come from vastly different backgrounds, with contrasting perspectives on what it means to be Asian and American, but also shared understandings. The lens is focused on a diverse group of individuals in a variety of places where we met, from Tokyo to Boston, San Francisco to Okinawa, Korea to Massachusetts.

The individuals chosen are activists, advocates, scholars, and teachers who challenge boundaries and borders. They are artists, performers, filmmakers, and writers whose lives are an expression of their identities. These are people whose stories express the wide range of diverse experiences of lives in which cultural, national, and racial worlds come together, sometimes colliding violently and sometimes blending smoothly and synergistically.

All the stories have an Asian connection, including Japanese, Okinawan, Korean, Chinese, and Filipino. They explore various borderlands, such as Chinese/Jewish, Japanese/black, Korean/Iranian, and Filipino/Mexican. They illuminate the liminal spaces where sexuality and gender meet race and culture. The stories have common threads yet are highly diverse. Mixing of people from different shores is often violent; the stories begin by highlighting the circumstances in postwar Japan. Many stories are of migration and tell of the individuals and families who came to America from the 1950s on. Transnational stories are also about returns and roots journeys to the United States or to Asia and back again. Finding community is a common struggle, and these narratives tell us of these challenges in being out of place and finding home. Complications of international and interracial families are clearly revealed through the stories of marriage, adoption, and nationality. The stories tell how identities are formed amidst the volatile environment of military bases, adding complexity to the concept of multiple identities. They tell of personal identity struggles as mixed heritage persons challenge the borders of existing ethnic communities and group identities and consciousness.

When Half Is Whole goes beyond the borders of traditional academic fields by examining the intersection of the United States and Asia through the stories of transnational and multiethnic Asian Americans. The many persons of mixed American and Asian ancestry who are now part of the U.S. landscape make up part of this account, while others have never left Asia; some have gone from here to there and back and forth between America and Asia. These stories examine how identities are formed within a context of politics and economies that transcend domestic systems and become transnational issues between states.

When Half Is Whole is based in research done over the past thirty years in Asia and the United States, examining historical material and highlighting emerging trends and movements. The stories reveal how identities develop amidst major evolutions in Asian countries and Asian American communities due to intermarriage between Asians or Asian Americans and others. The stories address the growing concerns of a population of mixed Asian American families and individuals, as interracially married couples abound and mixed Asians now constitute nearly 20 percent of the Asian American population. *When Half Is Whole* looks at how younger mixed Asians construct new identities in increasingly multicultural Asian social contexts and transform older stereotyped images of mixed race. The stories show the emergence of multiethnic organizations and the burgeoning of online communities that have transformed this issue, connecting previously isolated people in cyberspace and sometimes in person.

The subject of this book is timely in the sense that we are caught more deeply than ever in global cultural transitions and transformations. *When Half Is Whole* is grounded in an understanding that a transnational approach is required for comprehending the complexity of historical and contemporary issues. The stories that I present bring greater understanding to how identities today are flexible, inclusive, and multiple, and challenge the meaning of national and racial categories and boundaries. These lives demonstrate how the tensions in the borderlands and margins contain powerful currents that can illuminate and alter the mainstreams.

There was a time I realized that I could write this book for the rest of my life, or I could finish it. I decided on the latter, and here it is. I give it up to the world, no longer holding on to it with love and fear. Love, for it represents our lives and gifts I have received from others and now return. Fear, because I am afraid that it is incomplete. But it is my offering, my way of connecting to others and to life itself. These are just a few of the many stories that need to be told. Please read them and tell your own stories in your own way.

ONE

Flowers Amidst the Ashes

The end of the war liberated my mother. Like many other Japanese, for the first time she was able to imagine how she might make a life free from the oppression of the military state. It was a time when everything was in flux, presenting the opportunity to do things that had never been possible. Claiming she knew some English, my mother boldly sought a job at the U.S. General Headquarters, and when an American she met there asked her to date, she took a chance and went out with him. When he later asked her to marry, she decided that she was willing to take on that challenge too and accepted his proposal. My grandparents must have been moved too by the new space that existed in society, because they allowed the American to move into their Tokyo home. The American, who became my father, was also crossing boundaries and stepping into the unknown when he decided to marry a Japanese, have children with her, and live with her family in Japan. We, the children of postwar unions, were simply the products of our parents' revolutionary actions. Some of us were born unwelcomed into the world, while others were seen as flowers amidst the ashes—new life springing forth with hope and promise from the devastated land.

Parents like ours came together in a natural way as man and woman in an unnatural environment created by the forces of war and military occupation. Authorities on both sides tried to keep them apart, or at least keep them from marrying, but they came together anyway and offered each other what they could. For some the encounters were brief and utilitarian, but others endured and forged relationships that pressured the authorities to enable them to marry and travel freely to the United States as husband and wife and as families.

Norma Field's mother became one of these "war brides," marrying a man from Los Angeles in 1946 at the American consulate in Yokohama when such marriages were rare. A woman I met in San Francisco, Kazue Katz, told me that she was the first of these war brides in Occupied Japan. Her marriage would not have been allowed in California, one of many states that prohibited marriages between whites and "Mongolians" at that time. Kazue described her husband, Frederick H. Katz, as a persistent man who gathered twenty-nine supporting letters, including one from General MacArthur, to persuade the authorities to permit him to marry her. They had to overcome not only family opposition but also social disapproval and a legal system designed to prevent such marriages.

Recognizing that American men wanted to marry women they met during the war, the U.S. Congress passed the War Brides Act in 1945 to enable them to bring their brides home. But this applied only to European brides, not to Asians. Not until 1952 did it became legal for most Americans to marry and take Japanese brides to America. By then, the opposition had forced many couples apart and contributed to thousands of children being abandoned by their fathers, some also by their mothers. Exactly how many is unknown. Japanese officials wanted to publicize the children as a social problem created by the Occupation, but U.S. officials succeeded in crushing such unwanted publicity that would negate the image of a kind and gentle Occupation.

Unlike Kazue's and Norma's parents, my mother and civilian father were more like many others who tried to marry, encountering numerous legal hurdles and hassles and failed attempts at both the ward office in Tokyo and at the U.S. embassy. My parents' experiences were like those of the couple in the *Sayonara* story of the Michener novel and Brando film, in which the Japanese and American lovers have to run the gauntlet to get married. One couple decides a love suicide is better than the forced separation they are faced with, and in the book the Brando character, deciding that maybe the general was right in opposing his marriage, abandons his Japanese sweetheart to find an

American girl back home. But by the time the movie was made in 1957, three years after the book was published, Hollywood, like much of the U.S. government and some of the American public, had decided it was all right for an American like Brando to marry a Japanese woman, though we don't know whether they live happily ever after.

My parents stayed together, though it took until 1951 for their marriage to be legalized. By that time my father had been living in my mother's family home in Tokyo for three years and two children had been born. Nationality laws that made Norma an American because her parents were married made my two older sisters Japanese because my parents were not married. My sisters were registered in my mother's family register as Shigematsus. Since my parents were married at the time of my birth I received an American birth certificate with the name Murphy.

Marriage with an American meant new privileges, such as the use of St. Luke's Hospital in Tsukiji where I was born. I was the third child, and the extra mouth to feed increased my mother's secret journeys across Tokyo. My dad had military purchasing power as a civilian employee of the U.S. Armed Forces. Mom would buy goods at the PX and sell them at Ueno on the black market. She had to do this because food and supplies were scarce and because my father had trouble arriving home on Friday evening with his week's wages. On the way home he encountered not only bars but also people he thought were deserving souls with greater need. My *obaachan* (grandmother) called him *obakasan*, a "wonderful fool." He did manage to arrive home with some of his pay, some of the time, and with my grandfather's income as a Tokyo policeman we were a lot better off than the kids whose fathers abandoned them. Such children were scattered throughout Japan wherever there were Americans, and little is known of their lives except for the few who became famous athletes, musicians, and entertainers.

Tomoko, a girl born the same year as me, had been a baby bearing the looks of the father, whom the child was never to meet. He left before she was born and from her earliest memories the father she knew was a Japanese man her mother had married. She lived a quiet life in her mother's hometown north of Tokyo, growing up in a family surrounded by loving relatives, in an ordinary neighborhood, attending the local schools, speaking Japanese, and doing just what the other kids did. Rough boys bullied her sometimes, but friends would come to her rescue and protect her from their name-calling and insults. When people would rudely ask her whether she was American she would evade their question, pretending not to hear or making a joke.

Tomoko was adored in her large extended family and surrounded by love. Only occasionally was she torn from her warm feelings of oneness when she would be shocked to realize that she was different—she was the "American" in the family. Her favorite niece once stunned her by announcing to everyone in an innocent childlike manner, "I am Japanese and Tomoko is American." She never looked at her niece again without a twinge of hurt. When she stared at her own reflection in the mirror she was surprised to see that she did look different from others, as if she had never noticed before. But Tomoko wondered why she would always be the "American," when it was only her face and nothing else that made her American. Even when I met her as an adult, she was consumed with dreams in which only her face would appear.

Most of the mixed ancestry kids grew up in obscurity like Tomoko, encountering other problems later in life in marriage and employment discrimination. While some became celebrities, a few became nationally known for their deviance. One was a teenager convicted of several murders who professed hatred not only of women but of his own dark skin. His shocking story of abandonment by both parents and his life of fighting the prejudice and discrimination directed at him exposed the public to the reality of the tragic dimensions of such lives. While his case provoked reflection and perhaps sympathy in some, it also no doubt reinforced fears of the mixed blood kids as illegitimate and mentally disturbed children of prostitutes, further stigmatizing them.

Fortunately, these extreme cases were rare. The postwar era is characterized not only by tragedy but also by the inspiring story of Sawada Miki, the daughter of a noble family married to a man who was once ambassador to the United Nations. Sawada claims that her life changed dramatically one day when an apparently mixed race baby fell into her lap from the overhead luggage compartment when she was traveling on a train. The incident shocked her into action and she dedicated her property and life to establishing and running an orphanage, the Elizabeth Saunders Home, where more than a thousand mixed blood children were raised.

Sawada believed that the children needed to be separated from an unforgiving Japanese society and sheltered in her institution. She drew attention to the plight of these children, leading novelist Pearl Buck to establish a foundation in 1964 to help what she called "Amerasians," kids who were born all over Asia, wherever the U.S. military went. Her foundation helped Sawada to buy land in the Amazon area of Brazil and establish the St. Stephen Farm as a utopian place for the Saunders kids to emigrate and settle. Sawada's policy was to seek their futures outside of Japan either in Brazil or through adoption into American families. Although she was able to arrange hundreds of adoptions, only a few children ever made it to Brazil and most mixed blood kids were left to fend for themselves in Japanese society.

Hirano Imao, himself of mixed American and Japanese ancestry, was another advocate in the postwar period. Hirano's philosophy was different from Sawada's, and he focused his energy on integrating the children into Japanese society. Perhaps because he himself had to do so, he believed that they should and could live in Japan rather than seek another place in the world. Hirano helped by legally adopting many kids and offering individual and group support and guidance for them.

Sawada segregated her children because postwar Japan was not a welcoming place for the children who bore the stigma of being fathered by the American conquerors and occupiers. Some claim that the children were a painful reminder of American dominance and Japanese subjugation. Those without the protection of a father or mother's family were especially stigmatized and scapegoated. The Saunders Home children included commuters like those in the family of Suzuki Masako. She would escort cousins to the home for school and then pick them up and return them to their families in Yokohama. These kids lived in two worlds—the home in which they were surrounded by others whose faces were marked by the signs of mixed race and the neighborhood in which they were singled out as different.

While the story of Sawada's children has been told often, stories of those raised out in Japanese society are mostly tales of victimization. Norma's writing gives us a rare look into the world of a girl of the postwar era living in a Japanese neighborhood while attending school on a U.S. military base. I first encountered Norma in her classic *In the Realm of a Dying Emperor: A Portrait of Japan at Century's End*. In this book, and even more so in her subsequent family story, *From My Grandmother's Bedside: Sketches of Postwar Tokyo*, Norma paints a picture of a life I both knew and never knew. Her portraits of postwar, Occupation Japan and the life of a typical and atypical family living in Tokyo resonated with me so deeply that I began a correspondence with Norma as if I already knew her and she would know me. I have never felt more clearly the power of narrative, in which one person's story can touch others and enable them to bring forth their own story.

In Norma's house and in mine in Suginami-ku, our mothers' American husbands "squeezed into" our family homes. Norma's father stayed until she was in second grade and then "abandoned, or was expelled from, the family," ending an eight-year marriage. Her mother kept herself separated from the rest of the neighborhood after a bout with tuberculosis and the end of her marriage with the American. Norma's world was a mixture of Japanese and American, with sharp dividing lines. She felt that the bus that shuttled her back and forth between her Tokyo neighborhood and her American school was like a "space machine" that she would ride with a sense of wonder. The "chocolate-colored bus" carried her each weekday morning through the streets of Tokyo from her home to the military base and then at three o'clock in the afternoon went back through the gates, retracing the route to drop her off near her "unmistakably native house" where an "unmistakably native woman" would be waiting for her.[1]

Norma reflects on how she explained the native woman to her bus-mates. "Did I tell them she was the—my—maid? Did I wait until the bus turned in the dust before I crossed the street and passed through the gate?"[2] I too was a child wondering how to deal with such incongruities in the worlds of my home and school. And I wonder how the adults in my life dealt with these obvious differences that others, especially children, noticed all too clearly.

After we moved from Tokyo to Pittsfield, Massachusetts, my Japanese mother stood out wherever we went. Even her name was different, something no one had ever heard and no one could pronounce. The

Christian missionaries tried to call her "Theresa" but my dad got mad and told them they should call her by her name, Toshiko. I was not as bold, and when my classmate's mother asked me what my mother's name was, I told her I didn't know. When she persisted that surely I knew my own mother's name, I insisted that I did not. And when she asked, "Well then what does your dad call her?" I made her laugh and give up the inquisition by cleverly evading her—"He just says, 'Hey you.'" In my Catholic school the nuns taught us about Peter denying Jesus three times, and I wondered if I was just as bad. But how could I explain my mother to my classmates and their mothers? I wanted to be seen as American, but my face was a constant reminder to others that I was something else. My mother was an even stronger sign that we were foreign. How could I explain who she was to people who could not even pronounce her name—who didn't even seem to try?

Just as I knew I was not "a real American," Norma knew that she was not "a real Japanese" from a normal home and so shouldn't ask to play with the neighborhood children. She was stigmatized for having an American father, as was her mother for the relationship with the father and its demise. Norma bore the markers of his genes in her face. She reflected on what children like us may signify to others:

> Many years into my growing up, I thought I had understood the awkward piquancy of biracial children with the formulation, they are nothing if not the embodiment of sex itself; now I modify it to, the biracial offspring of war even more offensive and intriguing because they bear the imprint of sex as domination.[3]

Reading this passage I am reminded of a confusing incident in childhood. My Irish Aunt Margaret, who like several of my dad's siblings had never married or had children, delighted in dressing me up and taking me downtown to show off. One day we were walking down Main Street and a man stopped her and asked about my dad. She told him he was back from Japan and that I was his son, proudly beaming down at me. The big man looked down too and stared, at first with a quizzical expression and then suddenly breaking into a big smile as if he was recalling some fond memories. "I've got some kids over there myself," he boasted. Margaret's smile vanished and her sweet face became suddenly fierce. She looked him in the eye and said, "Well, my brother's not like that!" She pulled me hard by the hand and we walked away from that man.

My Irish aunts and uncles may not have understood our situation, but they struggled to help overcome the stereotypes and stigmas we faced. They taught us good manners and proper etiquette. They showered the priests and nuns with gifts of stationery from the paper factory where my Aunt Joanna worked, so that we were admitted to the St. Mary's School a year early, receiving a classic Catholic education steeped in tradition and strict discipline. Our aunts bought us only the finest clothes so that on Sunday we would be seen at church looking proper. They took us out to the fanciest restaurants, where we all ordered lobster, the most expensive item on the menu, so that we would not appear or feel small and poor. As we looked at the menu and noticed the prices, they would look at us and say with a smile, "It's okay, you can order the lobster." So even when we didn't want lobster, we ordered lobster.

The racially stigmatized need to work hard to overcome the stigma. By my behavior, I always had to show others how well I was brought up, how even a child like me, so marked by my race, could be a good boy, a smart boy, a credit to his family. I didn't realize at the time that I was also stigmatized by my father's alcoholism. My dad was the only man I knew who didn't drive a car, but I never fathomed what a social misfit he was, though I could sometimes sense it. In many ways, my Japanese mother was seen by society as the more normal one in the marriage, highly respected in the community as a wife for enduring her wayward husband's antics and as a mother for bringing up three respectable "half-breed" kids.

Norma's favorite aunt made sure that she was well brought up, and taught her some English so she could adjust to the American school. While she may have impressed with her manners, Norma's physical appearance would immediately overwhelm all other information received by the senses, rendering her a half-breed child more than anything else. Like my aunt, Norma's hoped that good manners and good grades would compensate for the disadvantages she was given.

Her aunt succeeded to the extent that Norma believed the neighborhood children avoided her because she was superior to them and not because she was a half-breed. Unlike some others from single mother homes, she still bore the signs of her parents' marriage, in her name and in her privilege of attending the American school. She could speak English, if anyone cared to know. And as if to prove that she really was Japanese she could show off her knowledge of strange kanji characters.

My father tried to convince me that kids disparaged me because they were ignorant. I came from a samurai family, he would tell me over and over, and how many of the snotty-nosed American kids could say that? I suppose his message got through, because I was always secretly proud of being Japanese, somehow balancing the pervasive influences in American society that also made me wish I was as white as my Irish dad.

In her Tokyo neighborhood, Norma stuck out as I did in my Massachusetts town. Many years later, she would marvel at how her grandmother could accompany her to the doctor and sit calmly in the waiting room as if Norma's curly brown hair was invisible, as if she was sitting next to a perfectly ordinary child. Near the end of her grandmother's life, Norma suddenly asked her, "You didn't mind taking a funny-looking kid to the doctor's?" After a long pause, without turning or opening her eyes, she spoke: "You weren't a funny-looking kid. You were a prize kid."[4]

My obaachan prized us too. Perhaps it was because we were her first babies. Unknowingly, she had married a man biologically incapable of fathering children. She had adopted my mother, her younger sister by twenty years, when my mom was five. My mother says that when we were born, Obaachan took control of us, telling my mother that she did not know how to raise children. Unfortunately, this period of mothering lasted only five years before we were all taken from her to our new home in America. Obaachan never recovered from the loss. She told me she cried every day for two years, and all the relatives say that she somehow remained psychologically frozen in time, continuing to live in that golden era when she was the mother of three babies. I am sure those were the happiest years of Obaachan's life.

We were lucky to be so cherished. We were less lucky in trying to figure out whether we were Japanese or American. How do kids make sense of such seeming dichotomies? We identify ourselves with one side or the other in complex ways. As Norma explains it, "I didn't want to be taken from Japan, but in the public world of school bus and playground, although I identified *with* puny Japanese against gigantic Americans, I didn't want to be identified *as* Japanese. . . . I think I simply and cravenly preferred to be identified with power."[5]

Such conditions breed ambivalence. For some kids like Norma and me there is a natural affiliation with the oppressed, the scorned, the downtrodden. We align ourselves with our weaker selves, loved ones, and minority group against the giants who oppress us. We also wish to escape the scorn and wrath of the oppressors and wish them to see us as one of them, not as one of the enemy.

Norma writes, "As a child, signs of American power and abuse stirred an atavistic anti-Americanism in me, the kind I felt as I rode the bus to the base school and tried madly to eliminate all traces of Japaneseness from my person and my tongue." She desired American things, like "American dresses and bobby socks and fruit cocktail," but her sympathies were with the "downtrodden Japanese."[6]

I am drawn to Norma's story because we have similar origins, yet our lives went in vastly different directions. We were both born in postwar Tokyo but Norma remained there through childhood and adolescence; I was raised in the United States. She came to America to live as an adult, marry an American, have another generation of mixed kids, while I went back to Japan, married a Japanese, and had mixed kids. Though I was raised on the other side of the ocean, I too sympathized with "defeated Japan, little Japan, weak Japan." A Japanese woman I once met who was married to an American asked me why I identified as Japanese. Her children, she told me, identify as American and are not interested in being Asian—worse, they reject it. I think that all children want to be part of the majority, but when they confront a barrier to acceptance, some try to blend in and others identify with the minority. I don't know why I identified with Japan. Perhaps it was loyalty to my mother, who otherwise was all alone. Maybe it was just a way of maintaining dignity by accepting who I was in others' eyes and being proud of it, at least privately in my own world.

Those complex feelings continue in adulthood. Norma writes, "American arrogance stirs up a tenderness for the unluxurious Japanese past that I can't repress, but knowing what it led to strips its innocence and makes nostalgia grotesque."[7] I too move constantly between romantic longings for an ancient Japan and repulsion at the dangerous consequences of nationalism.

For those of us who do not embody the Japanese child or Japanese adult, our views become distorted. We fight against accepting that there is anything uniquely Japanese, because that would exclude us. But we suspect that there is something Japanese, and that ironically we embody it. Norma illuminated this tension, which persists and changes in form over the years:

> The cultivation of essences, the belief that they exist, whether in nature or as artifact or character, is seductive and constraining. Drawn to its deployment in poetry and painting and performance, I long failed to recognize its power to stunt and deceive. Feeling betrayed, I became vigilant, in part out of shame over my blindness, and forbade myself pleasure in things announcing themselves as distinctly Japanese. Now words like "mederu" I find straying into my head. I roll them around on my tongue, still unvoiced.[8]

I too fight this battle. When I wrote "Multiethnic Japan and the Monoethnic Myth,"[9] my first academic paper, a reviewer gave a sharp comment on my first draft, claiming that my essay appeared driven by a personal agenda. I realized with some difficulty and discomfort that the reviewer was right. I was painfully aware that I was often cast outside the realm of "the Japanese" because the narrow conception of "Japanese" excluded people like me. It is not just outsiders who isolate and insulate the Japanese, but the country's own cultural essentialists and neonationalists who make a fetish of the supposed singularity of the national character. I asserted that there is no such thing as essential Japanese qualities. But in reality I am not only excluded, I am also often told by Japanese that they see certain essential Japanese qualities in me. "You are more Japanese than Japanese," these people exclaim. In other words, I have "Japanese essence." Even more confusing, I see these qualities in myself, almost reluctantly, but perhaps joyously? Now I try to capture what is Japanese about us, about me, with words. I permit myself to wear kimono, at least at home, and in public I do a storytelling performance, "The Celtic Samurai." I make miso soup and eat *umeboshi* whenever I feel like it. I think once I almost said "We Japanese."

But should we ever feel too comfortably Japanese we can always rely not only on complete strangers but also on lifelong friends and even on our own family members to remind us that we are something different. Norma's mother boiled her drinking water and dishes until she was ten, as if her father's genes had left her digestive tract different from her own. When Norma struggled with her mother over the use of the air conditioner, her mother told her that "you don't know how humid it gets here," seeming to forget that Norma has spent nearly every summer of her life in Japan.[10] We are aware, sometimes painfully so, that when our family talks about Nihonjin (a Japanese person) they are not including us.

There is something forever American about us, even to our grand-mothers, or to our mothers. I still foolishly struggle with Obaachan, though she is 107 as I write, trying to convince her I am Japanese. I show her my Japanese passport—surely this makes me Japanese! She smiles but is not convinced. I am forever her American grandson. Why do I care? This does not make me any less lovable, it is just the way it is. I am her favorite, she tells me, because I came back to Japan to be with her. I insist that I am American *and* Japanese. I am both. But how can she understand that a person can be both American and Japanese? Wasn't her life radically altered by the sharp dividing lines between two peoples who killed those on the other side of the line? Her daughter brought the two sides together by marrying an Ameri-can, but the children must be either American or Japanese, and to Obaachan we are American.

"Are you Japanese or American?" The question never seems to go away and to me always seems easily answered—"I am Japanese and American." But while we may come to know who we are, this simple and seemingly clear answer does not stop the question from being asked again or being answered for us.

This question acquired a new twist for Norma when she left Japan for college just as the country became caught up in a *konketsuji boomu* of popularity of mixed blood entertainers. Talent scouts descended on schools with large populations of mixed kids to scoop them up for modeling and acting. Norma left too soon to be told she was lucky to be *haafu* (half Japanese, from English *half*), as mixed people were beautiful, had long legs, and could speak English. Norma did not get to see the singing group "The Golden Haafu" on television popularizing the image of the fashionable mixed blood.

Like all the kids at her American high school in Japan, when she graduated Norma headed to the United States for college. She separated from her protective family and moved to the "fatherland" she had never known. She chose a college not far from where her father had been living for some years with his Scottish-immigrant mother in Los Angeles and met her American relatives for the first time. Norma continued to live in the United States but Japan was a place she would come home to every summer. She would remain close to Japan through her studies, her chosen major of Japanese literature sustaining her. Norma married, had children, and settled down to a life in the Midwest.

As Norma came to her father's land, I returned to my mother's land as a young man. Living with my grandparents in the city of Matsuyama on the island of Shikoku, I learned to speak and write Japanese. I met my Japanese family, some for the first time since childhood. Perhaps because I had grown up deeply romanticizing my connections with Japan, my homecoming involved a transformative development that my father referred to poetically as a "metamorphosis." I was empowered by connecting to ancestral roots, moving beyond my solitary self to a community of others. I found new meaning in my existence, eventually going back to the United States to embark on a new career by entering Harvard University, an unimaginable achievement after years of uninspired and unaccomplished living.

I heard stories like this from others who "returned" to Japan, even from people who were born in the United States. They talk of finding a world of new experiences—anticipated, unexpected, surprising, exhilarating, soothing, disappointing, disturbing. For some individuals it was melodramatic, while for others, such as this young woman, it was an unforgettable, transformative experience.

> I went with my mother to Japan. When we landed at Narita, knowing that we were there, together, gave me goose bumps all over. And

on the train from the airport we were sitting there holding hands—
we never held hands since I was little—just holding hands so tightly.
It was one of the most precious moments. That's when I began to
see—I'm Japanese too!¹¹

After the initial exhilaration there is a comforting feeling of familiarity and fitting in. There is also a growing awareness that one is
different, seen as different, and treated differently. Many eventually
go back to the United States, but I stayed, married a Japanese, had
children, and lived and worked completely among Japanese. As truth
is truly stranger than fiction, I became a professor at the University of
Tokyo, the flagship national university. I lived in a large housing complex for government employees and my children attended the local
public schools. I delighted in the dumbfounded looks on people's
faces when they found out that I, a mixed blood or a foreigner in their
eyes, was a professor at their elite university. Inside, I smiled with glee
when in response to their attempted put-down that I surely must be
an English instructor, I stunned them again, saying, "No, I am a professor teaching Japanese culture."

Japan has changed in many ways since Norma and I were born
there as mixed ancestry children during the Occupation. But as I write
now, controversies still rage, such as educators' questions as to whether
it is better to segregate or integrate. While dramatic cases of the need
for separation capture public attention, such as at the AmerAsian
School in Okinawa, the trend is more in the direction of integration.
Parents of children of mixed ancestry once sent their kids to international schools if they could afford it, regarding them as safe havens
from the prejudice and bullying the children would encounter in the
public schools. But now more mixed ancestry kids are getting their
education in public schools, even some who could afford the high
tuition of international schools. Their choice is reinforced by the generally more welcoming and accepting climate of public schools and
Japanese society in general.

The nationality laws that made Norma and me Americans in
Japan, and my sisters Japanese, have been stripped of their sexually
discriminatory feature and children born into the same circumstances

as we were can now become both Japanese and American. Although individuals are supposed to choose one nationality when they become adults, the Japanese government has been indifferent about enforcing the law. I give talks, write books, and appear on the radio in Japan advocating that children like these and adults like me should be treated the same as any Japanese citizen. If parents are unable or choose not to make their children Japanese citizens, I advocate for the protection of their rights to education and health.

Norma is a scholar whose voice is recognized as unique in its intimate understanding of Japanese and American worldviews. *In the Realm of a Dying Emperor* is an eloquent and insightful depiction of the condition of Japanese society at the time that Hirohito lay dying. She tells stories of her encounters with three extraordinary individuals whose fight for social justice against oppressiveness and conformity illuminate the tensions and constraints of ethnicity, gender, and class in turn-of-the-century Japan.

From My Grandmother's Bedside is Norma's tender family portrait, a touching and evocative reflection on postwar and contemporary Japan painted from childhood memories, mundane concerns, and poignant observations of political and social life as she cares for her slowly dying grandmother. For years Norma returned regularly to Japan, writing of the trials of a transnational family, caring for mother and grandmother living in another country. She refers to these journeys as "artificial homecomings" in which she again had to become daughter, granddaughter, niece in a "process akin to regenerating amputated limbs." Her writing captures the delicate subtleties of lives in the spaces where things come together and are torn apart into dichotomies. They are heartwarming and heartbreaking memories of family life, Japanese and American, delicately captured in sounds, smells, tastes, and sights, from an insider-outsider perspective. The book is an intimate series of portraits of a Tokyo family—a normal family just like mine. At least to me my family has always seemed normal, just another family. Like others, our families are concerned about putting out the garbage, relations with the next-door neighbors, and the price of eggs. In the summer we worry about surviving the heat, in the winter about keeping warm. We worry about growing old and the health care system.

Of course, we have other concerns as well. My grandmother is the same age as Norma's. I read Norma's stories with my grandmother always in mind. I identified with Norma as an adult, traveling back and forth across the Pacific to be with her grandmother, to return to her work and family in America, to bring her family in America to Japan to see her family there, to return to her work in Japan, endlessly back and forth.

Following her grandmother's death, Norma's mother came to live with her and spend her last years together, in a country foreign to her in every way, though she was enveloped in the love of her daughter and her grandchildren. Unlike Norma's grandmother who lingered for years in a semi-invalid state, Norma's mother went quickly one day from a healthy body to a spirit in another realm of existence, disappearing suddenly.

We imagined a similar ending for my obaachan and brought her here to the United States for a trial stay at ninety-nine. We envisioned her dying surrounded by her daughter and grandchildren. But after three months she announced she was returning to Japan. My sister, who doesn't speak Japanese, called me in Tokyo and asked me to find out whether that was what Obaachan really wanted to do. So I asked Obaachan in Japanese, *Dou shitain desu ka?* (What do you want to do?). She replied, *Anata no oneechan no tame ni kaetta hou ga ii to omou* (I think it is better for your sister if I leave). I relayed that answer to my sister in English, and she said, "I want you to ask her what *she* wants to do." So I tried again, and Obaachan said, *Oneechan no dannasama no tame ni kaetta hou ga ii to omou* (I think it is better for your sister's husband if I go back to Japan). After going back and forth a few more times, we gave up and realized that Obaachan, a woman born in Meiji Japan, just could not answer the question in the way my sister wanted.[12]

Our transnational family lives are full of painful separations, heart wrenching at times. Families are torn apart, some unable to come back together because of financial constraints or constraints of the heart. Many cross the great ocean never to return.

It is Christmas 2010. I am in California. A song comes on the radio, "I'll be home for Christmas." Home. Am I home now? Am I home in

Japan? Am I ever home? I think of Edward Said, the Palestinian-born literary theorist and passionate advocate for Palestinian rights. Said's memoir, *Out of Place*, moved me deeply.[13] Am I too always out of place? Is Norma out of place? Are we like Said, with our Western education and our dual heritage, forever trying to bridge the gap between the Western world where we have lived as adolescents and adults to the Eastern worlds where we were born and raised?

Some people never return home. I did not know Said, but I was touched by a conversation with Farhat Ziadeh, an aging Palestinian living in Seattle, about wanting to go home. He was in his seventies and felt drawn to spend his last days where he spent his first days. But he knew that he would not, reminding me of a compelling line used in a book title from my younger days, "You can't go home again." I repeatedly discover that this is true. Some say we want to go home as we approach death—we want to die where we were born, where we were children. I don't know if this is true. My mother does not want to go back to die in Japan. Growing up in a militaristic, emperor-worshiping, devastated, impoverished Japan was too much for my mother. For her, home is now America, and that is where she will die. I wonder if Said died peacefully in New York; was it his home? Or had he accepted being homeless?

Some say if we get to choose a last meal it would be like our first meals, food from childhood, soul foods, comfort foods. I would choose miso soup, rice, an *umeboshi* plum. Like Norma, I long for those distinctive Japanese tastes of *shiso*, *sansho*, and *myoga* when I am in the United States.

When I was a child I dreamed that there was a place for me, a home, a place where I fit in. Not where I was in Massachusetts. I imagined the magical place for me was Japan, the place where I was born. Though I had no memories I was certain that Japan was a place where everyone was like me and everyone liked me. It was a place where no one would ever call me a "Jap" and no one would ever hate me, a safe place, a place I could call home.

That was just a dream, I realized later. True, no one called me a Jap, but they had other names for me in Japan. I was more of an outsider there than I was in white communities of America. Finding a home is hard for some of us. Are we destined to be always "out of place"? Perhaps, but as a child, I dreamed of home.

The song ends, "I'll be home for Christmas, if only in my dreams." For some of us, that is the only way we will be home. But if home is where the heart is, I am always at home. When I was a child I asked my obaachan, "Where is God?" I wanted to see him. She pointed to her heart and smiled, "God is here." Is home also there? Does a world of fluid identities and borders represent a rich otherworldliness that erases the divisive binary on which dehumanization of others depends? Is home for some people a metaphysical and material position of displacement that one should embrace without romanticizing or denying its loneliness and pain? I think of my place in the world as more than just a state of mind or the ability to travel freely to and establish a sense of belonging in any given place, but as anchored in struggle and social movement. Mine is a paradoxical condition that develops out of being at home with a lack of home or total belonging, which brings a freedom from loyalty and subordination to specific ideologies, cultures, systems, worlds—homelessness as home.

TWO

We Must Go On

I got off the subway at Washington Street and walked quickly through the sleazy porno district known as the "Combat Zone" until I reached Chinatown. I stopped at my destination, 27 Beach Street, where I saw the sign for the Asian American Resource Workshop. The double doors on the street were wide open, and I could see all the way up a broad stairway to the third floor. I hesitated for just a moment before climbing up the creaky wooden stairs. At the top were two doors, the Chinese Progressive Association on the left and the Asian American Resource Workshop on the right. The door on the right was open. I entered a large, bright studio that looked like an abandoned garment factory. A young guy at a small desk looked up and smiled and we recognized immediately that we had something in common. I wanted to talk, but didn't know what to say, so I just asked to see their library. He took me in the back and showed me their modest collection and we started to chat. That was the beginning of a long friendship.

Peter Nien-chu Kiang was my first mixed Asian friend. I was his first mixed Asian friend too—we drew on each other for support, or maybe I should say I drew on him for help in entering the Asian American community. Peter was already in and I wanted to be in. It was 1980 and I had just returned from an extended roots journey to Japan, reconnecting with family and a vital source of ancestral and cultural knowledge. Reclaiming and recovering identities, I knew that I was Asian, I knew that I was American, and I wondered if "Asian

American" was a way of blending, balancing, or synthesizing. That's why I was in Chinatown. Peter was just out of college, a Harvard graduate living out his dream of establishing a grassroots educational resource center while subsisting on food stamps. I could not have met a better person to encourage me.

He was the director of the only community organization in Boston that was pan-Asian; all others were Chinese. The AARW was a small group of activists, artists, musicians, and educators, and at Peter's invitation I quickly became a member. Our goal was nothing less than to make fundamental social change through the development of Asian American awareness, pride, and unity. I became involved in the group's diverse activities, such as working to produce bilingual slide slows and develop curricula on Asian immigrant issues for adult ESL classes, train community members in video production for cable television access, organize coalitions to protest anti-Asian racist violence and police brutality, and convene conferences and professional development workshops for teachers about stereotypes and Asian American history. The office in Chinatown drew us from other parts of Boston, many of us from college campuses. I loved leaving the stuffy Harvard campus, where I spent most of my time as a graduate student, and taking the train downtown to my imagined Asian community. It made it easier that Peter had already paved a path that I could follow. A lot of people had already encountered what one guy called "an Asian who don't look Asian." Besides his looks, Peter was dealing with cultural differences in Chinatown among the Cantonese-speaking Chinese from Gwangdong, as his father was a Mandarin-speaking diplomat's son from Shanghai and his mother WASP.

"We were living in a suburb called Belmont, where we were the only Chinese family on our block. I think my father went through a lot in the early years after moving to that town. Neighbors wouldn't talk to him, kids would make fun of him. I don't know how he internalized all that, but it was clear that it was happening, because it was happening to me too.

"I started to feel it at an early age. It came out really strong in sports because a lot of kids had images of Chinese being really weak. Even then I knew it was wrong. Then there was this one kid who would draw these pictures of 'Fuji,' which was my nickname, but they wouldn't look like me at all. They were stereotypes with buckteeth and glasses. So friends of mine who at least respected what I could do, what my abilities were, made up a name for me which to them was kind of an endearing little nickname. I'm not sure what I thought—it was weird but at the same time it meant a kind of acceptance. So I adopted it, or at least wasn't angry when kids would call me 'Fuji.' The kid who was drawing pictures of Fuji would bring them over to me as presents. It was really wild. I didn't know any better, that was the really scary part. But this kind of big contradiction may be characteristic of 'half and half,' that much of your experience you internalize and feel alone and at the same time there's a certain part of you that strives for acceptance no matter what. Eventually the terms of that acceptance become very important, but when you're a little kid and you're isolated, alone with no kind of role models, no kind of support, those terms of acceptance will be for the most part stereotypes. Acceptance is a funny concept."

Peter's "Fuji" story is just like my own childhood among whites. My friends came in one Monday morning in fifth grade with what they thought was a terrific idea. They had been to see Elvis Presley's new film *Blue Hawaii*, they explained, and had come up with a nickname for me. Elvis had a Chinese servant named "Ping Pong," and it seemed appropriate that the name should be mine. I thought I should protest that I was not Chinese, I was Japanese, but I knew the distinction would be lost on my friends. It became my nickname, shortened to "Ping." I would have preferred "Elvis."

How ironic that Peter, who is Chinese, would be given a Japanese nickname, while I would be given a nickname that was supposedly Chinese. Americans didn't know and didn't care that Asia was not a country but a continent made up of many countries with vast differences, even contrasts as huge as colonizer and colonized. Of course, there have been times when it was important to distinguish, and *Life* magazine's December 22, 1941, edition carried a story complete with photos informing Americans of the crucial task of "How to tell Japs from the Chinese." The article lamented that "angry citizens were victimizing allies with emotional outbursts at the enemy." As happened throughout history, however, this flip-flopped a few years later when the Chinese became our new enemies when they went communist, and the Japanese our new allies following the Occupation.

This confusion of Asians became tragic for one young man in 1982, when Vincent Chin, a Chinese American, was beaten to death in Detroit by unemployed auto workers who, blaming Japanese competition for their lost jobs, targeted him because they thought he was Japanese. Vincent's shocking death forged a stronger bond between Peter and me, as both of us understood from our own experiences that in the minds of many Americans we were indistinguishable Asians. The way they ignored our differences and subjected us to the same treatment strengthened our Asian American identities, uniting us in shared understandings that forge the basis of a pan-Asian political consciousness.

Asian Father

While Peter and I connected quickly from presumed similarities, it was also apparent that there were huge differences. He was Chinese, I was Japanese. He liked long grain rice, I liked short grain. He ate with thick chopsticks, mine were pointed. The Chinese-Japanese distinction that eluded our American friends was so apparent to me, having lived in Japan. My grandparents had been part of Japan's colonizing settlers, living eight years in Manchuria. I heard them talk softly about Unit 731, the infamous, covert biological and chemical warfare research and development unit of the Imperial Japanese Army that undertook lethal human experimentation during the Second Sino-Japanese War and World War II and was responsible for notorious war crimes. When I had interviewed a few years earlier for a job in a Chinatown day care center, the director had told me over dinner that his first-born son had been killed by the Japanese. Then, when I had given up all hope of getting the job, he told me that he would hire me because I would be able to understand the Chinese children since I was Japanese. This weird experience symbolized my confused feelings about being Asian American.

The other obvious difference between us was that Peter had a Chinese family name and mine was stereotypically Irish. This gave Peter more legitimacy, as in an East Asian patriarchal tradition the children belong to the father's family. I sensed that an Asian family name made for easier entry and acceptance in Asian American groups, leading me to reflect on the power of names over identity and the difference between having an Asian mom or an Asian dad. I wondered about people of mixed ancestry who do not grow up with both biological parents, but like President Obama are raised by a single parent and experience one side of their ancestry—and have to develop their identity without the mirror and influence of their other parent.

My relationship with my father was obviously crucial in my development; I had to reconcile that I could identify with him in many ways, but not racially. He was white, I was not, or at least that was what I had been told. When I met Peter, I wondered how mixed kids with Asian fathers are influenced by them, and the differences between boys and girls. As I studied psychology I wondered how healthy gender identity development could require a boy to identify with his father and a girl with her mother, when so many kids were raised without their fathers.

I suspected that Peter's Chinese identity had been reinforced because to the Chinese side of the family, boys are better. Claudine Chiawei O'Hearn, the daughter of an Irish American father and a mother from Shanghai, writes of how she resented her brother for the ease with which he could slip into the culture, whereas she had to constantly prove and explain herself. He would be questioned about "what he planned to do with his life, when he was going to find a girlfriend, . . . while I was mostly treated with polite comments about the style of my dress and carted off to watch TV. . . . My parents were exasperated by my long face and didn't understand why I was bothered even as they had me pegged as the American one."[1] O'Hearn also claims that it helps to "look Chinese," and that was another reason she always felt her brother was more readily accepted as Chinese.

I was raised by an Asian mother, and the influence is clear. My mother intimately interacted with me in my formative years and passed on culture through our daily contact. Fathers usually have less contact with children than mothers and their impact is not as obvious, but can also be substantial. Peter's early rejection of his father's ways turned to understanding and appreciation as he grew older.

> "Since my father wasn't around that much it was a lot more subtle, and I only began to realize in junior high and high school that he had had a big impact on me, on how I developed, kind of just through example, not through things he would tell me. The things he would tell me I would tend to reject. I think he really exhibited the Asian characteristic of thinking about the group's interest first, rather than personal interest, that kind of lack of individualism that is so strong in American culture. It was something that I really appreciated and valued even though he never told me that that's a good thing to be . . . just seeing him and valuing him. And I think there were some other very subtle appreciations of tradition, history, and education, all those values that you find in most Chinese families was there in ours as well."

Peter's connection with his father was strengthened when they journeyed to China with his grandfather in 1982. Three generations of men: Yi-seng Kiang, Nelson Yuan-sheng Kiang, and Peter Nien-chu Kiang. The family had been away for half a century. For his grandfather and father it was a homecoming, a return to their motherland. For American-born Peter, it was a time of grounding his images of China in reality—the collage of stories from grandparents, photographs of relatives, distortions by the media, and history from schoolbooks. He vowed to return again someday with three generations of his own children and grandchildren, knowing they would all be proud.

Identity

One thing that Peter and I shared was growing up isolated as Asian. Neither of us knew any other Asians in childhood and adolescence, and we associate these circumstances with feelings of difference, isolation, and alienation. I interviewed Peter when he was twenty-four about his identity development.

> "I think there is a contradiction for 'half and half' growing up in a white community, because the external world is not Asian, though the

internal may be. That's an enormous contradiction. It may be true for other Asians, I'm not sure. I suspect that the degree of inwardness may not be as intense as for the 'half and half,' because for us one of the dominant feelings that we carry around with us all the time is a sense of being alone, and inwardness comes directly from that. Although there are some similarities with the general Asian experience growing up in white communities, that sense of isolation even in your family and the impact that has on the development of one's personality is potentially very different.

"The more I think about it, the more my life makes sense to me. Even that early period, the connection between that period and the next in junior high and high school which was one of intense alienation, . . . it all fits together, all these experiences, sometimes overt racism, seeing how people treated my father, all these things. The only way I had to channel it was into myself. It was all being internalized because there was no one to talk to. I think it might have been different if I had even an older or younger brother or sister who was also 'half and half' and was going through the same experiences. I was living with a sister from my mother's first marriage, and she was white and she didn't know . . . so not having any external support or understanding kind of by definition necessitated all of this being internalized. At times it came out in positive ways, at times it wouldn't. At all times there was a kind of individual, alone kind of feeling to it. And I think I had a lot of bitterness when I was younger based on those series of experiences as a little kid."

Growing up with such feelings, how does a child make sense of what is happening? Like Peter, children are often left on their own, internalizing their experiences. In her memoir *Hapa Girl*, May Lee Chai, the child of a Chinese father and Irish mother, writes of the isolation she felt, the inability of parents to provide support, and the comfort provided by a sibling.

> For all their wonderful qualities, my parents were never able to discuss race with my brother and me. . . . My parents could find no words to explain what was happening, and in some way I think my brother and I learned to blame ourselves. In fact, I know this to be true. I just never wanted to admit it.[2]

Now, when my father got angry, when we retreated to our rooms, we could sit in our closets and talk. When my mother came to look for us, we held our breaths, hiding in silence until she gave up trying to find us and went away. They didn't understand us, but we didn't need them. We had each other.[3]

My dad used to comfort me when I was taunted by assuring me that "Japanese are smart." I did try to do well in school and was rewarded for my success by my teachers' praise, classmates' respect, and my parents' satisfaction. But that small comfort of being seen as smart was overwhelmed by the negative images held by the children and adults around me that they absorbed from Hollywood's depictions of evil "murderous Japs" and neutered "Ping Pongs." This struggle may drive a child to construct a marginalized identity as an outsider, which may fit for a while, but will become constricting as one moves through adolescence into the adult world. This struggle was articulated by a young man named Lowry Cheng-Wu Pei:

> Somehow my upbringing stole from me a cultural identity and made me an outsider for no clear reason. Not for having a Chinese father, but for nothing. Because that was just the way it was. Being the outsider—outside of the majority culture and outside of the Chinese—became my strategy, my schtick. My way of knowing which I defended and clung to and despised; which I felt trapped in and afraid to leave; which left me nowhere to go. And then a struggle to get all the way into the world.[4]

This struggle to get into the world may be confusing and full of ambivalence. One may know what must be done, the way of self-healing, yet be fearful of the outside world. In our minds we may know the way to go, but our hearts are still afraid. Peter recalls:

> "In college I took courses in Chinese philosophy and internally I was relating very strongly to that, but externally there was still no way that I was relating to other Asians. I remember looking for a place to live that summer and one of the places that I called a woman answered and she clearly had a Chinese accent which I recognized right away and after talking with her I decided that I didn't want to live in

that house just based on that. . . . When I thought about that later I was really ashamed . . . but that's how deep self-hatred can go."

I was rescued from my ambivalence by my first encounters with blacks in high school. I felt valued by others as Japanese for the first time in my life. They included me in their group *because* I was Japanese, not *in spite of* being Japanese. I went to college ready and eager to become more Japanese, studying language, literature, and history. I felt like the writer Sui Sin Far (Edith Eaton), the daughter of a white British father and Chinese British mother:

> Whenever I have the opportunity I steal away to the library and read every book I can find on China and the Chinese. I learn that China is the oldest civilization on the face of the earth and a few other things. At eighteen years of age what troubles me is not that I am what I am but that others are ignorant of my superiority. We are coached by our parents to respond to taunts and put downs with such claims of superiority: "Chinese are better."[5]

While our parents tell us one thing, society gives us different messages, sometimes powerfully and dramatically. We construct our identities and develop our worldviews through these meaningful experiences, both proud and traumatic. We all endure moments of humiliation and isolation and engage in lifelong struggles to survive and transform oppressive environments. Experiences of racism in his youth had a great impact on young Peter, especially an incident playing football when a big kid roared, "Kill the Chink!" He was struck that no one intervened or even seemed to notice or care, and he realized he was completely on his own. Reflecting on that transformative moment in his life, Peter explains:

> "I think my competitive drive was fired by experiences like that. There was a striving for quality, for the sake of quality, but also proving that I was good or better than they were. It became very intense, not having a close community and family. . . . I felt like I needed to resolve, to figure out, to analyze and synthesize all these things from my past, my family, my Chineseness, my conflict between science and art, where I fit in."

In his search Peter found himself gravitating to a third space, the counterculture of the time. He felt more welcomed at first, but gradually discovered that he found no room there for his Asian identity.

"Entering the counterculture was made easier by having the half and half experience of difference. But what I finally realized was that even in those movements, even in the counterculture to which I had gravitated to find acceptance and to deal with my alienation, even within that I felt intensely alienated, all the feelings of being different, feeling alone, like I didn't belong, like I couldn't relate to other people, feelings that the values were very different."

Community

I met Peter in Chinatown because I was searching for community. It was exhilarating to meet him because he was energized from his adventures, much like Obama when he worked in Chicago as a community organizer. Placing ourselves in a context of a larger group brought us out of our self-absorbed identity consciousness, which was overcome by a sense of identity won in action. Peter's discovery at twenty-four was that community was a way to connect with self and others, synthesize one's experiences, and find one's place in the world.

"Artistic introspection, expression, and creation I saw as means of overcoming my alienation. I recognized a strong commitment to changing things, having seen a lot that was wrong, and finally realizing that was something I couldn't do by myself. Reflecting on all this alienation was important but not enough. My sense of myself and what I had to do with my life I could no longer see simply as an individual, and it became very important to start to place myself within the context of a group of people, a community, a sense of collective history.

"This was a huge breakthrough because as I have said, I think growing up 'half and half,' growing up in a white neighborhood, you always have this sense of being alone, and that becomes a dominant sense to your whole life, your whole outlook, and I think at least for me, and I would say for other people too, it's really critical that that be overcome and I think that can only be done by placing oneself within a context of history and community. I think it's important for the 'half and half' to realize their vital connection to Asian American history and to see that their identity is related to history. It's also important to identify with other third world communities. Any hesitation that I felt because physically I could be perceived as white was overcome through working with people."

Seeking a place where he could express his blossoming Asian identity led Peter to direct his energy toward the "Third World" in acts of collective engagement. While still a Harvard student, he poured his anger and alienation into activism, enlivened by the connections he made with comrades outside the Asian American community and invigorated by solidarity with other activists who were into decolonizing and liberation.

Peter also connected more directly with the Asian American community. As for others, the connection energized and empowered while also bringing on a struggle to be natural and authentic, making us sometimes confused and artificial. Even though he himself was not one, in his early days of activism Peter took pride in his identification and affiliation with the FOBs (fresh off the boat), perhaps because his connection to China was more recent than many ABCs (American-born Chinese) and he was empowered by his studies of Mandarin and Cantonese. One day I heard him teasing our friend, who was ABC, about his lack of Chinese knowledge, calling him Jook-sing, a pejorative term indicating he was Chinese on the outside but hollow on the inside. Our friend retorted, "Well what are you?" Peter countered that he was "only half Jook-sing." But the other guy struck back with the trump card, rarely played among friends: "Yeah, well what about the other half?"

These games of authenticity bring out our vulnerability but I play them anyway, if I want to prove how Asian I am. This is often just a game, but sometimes more than that, such as the time a guy was hired over me for a position as a counselor for Asian American students. A friend who knew what had happened told me that the other guy got the job because he appeared more authentically Asian to the interviewers. I was incredulous, insisting to myself that I was way more Asian than he was. I could speak Japanese, I was born in Japan, I lived in Japan, I was called a Jap more times than he was, and I love *natto*, the slimy fermented beans that are the ultimate test of authenticity. But I knew that all of this was irrelevant and that my looks and my name had doomed me to the doubters who questioned how Asian I was.

Because it is so hard to prove we are Asian, some profess it is easier to be white, dwelling in a comfortable place where color does not exist. Is this why so many Asians of mixed ancestry become invisible and unheard from, at least in ethnic circles, claiming, if questioned, that race, ethnicity, and culture have no meaning in their lives? Is it too much for us to be Asian, to figure out what it means to us and others? O'Hearn writes:

> It's easier to be white. To be Chinese, to be half Chinese, is work. I often find myself cataloguing my emotions, manners, and philoso-phies into Chinese and American, wary if the latter starts to outweigh the former. Three points Asia. How can I be Chinese if I prefer David Bowie to Chinese pop, if I can more easily pass as an Ameri-can, if I choose to live in New York and not return to Asia where my family still lives, if English is my first language and Chinese remains a distant second? How can I be Chinese when I struggle to commu-nicate with my grandparents? I am unable to tell them about friends, boyfriends, life-altering experiences, beliefs, new jobs—to tell them about my life and who I have become—and the result is they don't really know me. I'm ashamed to admit that there have been times I dreaded visiting them because of the humiliation of having to resort to hand gestures and second-grade Chinese.[6]

It may be easier for some people to be white, but not for Peter. He always made it clear to everyone that he was Chinese American, without apology or explanation. I loved that about him. He knew that people were looking at him thinking, "Who is this guy Kiang?" but he never let on that it bothered him or that their questioning of him deserved recognition. I tried to do the same but found that my name was clearly a handicap. I envied those like Peter whose Asian fathers had endowed them with family names that enabled them to be accepted in the patriarchal Asian communities. My solution was to give myself an Asian name, with the obvious choice my Japanese family name of Shigematsu. Armed with my name I went forth into Asia and Asian America declaring boldly who I was, should anyone care to know.

Sharing Voices, Crossing Boundaries, Building Communities

My young friend Peter became a college professor who is redefining what it means to fulfill that role in the academy. Peter sees much of his work as a researcher and teacher centered on integrative themes of sharing voices, crossing boundaries, and building communities as a way to frame his commitments and contributions to create contexts in which immigrant voices, student voices, women's voices, Asian American voices, and others can be expressed and appreciated. The focus of his research and writing is to document and validate student and community voices as a way to challenge the dominant paradigms and to ground alternative theories.

The structure of his faculty appointment and teaching responsibilities purposefully crosses disciplinary and institutional lines. His day-to-day practice is multidisciplinary on many levels—reflecting the nature of his dual professional fields in Asian American Studies and education, as well as his commitment to seek connections across boundaries that isolate subject matter or separate people. He credits his organizing experience, biracial background, and experiences at all levels of education with enabling him to move comfortably and productively across boundaries of race, culture, gender, and class to facilitate collaboration and forge coalitions in his relationships with colleagues and communities.

Nearly every aspect of Peter's research, teaching, and service relates to community building. His studies in Boston Chinatown or with Cambodians and Latinos in Lowell, Massachusetts, for example, explicitly examine the dynamics of immigrant community development. His research and service within educational institutions invariably point to the importance of communities as a survival strategy to address student needs or as an anchor for curriculum transformation.

His work as a teacher is about building community in the classroom through respect, mutual understanding, and creating spaces for his students' strengths and struggles to be recognized.

Healing and Transformation

Peter's visions of community expanded from his younger days as an angry activist who sometimes sharply divided his world into "us" versus "them." He has become inclusive, forging connections in innovative ways, seeing relations and associations where others see differences and conflicts. He formed a connection with the Joiner Center for Vietnam veterans, creatively uniting their efforts with his in the Vietnamese community. In a life-changing research project, he listened to the stories of Asian American veterans and learned more about the meaning and process of healing from them.

Although early in his career he defined his work as a means to share voices, cross boundaries, and build communities, he later came to see the themes of healing and transformation as even more meaningful signifiers of how he views his role and responsibility. In a poem written in 1988, Peter spoke of how he works with students. Here are a few lines taken from "Your Words":

> My students now
> like Ely and Thanh
> slowly shed their silences.
>
> I tell them—
>   Writing is healing
>   when the walls hide war and devastation
>   Writing is transformation
>   when the walls are white and echo English Only.
>
> I tell them—
>   Write from the past
>   But write for the future.
>   Every word
>   is a lesson in survival.[7]

Peter would probably say that his students' needs led him to his place in the world. Despite his pedigree as a Harvard graduate and his distinguished career, he has chosen to devote himself for more than twenty years to an urban public university where the students are mostly working-class. Many of his Asian American students are from local Boston communities, often Southeast Asians with traumatic family backgrounds. Peter's classes are designed around the belief that there are strengths to be shared and lessons to be learned from these students, especially in facing and overcoming obstacles. He is both affirming and honest in analyzing issues together, even if dynamics become difficult emotionally and seem out of control pedagogically. His work is guided by a belief that the reality of oppression already defines much of his students' daily lives as working-class, predominantly non-white immigrants, and that those experiences represent rich resources for meaningful teaching and learning.

Peter began to see himself as a faculty person of color as playing a unique and desperately needed role of facilitator of healing and transformation within universities and communities. This unstated, undervalued, and constant commitment to facilitate healing and transformation is central to his work. "Educate for life" is another way Peter envisions what he does, his role within his particular time and space. He sees himself critically analyzing narratives, flashbacks, and research agendas, honoring the voices, pedagogies, and tears of his students. One powerful way Peter does this is by asking students to write a letter to a real-life individual important in their lives, describing something specific and meaningful they learn in his course. He asks his students to go to places they are afraid to go, inside themselves, touching their own wounds and those of others. They may tell him they hate it, that it is too hard to recall so many sad and negative images, things that they try not to remember deeply. But they also say things like this Vietnamese student did following a trip to the site of the Tule Lake internment camp for Japanese Americans, used during World War II:

> If I don't remember the past, I won't be able to tell why I have to leave my homeland, I won't be able to figure out what I expect from

myself while staying here to pay back to the sacrifices of my parents. . . . I think we all, as Asians, should know it, should make other people aware of it and remember it. . . . We must remember and tell it; we must acknowledge it and tell it.[8]

Another Vietnamese refugee student wrote:

I tried so hard to bury the pain and hopelessness of the escape for years. I thought that my wounds had heal but when I watch the video and do the reading, I felt like someone had took a knife and slash the healing wound open again. I felt that my tears were no different from the blood that was running down from my wounds. Although upset, I was glad that the professor showed the video and have such reading. If it wasn't for that, our struggles and hardships would forever remain silence and no one would ever understand what we had to go through.[9]

Healing and transformation are not confined only to immigrant or refugee students. Others, Asian American and from other backgrounds, find healing and transformation as well. One student's letter addressed the silence surrounding her brother's death and how the class gave her the strength to write to her mother in Korea. She wrote of how she learned from the class that rather than avoiding one's pain, it can be good to talk to someone and cry and let your feelings out. In attending to her own capacity to suffer, she uncovered a profound connection between her own vulnerability and the vulnerability of others. She developed greater resolve to be thankful for what she has and to try to heal her feelings so that she was able to talk and turn her negative feeling into a positive energy that would help her in the future.

Toronto Reunion

I last saw Peter in the summer of 2009 in Toronto. He had been selected to receive an award by the Asian American Psychological Association. I was there as a keynote speaker. Our invitations had been initiated by Karen Suyemoto, who was the president. So there we sat, three Asians of mixed ancestry, one the lifetime contributions award winner, one the president, and one the keynote speaker. How things have changed, I thought. His acceptance speech was classic Peter, he never said a word about himself, just told stories about others, including me, telling others of our contributions to Asian American communities.

I wondered at first why Peter, known as an educator and not a psychologist, was being honored by a psychological association. But I realized that Peter had become exactly what I had hoped to be, a community psychologist. It was fitting that Peter receive the award, as his work has been so much about healing and transformation. His work has been not only on the individual level but also on the community level and across communities.

Our meeting brought back many memories. Although we remained roommates for several years, I had sensed a growing rift in our relationship. Peter was becoming a hard-core community activist, trying to use his involvement in communities as his credentials for doing Asian American studies, resisting the need to validate himself with degrees from institutions. Peter still hoped to revolutionize the world, I felt, in a naïve manner, while I thought he saw me as too cynical and pessimistic about what we could do to change the world. I entered a doctoral program in counseling and consulting psychology, where I sought to be a clinical and community psychologist doing internships in San Francisco with Asian Americans and in Boston's black neighborhood of Roxbury. My studies at Harvard were with a teacher who used words like "healing" and "education as transformation," but I don't recall sharing much of this with Peter. I guess I thought Peter saw my work as a counselor as too individually oriented—too centered on the self—and disconnected from the larger issues of social justice and equality. Following my graduation I moved back to Japan and Peter and I drifted apart.

I had always thought of our relationship as unbalanced. I saw that Peter had helped me and I was grateful for his trailblazing. His dedication was inspiring. I had been encouraged by his trust in me. But in Toronto he surprised me by saying, "It was you who encouraged me to go to graduate school." I dismissed his statement at the time, but realized later that Peter had tried to tell me something, sincerely expressing gratitude for the role I had played in his life. I had never thought that I had influenced him. At the time I was a graduate student Peter was determined to be a community activist. But he told me he realized that to accomplish his goals he needed to adopt the strategy of legitimizing himself through the accepted means of a doctoral degree and use it to get into a position where he could have the kind of impact he wanted to have, just the way I had described my motivation in getting an advanced degree. In any case, Peter returned to school and got his doctorate at Harvard, his alma mater, and began to use it.

In midlife, Peter still seems to have dreams of helping young people be aware of what is going on in this society, to get involved in fighting for their beliefs, what they think is right, for justice and equality, to set up programs to help the younger generation to get higher education and help their people. For Peter, healing and transformation are never simply individual acts, they are inseparable from sharing voices, crossing boundaries, and building communities. He writes of how he was affected by a particularly inspiring student who faltered in her project presentation and began to cry quietly, but recovered and told the class, "I want to go on."

> I too have tried to go on—as a teacher, advocate, and organizer across the fields of education and Asian American Studies. . . . In the end, healing and transformation must intersect with justice and equality. We have many legacies to uphold and more pathways to create.
>
> We must go on.[10]

THREE

For the Community

I learned early in life that others were eager to figure me out, catego-rize me, label me, even name me. They saw what they wanted to see, what differentiated me, what bothered them about the way I looked. In my earliest memories of my life in the United States, I sensed that people saw me as "Oriental," different from them, and that they in-terpreted my difference as weakness. The "Orientalism" I experienced was aggression and judgment and I realized as a child that I had to be vigilant, project quiet strength, and be brave and ready to fight. I found that I could use Orientalism to my advantage by cultivating an air of mystery and unpredictability that quelled potential attacks. Aggression was mostly verbal: taunts of "Ching Chong Chinaman" or "Chink," amusing now for their mistakenness, at the time stung as badly as the more appropriate "Jap." I never let on that any words penetrated the samurai armor protecting my Japanese heart.

I would have chosen none of these labels for myself, and the inad-equacy of any term to fully explain who I was continued throughout my life. Japanese, American, Japanese American, or Asian American all fit but did not describe everything about me. Amerasian, Eurasian, *haafu*, hapa, or half Japanese and half Irish described more completely but none were satisfying. I longed for a word that would easily an-swer the question "What are you?" I wondered what control I had to say who I was? When my friends in high school declared themselves "black," I had rejoiced with them, all the while longing for my own term of self-definition.

In 1984 I moved to San Francisco to experience a Japanese American community and a more pan-Asian environment than Boston offered. A lively debate at that time regarding the term *hapa*—borrowed from Hawaiian—included a spirited article by Lane Hirabayashi in the local Japanese American newspaper. He pointed out that the term itself was not what is most important and that a crucial issue was being buried in the arguments focused mainly on terminology.

> I believe the critical point being overlooked has to do with the right of the "insider" to define and conceptualize his or her own experience, and then develop a perspective which reflects this. This is not to say the insider's point of view is necessarily the most accurate or "truthful" (whatever the truth may be). My point is that—as a person of biracial, bicultural ancestry—I have to develop a way of looking at and understanding myself that fits my reality and needs.[1]

I loved the message that "we" had the right to self-definition. Just the thought that there was a "we" was exhilarating. Lane pointed out how an outstanding dimension of the debate was that the people who wrote to protest the term were not persons of biracial, bicultural ancestry. He took on respected community leaders Karl Yoneda and Raymond Okamura for their rejection of the term *hapa* and their unwillingness to extend to us the same rights to self-determination they have insisted upon for themselves as Japanese Americans. Lane rejected their assertions—that we just need to think of hapa as "beautiful human beings" or simply as Nikkei (members of the Japanese diaspora)—as smacking of paternalism and forced assimilation. "If I accepted it, I would lose myself," he wrote. He also wrote of the rejection he has experienced not only in the larger society but in the Japanese American community as well, such as being challenged by another Sansei over his right to teach Asian American studies. Lane explained how the debate left him feeling outraged and alienated. He defiantly wrote that he still called himself hapa and rejected outsiders' attempts to define his experience and identity on their terms. He identified the key issue as power.

Lane was one of the first people I wanted to meet when I got to San Francisco. We hit it off right away as two young men similarly consumed by our identities, community connections, and scholarly passions. I remember we talked one night while parked outside my apartment in his yellow VW bug. He got heated up as I tried to explain that identity development theory seemed to suggest that we would be considered more psychologically adjusted when we stopped insisting we were Japanese American and accepted a mixed identity—that we needed to get over our anger that we weren't accepted or understood by others and just integrate everything into a biracial identity. "Okay, so I might be less developed according to psychological theory, but this tension is what keeps me going, drives me to do things," he exclaimed. I wondered what would happen to Lane if he lost his tension. Didn't some people just seem to disappear from the struggle when they got it all together, mellowing out in their bland suburban homes? As a student of psychology I got the impression that humans were supposed to proceed through distinctly marked stages of development, becoming better and mellower as they reached higher and higher stages. When I saw psychological tension in people I assumed it meant that they were less developed than someone without such tension. Lane had tension. Was it coming from his position as a self-identified Japanese American who might not appear to be Japanese to others? Was it because he did not acquiesce to their definitions but asserted himself as both Japanese American and mixed race? Did the tension come from the conflict he encountered as he challenged the limiting perceptions and judgments of others and butted heads with respected elders?

At the time I was absorbed in reading Erikson's work on identity and was struck by his description of ethnic writers as "martyrs of self-chosen or accidentally aggravated identity consciousness who must sacrifice the innocent unity of living to a revolutionary consciousness." Erikson explained their preoccupation with identity as "not only a symptom of alienation but also a corrective trend in psychosocial revolution." I felt understood and empowered when he admonished that "a certain painful identity consciousness may have to be tolerated in order to provide the conscience of man with a critique of conditions, with the insights and with the conceptions necessary to heal himself of what most deeply divides and threatens him . . . namely, his division into pseudospecies." I saw myself and perhaps Lane too as one of those whose identity consciousness was "absorbed in actuality, lost in the intensity of the struggle." Was my "identity consciousness overcome through identity won in action"? Were we destined to be "spokesmen or prophets of identity confusion"?

Lane's identity consciousness led him to voice his opinions and state his position for himself and for a whole group of others. *Hapa* has since become popularized as a term embraced widely by mixed Asian Americans and a symbol of their identity and empowerment, but few people who now use it know the debt they owe to Lane for advocating the term at a time when it took courage to speak out. I wondered whether Lane felt any reservations in voicing an opinion against community leaders. I asked him some years later whether at that time he was aware that his style of publicly opposing respected community elders might be perceived as "un-Japanese" and be used against him as an indication that he was not authentically Nikkei? Did he worry that he would be chided for not showing enough respect for elders, for not understanding Japanese common sense or cultural values such as *enryo*? Did he know all this and persist anyway, emboldened by the examples of the men in his family, his father and uncle, who publicly protested injustice?

> "I think I remember worrying a little bit about all that. In the Japanese American community in those days you didn't take on "elders" too casually because you knew that—right or wrong—there would be retribution, especially if you made anyone look bad. So if I didn't have the support of you guys on the one hand and the [San Francisco Center for Japanese American Studies] folks on the other hand I might have been more inclined to keep my mouth shut. In retrospect, I'm appreciative of everyone's support because it enabled me to express exactly what was on my mind. Here, I should also say that I had known the Yonedas and Ray Okamura since I was a kid because they were always at Center programs, and so, yes, they were community elders, but they were also like extended family. The other thing is that I leave clues all over the place that I am who I am."

Lane's family also had a special place in the Japanese American community. His father James was prominent in the San Francisco community and his uncle Gordon was nationally known. Both were part of a family that was taken to the WCCA (Wartime Civil Control Administration) camp at Pinedale, California, following the December 1941 bombing of Pearl Harbor and then forcibly incarcerated at the WRA (War Relocation Authority) American-style concentration camps at Tule Lake in Northern California. His grandparents hated camp and tried to leave as fast as they could. James, the eldest child, was sent out to Weizer, Idaho, to harvest sugar beets and save money. His father joined him soon after and they both worked in the fields for about a year to get Jim's mom and the two youngest children out of Tule.

Lane's uncle Gordon, then a twenty-three-year-old University of Washington student, turned himself in to federal authorities in Seattle rather than be moved to a camp. His grandmother begged her oldest son not to defy authorities so that the family would not be split up, but Gordon felt very strongly that he needed to do it. He was protesting mass removal as well as mass incarceration, and his intent was to protest the American-style concentration camps themselves. In the end, the government's lawyers hung the curfew charge on him as a way to avoid having to address fundamental constitutional issues that Gordon wanted to raise. He was convicted of violating military law and did time in Arizona on that first conviction. Shortly afterward, he was tried again for refusing induction—he was a conscientious objector—and was sentenced to McNeil Island Federal Penitentiary on a second conviction.

Gordon's case became one of three major U.S. Supreme Court cases that challenged the substance of Executive Order 9066; the Supreme Court ruled in favor of the government. But in the early 1980s the redress and reparations movement brought the spotlight to Gordon when petitions of *coram nobis*—legal efforts to highlight errors of fact in court—were filed on his behalf and that of two other Japanese Americans who had challenged the incarceration, Min Yasui and Fred Korematsu. The petitions brought to light legal flaws in the imprisonment and in 1987 the U.S. Ninth Circuit Court of Appeals overturned Hirabayashi's conviction. The next year, President Reagan signed the

Civil Liberties Act of 1988, which blamed the incarceration on racial prejudice and failed political leadership.

Gordon's bravery in the height of wartime hysteria impressed his young nephew. Lane was also heavily influenced by his father, a pioneer in his own right. James was a high school senior in 1942; after the war ended he resumed his education and eventually received a PhD from the Department of Social Relations at Harvard University, where he studied with some of the great scholars of that generation. His marriage with a Norwegian American woman was just a year after the 1948 repeal of a California law that prohibited marriage between "whites" and "Mongolians," and many years before the 1967 U.S. Supreme Court decision that struck down similar laws. Lane's mother Joanne left her traditional Norwegian American family and community to marry Lane's father. Like James, she was an anthropologist interested in Asian cultures. They spoke English at home, ate Japanese food with Japanese dishes and utensils, and Japanese books, games, and cultural artifacts were always around. James's influence on his son was enhanced by his professional focus on Japan and the time the family spent there when James was a researcher at the University of Tokyo.

James became dean of the nation's first school of ethnic studies at San Francisco State College. Lane credits his father's developing perspective with influencing him to get involved in ethnic grassroots organizations and join a number of Japanese American youth groups in San Francisco.

"The 1969 strike at San Francisco State had a huge impact on me. I was a junior in high school. My parents were already divorced but I saw my dad almost every weekend over in the city. Jim was tenured faculty . . . but students and colleagues in the Teachers Union convinced him to go out on strike.

"It's when and how I started getting involved in community-based organizations like JCYC (Japanese Community Youth Council), adding a new political level to my sense of Japanese American identity. (This was especially the result of meeting people who were active in the Asian American movement of the 1970s.) For a hapa kid from Marin County, seeing the strike and then hanging around J-Town and Chinatown fully introduced me to the idea of empowerment, in which the principles of autonomy and self-definition were key components. . . . It was a matter of simple extension to think: if those tools could help free me in terms of my identity as a Japanese American and Asian American, the same tools would surely be of use in understanding myself as a mixed race person. The great thing was the folks around the old San Francisco Center for Japanese American Studies were very supportive of this line of thought.

"Then around 1980 I met you, Grace Fleming, George Kitahara Kich, and we formed a network within the Center that resulted in a series of influential panels and community presentations in San Francisco and at the CJAS conferences at Asilomar. So for me, . . . these were terrific developments because it meant I could still participate in the Japanese American community even as I became more aware that I'm not exactly a Japanese American per se; nor am I a Norwegian American. My experiences encompassed elements of both sides."

Lane also organized a groundbreaking panel at the Association of Asian American Studies at San Francisco State in 1986 that featured George Kitahara Kich, Cindy Nakashima, and myself. George was a pioneer in mixed race research and wrote one of the first doctoral dissertations on the subject. He also was a founding member of I-Pride, a community group that advocated for mixed race families. George's study on mixed Japanese-whites promoted a three-stage model of identity development. In the first stage, biracial people are either seen as different or feel themselves to be different from others, often in a negative manner. A struggle for acceptance by others occurs in the second stage, in the context of school or community settings. The third stage is characterized by self-acceptance and assertion of an interracial identity, in which the biracial person creates congruent self-definitions rather than be determined by others' definitions and stereotypes. George described development as a lifelong task, which seems to repeat at different levels of complexity during major crises or transitions throughout the life span.[2]

I was encouraged by George's research to pursue my own study, especially to understand the "roots" journey to Japan and search for community as Japanese American, both of which were transformative personal experiences. The Association of Asian American Studies seminar that Lane organized was a major breakthrough for me as I sought to assert myself in the field, and I was thrilled when my paper "Addressing Issues of Biracial/Bicultural Asian Americans" was published in the book that came out of the conference, *Reflections on Shattered Windows*.[3] It was one of the first published papers I know of to advocate the inclusion of these issues in Asian American studies. Besides the obvious demographics of rapidly increasing numbers of intermarriages and therefore mixed ancestry children, I asserted that we could play a special role in Asian American communities. Since we are oppressed not only by whites but also by other minorities, including Asian Americans, we are a reminder of how all oppressed people may also be oppressors. I maintained that facing the issues that confront biracial Asian Americans can help all Asian Americans reconsider a simplistic view of racism as emanating from whites only—to move beyond this to a broader awareness of the racial prejudice and discrimination that are institutionalized and exist in all of us.

I felt that it was necessary to write the article because inclusion of mixed race Asians in Asian American studies or communities was not an accepted idea at the time. I was confronted with this reality when Lane invited Grace and me to present in his Asian American studies class at San Francisco State. I had not been speaking very long before a student interrupted me: "Are you Asian?" I bristled but decided to make this a teaching moment. "Why do you ask?" The student retorted, "Because you don't look Asian." I was stunned by his brashness and staggered around for a while though I am unable to recall how I responded. Many years later, I wonder why I became so frazzled by that simple comment. I guess the trauma goes deep because looking Asian was a source of childhood pain. White kids picked me out and peppered me with racial taunts, so to be told by Asians that I don't look Asian is experienced as rejection—once again. When we processed the class in his office, Lane told me that the hostility I experienced was probably indirectly aimed at him, but since he was the instructor the students felt frustrated in their inability to challenge him, instead accusing me of being an inauthentic, illegitimate Asian.

That was 1985. Two years later I was living in Japan, where I would stay until past the turn of the century. I wonder whether I suffered from "ethnic fatigue" and was tired of living as an Asian American. But if so, why did I go to a place where I would be challenged even more as Japanese? Perhaps this had become my way of living, on the margins, in liminal spaces. I eventually returned to the United States unapologetic and self-confident in my "Japaneseness." I had become Japanese, much like Obama became black. I had paid my dues. No matter what anyone said, I knew I was Japanese, simply based on lived experiences.

Lane's reflections on his identity development preceded what would become much more common in later years, as people of mixed ancestries started to publicly share their thoughts in anthologies, memoirs, and other autobiographical writings. In 1982, Lane published a self-reflective essay.[4]

> An identity crisis? Who me? The best of both worlds: YELLOW and WHITE? Well . . . But if you were to ask about the inner perceptions, the inside life of an out-marriage child, what would there be to tell you?
>
> As a child there were the small dilemmas. A household life: never painful, and now they seem almost silly. What's for dinner? When it was my turn to set the table I'd wonder: who's cooking tonight, mom or dad? What will we be having: gohan or potatoes? Should I put out hashi and rice bowls or the knives and the forks?
>
> This was the "me" as I felt inside. Momentarily puzzled at times perhaps but definitely a whole. There were no splits, no divisions, to confuse or mar my world. My parents were my parents, my friends were my friends, and I was myself. But there was also the "me" as other persons perceived me. This was where the dilemma of identity seemed to begin.
>
> My last name, a nihonjin name, always made me feel Japanese. There it was. I couldn't have run away from it, hidden it, gotten rid of it, or denied it. I was stuck with it, but never completely displeased, even when they laughed at it: my childhood friends in games of name teasing.
>
> "KAWASAKI, HONDA, HIBACHI; KAWASAKI, HONDA, HIBACHI." My face would burn, my eyes fill with warm, heavy tears. But later I would feel unrepentant as if with my name I could defy the world around me . . .

As I looked out at the world, and that world looked back at me, people perceived me differently. I found out that there were two parts to me. One part evoked the response, "OH, ARE YOU JAPANESE?" The other drew the reaction, "HEY, I KNOW YOU'RE AN ORIENTAL."

Once an elementary school teacher—upon seeing me at the back of the classroom where I was peering intently at the assignment on the blackboard—asked me: "Will you stop squinting like that?" "What's the matter? Do you need glasses?" I was silent in confusion. Had I been squinting like he said? I was still too young to realize then, to tell him straight to his face that I wasn't squinting. That was just the way my eyes were.

Later on, in high school, I was to hear the other story, the flip side to the Eurasian coin. The ex-army typing teacher would smile and greet me: "Konnichiwa" he would say in some half-forgotten G.I. Japanese. "Ikaga desu ka?" I stopped, taken aback and not knowing how to reply I turned around and walked away. What could I have said that would have reflected my own feelings, or that would have unmasked his assumptions?

WHO ARE WE? the children of out-marriages? The EURASIAN, HAPPA, KONKETSUJI, HAFU, MIXED MARRIAGE children? Is it true that we are either strikingly beautiful—skilled as the models, singers, entertainers . . . the prostitutes of all-night honky-tonks and red-lit bars? Or are we somehow the awkward and homely—an unfortunate combination of mis-matched pieces? Are we the ainoko of unacknowledged, unidentified parenthood; the children of sin and shame, or even polluted blood? Or will the mixing of genes and heritage make us the leaders of a new and proud cosmic race? Is it true that we are marginal men and women trapped and torn between two peoples, two cultures, two worlds? Are we excessively self- and race-conscious, inferior, hypersensitive, hypercritical, and even worse? Are we bi-racial, bi-cultural, and restless with the consciousness of having dual citizenship to personality and identity? Or do we simply decide to avoid the issue by becoming 100 percent WHITE or YELLOW?

"Stereotypes," you may think, but let me ask you: Why is it that so many of us are slipping into the mainstream—passing? Why is it so much easier to flow with the current, to adapt, to assimilate, *even* if we have to deny a part of ourselves?

Lane's essay makes me wonder why for some people their ethnicity is the central guiding factor in their lives, while for others it is just a fact of life that has little effect on them. This is apparent even among siblings. In my family, it has been a salient aspect of my life from childhood to now, while my sisters have lived their lives with ethnicity mostly a matter of minor concern or relevance. As Lane interacted more with other hapa he wondered what factors make people more or less interested in their ethnic heritage. He wrote about it—experimenting with a spelling of *hapa* as *happa* to set it apart somewhat from the original Hawaiian term.

> I once sat down and compared experiences with a happa woman I met at school. She too grew up in white middle-class suburbia. She had a comfortable home and loving environment, but her parents did not put any emphasis on Japanese or Asian culture. There were no relatives nearby and most of her friends and boyfriends were Caucasian. She told me while she didn't reject the "fact" that she was Japanese American, she didn't think much about it and it didn't affect her day-to-day life. As we talked I realized that, given a slightly different set of circumstances, I could have easily been just like her. Because of my background and experiences, however, my values, style of interaction, identity, and lifestyle have been profoundly shaped by the strong psychological ties I have to my father.
>
> In this sense—having to deal with issues which are not fully understood by either Japanese Americans or North Americans—the process of developing a positive sense of self and of identity has been filled with obstacles and struggles for me. Since I do acknowledge that important aspects of my self-image are tied to things Japanese American, though, I feel a strong need to identify as a Nikkei. Otherwise I would have to deny and reject central relationships in my life.[5]

These days, many young hapa claim to have gone through their lives without much trouble. Rocky Kiyoshi Mitarai, however, wrote of his traumatic experience with hate crime in San Francisco's Japantown, where in 1997 he was attacked and nearly killed by a group of Asians because he was hapa. Their reaction to a good luck charm he was wearing with the character for *fuku* (happiness) started the violence. Just before they started to beat him he heard one of them say, "Why is he wearing that necklace? He doesn't even know what it means!" Another yelled, "You see Bruce Lee movies and you want to be Asian, huh!"[6]

Rocky wrote, "Things have gotten to the point where I am almost killed by other Asians because of my way of life. I can't just stop being Japanese. I have worn that necklace for many years and it reflects who I am, and that I am proud of being Japanese. I have just as much right to wear it as anybody else."[7] While his traumatic experience on that day was an extreme case of violence, Rocky also mentions some daily harassments that might be labeled as microaggressions. He hears remarks like: "Why do you try so hard to be full Japanese?" "Why is your last name Japanese?" "You shouldn't be in the Japan Club—you aren't a real Japanese." "Eating rice today, huh? Are you getting in touch with your Asian side?" "Look at this guy—the Asians don't want him, the Caucasians don't want him. He might as well be a Mexican."[8]

> I am often criticized for doing "Japanese" things, such as eating with chopsticks, practicing martial arts, or even making a simple trip to Japantown. People ask me why I do these things and some people even tell me that I shouldn't do them. I was raised doing them, and now that I have grown up and people can't see my Asian physical characteristics, I am criticized about the way I live.[9]

Being challenged on one's right to be Japanese especially grates on those who have also been denigrated for being Japanese. When Rocky was growing up in a mostly white town, people made slanted eyes in front of him, called him names, and since he was fat, asked if he was going to be a sumo wrestler. He endured his classmates' and teachers' racist comments: "I kind of accepted it and made fun of myself too, so that I would fit in." But he also observed perceptively: "Things like that hurt me while I was growing up, which is probably why I denied my Caucasian side after grammar school and identified myself as full Japanese."[10]

The desire to be part of the majority is natural but when our desire is thwarted some of us react as Rocky did and defiantly identify with the minority. This action is both acceptance of others' labels and self-definition that allows one to preserve dignity and self-respect. In his "Happa Experience" essay, Lane expressed his anger at those who deny our identities:

> When I encounter people who argue that happa are not truly Japanese American I always get angry. Although they may not realize it, such persons leave no room for the happa who have to struggle against all odds to positively conceptualize and integrate their feeling that they belong to the Japanese American experience in North America too.
>
> So a spirit of tolerance and understanding is essential and these words constitute a plea for others to respect the diversity and complexity of the happa experience. It is true that identity is something that evolves and changes over a lifetime, but acceptance from others is necessary for the happa who chooses to identify as Japanese American. Such an acceptance can constitute both an end and a new beginning, since the question of identity must be dealt with before other kinds of thought and action can take place.[11]

When we first met, I was drawn to Lane's youthful anger. While peacefulness is ideal, the reality is that there is a lot to get angry about in this world. There is a place for righteous indignation when we see human rights denied or a lack of respect for human dignity. Rocky fights back in his own way, refusing to be deterred from valuing his connections with his ancestry and continuing to assert himself not only as hapa but also as Japanese American.

> Many hapa people's experiences today are similar to those of the Japanese Americans about thirty years ago. Many of them had an identity crisis because their knowledge of Japanese language and culture was limited because their parents tried to mold them into "Americans" for their own good and protection. At the same time, people were constantly questioning their knowledge about the United States and their ability to speak English. They were judged by their appearance and nothing else. I know that the oppression I have been subject to is not at all equal to what my father and Japanese family went through during the terrible internment experience. But the rejection, the necessity to prove my "Asianness" and being hated because of my multiethnic

background are things that weigh heavily on my mind every day. People may choose not to accept who I am because I am hapa, but this ignorance cannot change me. Nobody can take my heart and spirit away from me. I am a very proud Japanese-American.[12]

Young people like Rocky contest the dire pronouncements of the death of the Japanese American community. Lane has been fighting this negative prediction for many years. In a 1993 article he took on Harry Kitano, perhaps the most respected Japanese American scholar, for his assertion that "the Japanese American community . . . thriving today will be 'no more in 2050' in the face of the rising rate of intermarriage."

> Simply put, Dr. Kitano seems to assume that the survival of Japanese American culture and community revolves around the purity of Japanese "blood" down through the generations. . . . Now, contrary to this view, most contemporary social scientists agree that culture is learned. In turn, learning one's own culture has to do with exposure within the family context as well as in institutions where the values, norms, and typical practices of a given group are enacted, whether this be a school, church, club, interest group, or even a "slo-pitch" league. . . . Given these points, I submit that all of us who are involved in Japanese American community-based organizations need to consider the issue of inclusion: that is, the kind of opportunities and spaces available for folks of part Japanese ancestry to participate, to become involved, and thus to retain critical linkages to their Japanese American heritage.[13]

Communities grapple with this issue of mixing in strange ways; some decide on blood quotas to determine who is a real Japanese American. Rebecca Chiyoko King-O'Riain has written on the ways in which beautiful bodies express the shifting boundaries of community.[14] The gatekeepers emerge at events such as the Nisei Week Queen pageant in Los Angeles and the Cherry Blossom Queen pageants in San Francisco and Honolulu. They decide that given the reality that marriages between Japanese and other Americans have been extremely common for many years, 50 percent is good enough to qualify. That means my sisters would qualify as Japanese American, but their children's 25 percent would not be enough. But how do the gatekeepers know how much blood one needs to be authentically Japanese? I wonder about Scott Fujita, the professional football player who is o percent by blood but was raised by Sansei adoptive parents and says he feels like he is Japanese American, because of the affinity for the cultural background he acquired through socialization in his family. I recently asked Lane what he thinks.

> "To me, if he wants to assert he is 'Japanese,' it doesn't really bother me. I guess we have a case like this in terms of Tai Lan (my young sister). Jim has never denied she was Chinese, and he and Chris did everything they could to give her a chance to relate to her ethnic background—took her to Mandarin lessons, enrolled her in a Marin County Lion Dance troupe. . . . Yet, because she's being brought up by my father, and because she's hung around many of the same Japanese American people and groups that I have when I was growing up, I would defend her if she said that she was as Japanese American as anything else, if anyone in the community objected."

Author Stewart David Ikeda, himself of mixed ancestry (and whose family includes Mariana, a young adopted child from Guatemala), writes of his belief that a distinct Japanese American culture can and will survive, but perhaps in an unexpected form.

> It will be preserved only very purposefully as family heritage, not automatically as a geographic accident, racial legacy, or birthright. There may be more of us in this century who don't in fact "look Japanese" or speak Japanese than those who do. If most JAs will look like Mariana and me, we must accept that the JA experience is inherently multicultural and changing—something different from our Japanese roots that we are making up as we go along.
>
> I've been thinking about this, too, because in the past few years, two sansei relatives and another family friend have all adopted children, as it happens, from China. As it also happens, all are in interracial relationships. These children will look superficially more like their mothers, and thus like a "traditional" JA family. They will also stand out in any gathering of their much more numerous hapa cousins.[15]

Ikeda reflects on what "the little yonsei from Guatemala" means to him both personally and for Japanese America, which everyone recognizes has been changed by high outmarriage. He points out that much is made of the "diluted blood" of mixed race youth, but there is less mention of how collective wartime upheaval and subsequent assimilation have left even "pure" Yonsei—the great-grandchildren of immigrants— just as "culturally diluted." He cautions, "As a diasporic people—like the Jews, forcefully dispersed, wandering, surviving in our separate ways—we face a mounting struggle to maintain our distinctiveness, stories, and heritage."[16] He asserts that we're all hapas now—twenty-first-century Americans of every background—psychically and culturally, as globalization and our increasing diversity have rendered us cultural if not racial hybrids.

Lane also feels that the struggle for community demands commitment and contribution.

"I'm always much more interested in who is contributing what. If they do something in or for the Japanese American community, then to me it's a matter of personal preference and identity and that's their right. What counts to me is what people contribute to community building and culture building. That's something I value, and it's not a matter of genetics or of being of Japanese ancestry. If people who are not of Japanese ancestry want to contribute something, and they are sincere and effective, then I am happy to work with them. I might even value them more, in terms of the community, than someone who is of Japanese descent but isn't interested in participating.

"This is where my perspective intersects with the questions of whether happa folks or mixed race folks, are part of the Japanese American community. To me they are, if they contribute. But same with Japanese Americans who have other Asian or non-Asian partners. Those partners are in if they contribute. I agree with those who say that if we hold this kind of attitude, first, it is healthy; and second, that way the community can keep on growing.

"Inclusion in Japanese American community affairs has reaffirmed for me the fact that the kinds of cultural, spiritual, and political resources that the Japanese American community offers are a precious heritage that we can draw from to meet our ongoing needs—whether we are of full or part Japanese descent and, for that matter, whether we have any "Japanese" blood in our veins at all.

"The Japanese American community will change but not end if we who are involved decide otherwise and act accordingly to develop the kind of community that can help us recognize and meet the challenges of an increasingly multiracial, multicultural population and society. In short, rather than intermarriage rates, our own perceptions, choices, and actions will play the deciding factor in whether the Japanese American community still exists in 2050 or whether it will indeed have vanished."

Lane has taken his own place in Japanese American cultural history as the George and Sakaye Aratani Professor of the Japanese American Internment, Redress, and Community at UCLA. The chair was created by George Aratani, a man who lost his family's fresh produce business while he was incarcerated during World War II. Many other Japanese Americans lost all they owned and Aratani's hope is that something like that never happens again. The new chair was created as the U.S. government faced many of the same wartime pressures that can isolate a racial or cultural group—in this case, Arab Americans. Lane's mission is to teach, do research, and publish on these themes, and to use the endowed chair as a vehicle to educate the public about the injustices of mass incarceration and about how Japanese Americans drew from community resources to fight for redress. His work focuses on the United States, but he has looked beyond U.S. borders into other worlds since his doctoral training at Berkeley in anthropology and Mexican studies. He was involved in the Japanese American National Museum's International Nikkei Research Project in the 1990s and began to think more systematically about people of the Japanese diaspora in places such as Mexico City, Lima, Buenos Aires, and Havana.

In spring 2010 I went to San Jose to hear Lane speak about his new book with Kenichiro Shimada of the photographs of Hikaru Carl Iwasaki, *Japanese American Resettlement through the Lens*.[17] When a questioner challenged the rosy picture created by the photos taken when Iwasaki was in the WRA's photographic section between 1943 and 1945, Lane deftly countered that this is one view of what happened and encouraged the person to tell his own equally valuable story. I watched Lane in front of an audience and I observed the painfully familiar shyness of a retiring personality like my own that shuns the spotlight. He has become a professional who I know is not up there for himself but for the community he serves. Lane exudes a passion as he talks that is captivating and inspiring. Listeners are moved by his dedication and commitment, which are not only for the Japanese American community but also a deeply felt family obligation. People of other communities are inspired to see the importance of Lane's work to encourage that lessons be learned from the Japanese American experience and applied to current and future situations.

To me, Lane will always be the guy with whom I bonded at a time when it was important to be accepted as Japanese American on my own terms, as a person who was Japanese and something else. As someone already putting himself out there in that way, he was a valued ally. Reminiscing recently about the old days, Lane reminded me, "The key thing we were working for was authenticity and self-definition, and the self-acceptance that comes with that." Now I wonder how to understand the struggles we went through in the process of moving toward self-acceptance. Would it not have been easier to be white, marry white, and disappear among colorblind, liberal friends? The tension Lane described when we met as young men came from self-identifying as Japanese American, inviting others to challenge him, and not acquiescing to others' perceptions, definitions, and judgments but asserting himself as both Japanese American and mixed ancestry. Lane created more tension when he questioned respected elders.

The tension and anger in young Lane that drove his activism may have come from painful identity consciousness, but it was his choice to engage in struggles that further aggravated that consciousness. His preoccupation with identity was a moral decision that went beyond complaint, exposure, and personal alienation, bearing meaning for a community. As a spokesman for identity questions he has provided a community with transformative insights needed to heal the wounds that divide and threaten us—insights needed so that we open our arms to welcome and include.

FOUR

English, I Don't Know!

"Fija Byron desu. Chichi wa Amerkajin de, haha wa Okinawajin desu. Dakara hanbun Amerika, hanbun Okinawa. Jijo ni yori, chichi wa mattaku shiranai no de, Eigo, I don't know." (My name is Fija Byron. My father was American, my mother Okinawan. So I am half American, half Okinawan. But I never knew my father. So English, I don't know!)

People laugh and the tension eases. These days Byron always announces right away to his Okinawan audiences that he does not speak English. He even tells them that his father was an American whom he has never met. He answers the questions he knows are on everyone's minds.

"Are you a foreigner in Okinawan clothes?"

"How did you learn to play the *sanshin*?"

"Why can you speak Okinawan language?"

There are more questions, of course—seemingly never-ending questions.

"Why don't you know your father?"

"How come you look like that and can't speak English?"

Byron stops short of addressing all the unasked questions in their minds, hoping he has answered enough for them to allow him to proceed with his performance. He used to just begin playing, but found that there was a tension in the room that permeated the air. Eventually, someone would ask the inevitable question: "Why is a foreigner like you so good at acting like an Okinawan?"

This would throw Byron off because in his own mind he is only an Okinawan. The question reminds him that this is not the way others see him and he has to deal with that dissonance once again.

These days Byron has become a walking and talking symbol of an Okinawan who does not "look Okinawan." He is an Okinawan who "looks foreign" but does not speak English. Byron defines himself not only by what he lacks but by what he has. He is an Okinawan who can actually speak the native language. He is an Okinawan who plays the traditional music.

Every day Byron dresses in traditional Okinawan kimono and zori sandals, as if he is expressing or performing ethnicity in daily life. Emerging as an entertainer and educator, he hosts a radio show where he speaks in Uchinaguchi (Okinawan language), writes a newspaper column where he introduces words and expressions, and teaches language classes. Byron also emcees wedding ceremonies and special events, mixing animated talk and humor with live folk music that he sings and plays with his sanshin, a snake-skinned, traditional three-stringed instrument similar to the Japanese shamisen. His appeal is his effervescent personality, but that is not all. Although Byron, like many so-called Amerasians, is seen as foreign and has been targeted in anti-U.S. movements, he has also been exemplified as so Okinawan that people shake their heads in wonder and say, "He is more Okinawan than Okinawans." So while he may be regarded as a symbol of the U.S. military presence, he is also, in a more complex and metaphorical way, seen as a symbol of Okinawa itself, with its identity now strongly marked by the United States.

The more famous he becomes, the less necessary it is to explain each time who he is. One night when we were dining out, he was recognized by the owner of the restaurant.

"Aren't you Byron-san? I'm a fan of your radio show."

But when the owner introduced the special customer to his younger staff, who had never heard of him, Byron had to respond to their awkward attempts to speak English by insisting in Japanese, "Sorry, English, I don't know."

A New School

When I first met Byron in the fall of 1999, he was at a different stage in his life. I had come to Okinawa to visit the newly opened Amer-Asian School and to give a public talk to lend my support. In February, I had been struck by a front-page story in the nationally circulated *Asahi* newspaper—and in the months that followed, by more articles in newspapers and magazines—describing current educational, social, and psychological concerns of Amerasians. I watched with surprise as television networks then picked up the story of the formation of a new school. For the first time in many years the mixed ancestry Amerasians of Okinawa were a focus of national attention.

The AmerAsian School in Okinawa was the first of its kind, founded more than fifty years after Amerasians first became numerous after World War II. I was asked to endorse the new school and join a new study group because of the research I had done on the social and psychological issues of Amerasians.[1] My studies showed how Amerasians have been used by others to embody political, social, and psychological tensions existing around issues of racial and national identity formation in Japan and in Okinawa in particular. Amerasians were useful in representing the difficulties in transnational situations posed for political states such as the United States and Japan and for ethnic communities such as Okinawa.

I found that, by all visible signs, the lives of Amerasians had become far less problematic than in the past. The infamous areas of bars and prostitution around military bases in places like Koza where Byron was raised had been cleaned up. Improved economic conditions had given other jobs to local women. The power of American men had diminished so much that there were cases of American men trying to swindle Okinawan women. Readily available abortion had eliminated most unwanted pregnancies, and the military that once actively harassed soldiers who wanted to marry local women had even asked me to conduct cross-cultural marriage orientations.

Despite the troubled history, the time I lived in Okinawa in the late 1980s and early 1990s was characterized by a positive feeling about the status of Amerasians. The successful movement to revise the nationality law had provided Japanese nationality for nearly all Amerasians and practically eliminated the problem of statelessness. The Japanese government had gradually provided social benefits to Amerasian children regardless of nationality, such as the rights to education, health care, and other social services.

The Amerasian children themselves seemed to be disappearing into mainstream society. Christ the King School once had hundreds of mixed kids but closed years ago. The neediest children also seemed to be dwindling in number. During my research, the Pearl S. Buck Foundation, which once had an active file of nearly six hundred children, stopped its activities when the caseload dropped below one hundred. International Social Assistance of Okinawa also closed its doors, having provided services for many mixed couples and their children, including dealing with problems of statelessness and arranging hundreds of adoptions.

But the problems of Amerasians continued, including prejudice, discrimination, poor educational attainment, low socioeconomic status, and identity concerns. Amerasians continued to be scapegoated when the political conditions in Okinawa related to the military bases became volatile and a sacrificial lamb was required. Incidents such as the B-52 protests in the 1980s and the internationally publicized and politicized rape of a schoolgirl by American servicemen in 1995 generated considerable hostility toward Amerasian children, simply for bearing the genes of some American soldier. The bases house tens of thousands of military personnel and occupy 20 percent of the main island—a permanent political, economic, and social issue in Okinawa. Ironically, continuous peace education efforts are also a source of violence that targets the Amerasian as a vulnerable and handy symbol of the U.S. war machine.

Meeting Byron

Shortly after I arrived in Okinawa for my talk, I received a call from Professor Noiri Naomi, a passionate supporter of the school. We had met in Tokyo; she welcomed me to Okinawa and told me that Byron, a young man who worked for the school, was eager to meet me. I called him on the phone and he enthusiastically agreed to come to my hotel. It occurred to me after I hung up that we didn't bother to describe ourselves, both of us clearly aware that as two half-breeds we would have no trouble recognizing each other. Later, I saw him when he walked into the restaurant and watched as he scanned faces at the tables. I observed the instant glow of recognition and his smile when he saw me and walked over without hesitation. I couldn't help but reflect on a lifetime of experiences with the mixed blessings of a face that often stands out in a crowd.

Byron launched swiftly into his story. His mother met his father while studying English in the United States but returned to Okinawa alone and gave birth to Byron in 1969. She decided she was unable to raise him as a single working mom and gave Byron to her older brother and his wife to bring up. Though Byron grew up with two parents, his home life was chaotic and the family dysfunctional. Byron remained in their household throughout his school years, fighting constantly with those who tried to bully him, particularly when tensions flared between the locals and their American occupiers.

The name "Byron" branded him as the child of an American. Though he lacked the American family name that would announce to others that he was the child of a legally married couple, the American first name lent a certain air of legitimacy. It also set him apart from his classmates, though it allowed them the comfort of calling him by a name that they felt fit his face.

Byron still doesn't know his father's name. Despite his pleas, his mother went to her grave with her lips still sealed. Fantasies of meeting his father one day that permeated his childhood and adolescence have now vanished, reappearing only in his dreams. Still, the hurt remains. He tells me, "Can you imagine, not knowing your roots? There is nothing more painful."

In daily life Byron still deals with his unknown father's legacy, manifest in his face. From childhood, Byron has been treated like a foreigner on his home island. Conversations begin with "What are you?" People praise him condescendingly: "You speak such good Japanese!" He is infantilized regularly: "You are so good at using chopsticks!" He explains simply, "I am Japanese!" "I am Okinawan!" Such experiences are exasperating and have fed Byron's identity questions.

Byron went through a period in which, like many other Amerasians, he dreamed of his escape from the islands to the United States as a way of leaving discrimination behind and being in a place where he fit in. So at twenty-two he picked up his guitar and went to Los Angeles to become a rock star. As he had hoped, he found that physically he fit in easily for the first time in his life. That was such a relief. But as soon as he opened his mouth, he became a foreigner. Americans asked him, "What are you?" He felt like an alien. People couldn't figure out why he couldn't understand or speak English. And they were puzzled further when he explained that the reason was because he was Okinawan. He then thought it might be easier for Americans to understand if he said he was Japanese. But it didn't help at all. "You're Japanese?" was all they could say. After a few years of living like this, once again a "foreigner," Byron reluctantly abandoned his dreams of becoming an American and returned home to Okinawa.

He wandered aimlessly for a few years until the day he heard about the new school. An Amerasian school was like a dream come true. This was the school he wished he could have found as a youth. He imagined that contributing to the school would give his life meaning and help other young people survive better in their tough environment. He could be a mentor for kids like himself and guide them from the lessons he had learned growing up in Okinawa. He could be a big brother and they could be like the younger brothers and sisters he never had. Byron saw the school as a way out of his solitude, a community he could be part of for the first time in his life. He rushed over and offered to do whatever they wanted him to do, and so became the bus driver and all-purpose handyman.

I got to see the school the day after I arrived. Byron picked me up at my hotel and drove me up the coast a few miles to the city of Ginowan. We had another chance to talk as we were soon stuck in traffic. Okinawa is the only part of Japan where the famed train system does not exist, so we were in a car like everyone else on the island. We soon came to the familiar barbed wire–topped fences and passed the gates of Camp Kinser on the left, one of the military bases that spread all over the island. One is never far from either the ocean or a military base. Winding down a back road we came to a small sign that announced the AmerAsian School in Okinawa, and I saw a small, white, two-story building.

Once inside, we walked down a hall and opened a door to a small classroom. Kids with clearly mixed faces like mine looked at us, some fascinated, others disinterested. I felt connected to them and yet conscious that I was also different, more American than most, not Okinawan at all, and only there temporarily. But I imagined that this is a place where I might find meaning too, if not to the extent that Byron seemed to have found a home.

Victims, Hybrids, and Pure Bloods

That evening I gave a public talk with Tanaka Hiroshi, a nationally known figure in the movement for rights of Korean residents. I was honored to be on the same program with such a distinguished activist scholar whom I admired. I was surprised that it was me whom the media put in the spotlight: a local newspaper had interviewed me and carried a full-page spread with huge photos the day before the event. Apparently my story was seen as attractive to readers: a successful Amerasian, a Harvard graduate and Tokyo University professor who publicly talked about the issue. The next morning's daily again gave big coverage of the talk, including my major arguments. One was that the school is good for what it does, providing a refuge for kids being bullied at public school. I also voiced my objection to the school becoming a place of segregation where the Amerasian children were isolated, and said that the national government had to take responsibility for providing multicultural and bilingual education and a safe place for all students to find dignity in diversity.

Following my lecture in Naha, a woman in the audience asked a simple but challenging question: "Why is this issue important for Okinawans?" I answered that American Okinawans are a minority within a minority and can provide majority Okinawans with a different view of themselves. With a long history of oppression, Okinawans understandably have a collective victim consciousness. But as objects of discrimination by majority Okinawans, Amerasians can teach majority Okinawans about their own racism. I am not sure how my message was received. I had touched the taboo subject of prejudice in minorities. Some in the audience nodded, others looked puzzled, and some were clearly perturbed. I have only heard one Okinawan express this idea—Oshiro Yasutaka, former director of International Social Assistance of Okinawa and Okinawa University professor.[2]

After the talk, Byron took me out to a pub for some late night food and drinks. We were accompanied by Uezato Kiyomi, one of the mothers who founded the new school. She is different from the others, as her child's father is a prominent Okinawan and she herself was once considered for the office of vice governor by Ota Masahide, an esteemed scholar of Okinawan history who became governor. I knew of Kiyomi because she had authored a book, *Amerajian: Mou hitotsu no Okinawa* (Amerasians: Another Okinawa), which explains how the school's use of *Amerasian* places the situation in Okinawa firmly in the context of American hegemonic power in Asia and the widespread military bases, for which Amerasian children become a "social problem."[3]

It took a while, but Kiyomi finally told me that one thing about my talk bothered her: she cannot tolerate hearing Okinawans described as aggressors. "To me," she said earnestly, "Okinawans are victims."

The problems of identity that loom so large for many Amerasians are complicated by the complexity of identity for majority Okinawans. A history of oppression includes the subjugation of the Ryukyuan kingdom by outside forces and the horrible atrocities and pain suffered in World War II. The massive U.S. military bases provide eternal fuel for an Okinawan metanarrative of oppression that erases contradictory memories, disparities among the population, and intimate connections with Japan. It is similar to a Japanese national narrative of victimization, Japanese to Americans, that dangerously induces amnesia of Japanese aggression in Asia and the suffering it caused.

In my negotiations with a major Tokyo publisher that released my writing on Amerasians, my editors reminded me of the need to be sensitive to the feelings of Okinawan readers. As with any minority group, it is extremely difficult to talk of prejudice and discrimination related to Okinawans except in a way that shows them as victims. Glorification and romanticization of Okinawan tradition and customs are promoted, and of course, raving about the blue sea, tropical fish, and white sandy beaches is also allowed. This delicate and celebratory treatment is one way to try to mollify the anger and resentment Okinawans feel about enduring the burden of the military bases for the rest of Japan for more than sixty years.

Some Okinawan teachers still reveal the tendency to paint everything in terms of victimization even as they take a new approach to using Amerasians for educational purposes. They do not completely shun the Amerasians—some even have their classes visit the AmerAsian School. But the purpose is to show students the "pathetic" children who have been abandoned by their callous American fathers. "Why aren't you sad?" a student at the AmerAsian School told me she was asked by a schoolgirl visitor who was apparently surprised and upset that the Amerasians weren't all crying or morose. The visitor's confusion shows that her teacher had failed to tell her class that the reason Amerasians are in their own school is not because their fathers abandoned them but because of discrimination by majority Okinawans. The teacher was denying this disturbing reality, and instead used Amerasians as a teaching tool to raise consciousness against the U.S. military, a role that Amerasians have played for many years.

The problem of victimization is also significant for Amerasians, who may be seen as lying at the bottom of a line of aggressors: Americans oppress Japanese, Japanese victimize Okinawans, Okinawans subjugate Amerasians. Some of my earlier writing depicted Amerasians as lost in the "shadows of oppression" and caught "between a rock (the United States) and a hard place (Japan)," asserting that Okinawans replicate the structure of domination and exclusion that has been so oppressive for them.[4] But I have met Amerasians like Byron who recognize that victims—whether on an individual or group level—are prevented from achieving maturity. To change their lives Amerasians need to overcome a self-image as unfortunate victims of their American fathers or Okinawan society. That way of thinking gives them someone to blame for their misfortune, but doesn't help them to rise above the situation.

Byron resists defining himself as a victim of hostility or neglect—although those influences are manifest in his life—and involves himself in activity that is positive and affirming. Struggles with identity involve efforts to overcome old limiting stereotypes and embrace alternative and empowering images. Amerasians and other mixed ancestry people in Japan today can draw on growing positive expressions of the value of mixed identities in both the United States and Japan. New images of hybridity and creolization celebrate the worth and meaning in living in borderlands or crossroads of cultural worlds. Across Asia, the mixed look has become fashionable and desirable. "Transnational" persons are considered to have experiences and sensitivities that can lead them toward understanding how to live in this century. Amerasians may attach themselves to these images as a way to appreciate their diverse backgrounds and make sense of their place in the world.

Class becomes a dividing factor in determining which Amerasians can acquire the necessary tools to fit this ideal image. Some can wield English ability and multicultural knowledge as weapons. But these new images pose difficulties for many like Byron who find it impossible to join in the celebration of their hybridity. They may struggle with the new images as much as the old and still be perceived as deficient—an Amerasian who can't speak English.

I am an Amerasian who can speak English. When I was tempted to think that "we Amerasians" were alike, I was surprised to hear Byron admit that he had described me to his friend as "Amerika." This meant that I was not one of "them," but one of those who had been privileged to receive an English education while living in my father's home and in my father's country. "They" were the children raised among Okinawans, deprived of their fathers, deprived of English, and scorned by others. Their inability to respond to the demand to "say something in English" was the telltale sign to others that they were not only undoubtedly illegitimate but also without specialness—no different and even less significant than the Okinawan next door. In the United States, it is commonplace for Japanese American kids to be monolingual, English-speaking, with no sense of stigma or shame that they cannot speak Japanese. But in Okinawa, being monolingual in Japanese and not speaking English is a distinguishing characteristic, usually determined by class, that stigmatizes a mixed ancestry person.

Byron's labeling of me as "Amerika" showed the gap that exists between the "privileged" Amerasians and those who are considered by others and often by themselves as "disadvantaged." Others reminded me that my imagined community of "us" didn't exist. A public school child told me that those at the private English schools lived in another world that he could only dream about. And a boy with a black father claimed that those with white fathers had entirely different experiences than his and far less painful. The encounters of American-raised Amerasians like me with *shima haafu* like Byron are permeated with deep misunderstanding, as our longings are completely opposite. Amerasians from America who return to Japan long for things Japanese (or Okinawan), while the *shima haafu* long for their idealized image of America. We may gaze at each other with wonder, envy, and resentment.

But the connections may also be felt. Some Amerasians I met seemed to wish that we mixed bloods were all somehow united. A boy from the private Christian school raised by both parents declared affinity with those raised by single mothers, and a girl with a white father told me that she regarded those with black fathers as part of the same group.

The day after my lecture I got together with Byron and two other Amerasians at a coffee shop. All three speak Japanese, but only a little English. They talked of how they first experienced the empowering aspects of regarding themselves as *daburu*, the ideal image of the Amerasian promoted by the school and by Okinawan society as well. *Daburu* is a double identity, American and Okinawan, developed through dual education in English and Japanese. But this identity became problematic for them because if *daburu* was the ideal way of being Amerasian, then didn't that make them deviant? We talked of there being different and equally valid ways of being Amerasian, and as the discussion heated up, Byron declared, "We should get up in front of a whole auditorium full of Okinawans and say, 'We are *haafu* and we don't speak English!'" Then he looked at me and said, "You should be our leader!" I wondered whether the boundary between "us," the *shima haafu*, and "them," the American *haafu*, while not removed, had been permeated, and I was accepted as a soul brother or respected elder.

The kind of movement that Byron advocates is hard for Amerasians to engage in, and most visible social action has been initiated and conducted by others, usually their mothers. The AmerAsian School is one example, but mothers have also organized to protest their treatment by the media, particularly in certain books that they felt were especially damaging to their image and that of their children. The inability of Amerasians to get together shows the effects of their isolation and avoidance of each other as a means of evading the disturbing reflection gazing into a mirror. One of the women at our coffee shop meeting, Tomiyama Maria, attempted to start a group in 2000 called the Children of Peace Network but it suffered a swift demise from lack of participants. The ones who did contact her were only interested in finding their fathers. Byron now has the goal of starting a nonprofit for Amerikakei Uchinanchu (American Okinawans)—the term he advocates—believing that the need is there and people will come if they find a safe place to be together.

Though he lacks the support of a group, Byron asserts that while a double identity is appropriate under certain conditions, it is not universal. Yet *daburu* is often promoted as the only way to be a well-adjusted Amerasian, with deviations seen as deficient. Those like Byron who want to shout out "We are *haafu* and we don't speak English!" declare that there is no such thing as an Amerasian identity that must be nourished as an essential, fundamental, and genetic property of all Amerasians, possessed by all Amerasian children, whatever their background. He tells us that class, culture, and gender are integral components of identity rather than something added on to a basic ethnic identity.

Byron eventually split with the AmerAsian School, feeling that he was not seen as a role model and was in fact a symbol of just the kind of Amerasian the school did not want their kids to become.

> "I realized I'm not daburu, and can't become daburu. I don't have the American culture, how could I? And I don't want it. This is all I am, Uchinanchu. There's nothing wrong with haafu like us, we can't speak English, that's all. Even if I couldn't be daburu I'm still a whole person, not half but completely Okinawan."

The Sound of Sanshin

The loss of the AmerAsian School from Byron's life left him once again on his own. His five-year period of trying to be American had ended and now his dream of being *daburu* was also over. He still felt confused every day about who he was. One day he had a life-changing transformation.

"One night at a pub I heard the sound of the sanshin, and it was like being hit in the head with a hammer. The impact was like a bolt of lightning! The song was 'Juban Kuruchi,' and the lyrics tell the story of how in life there are things that each of us is born to do. I realized that I had been trying to erase the reality that I was born and raised here on this island. Suddenly as I listened to the music my hardened heart melted and I was freed."

Byron put away his electric guitar and devoted himself to study of the sanshin. He set out on a road of discovery, immersing himself in the study of Ryukyuan *minyo*, traditional folk music. Music led him to language, as he wanted to understand the words of the songs he was singing. But the Okinawan language is a language no longer used in daily life, understood only by the middle-aged, spoken only by the elderly. Byron felt anger at the society that did not value its own language, though he understood the history of oppression, forced assimilation, and self-chosen accommodation that had drastically reduced the use of the language. He sought out his elders and listened to their stories about learning Japanese and how they developed shame about their own language in schools where teachers hung the *hogen fuda* around the neck of the unfortunate child caught speaking his native tongue. Byron learned about the politics that labeled the Okinawan language a dialect, indicating it was "a language without an army." I asked Byron what the language means to him.

"I have always been asked, 'What are you?' To show people who I am, I studied the language. I have been discriminated my whole life—'You're not Japanese!' 'You're not Okinawan!' 'You're not American!' I felt like I was always out of place. So to make my own place, I used language. This face tells people that I am a Westerner and should

speak English. And people can't imagine I can speak Okinawan.
But the reality is I was born here. I am Uchinanchu. I strongly wish
people could understand my situation. By using Uchinaguchi maybe
they can."

Byron's wife Yoko explains:

> "His background, born and raised here, is no different from others,
> but people ask, 'How long have you been here?' and it hurts to be con-
> stantly treated in that way. At times he rebelled and fought back. Then
> he realized he could defend his identity through language. He wears
> it as armor. It became tiring to keep saying, 'I'm Uchinanchu!' 'I'm
> Uchinanchu!' 'I'm Uchinanchu!' 'Don't discriminate against me!' Now,
> rather than having to declare it, he lives it, he embodies it."

Byron has dedicated his life to being Okinawan. Seeing the power
in words, Byron diligently studied a language that is known by only
a few people his age. Yet it is a symbol of ethnic pride in the face of
assimilation to mainstream Japanese ways. His ability to speak this
language proclaims his authenticity. His family name is also unique, as
he proudly pronounces it in its original form of *Fija* rather than *Higa*,
which is the way the Japanese taught islanders to say their own name
many years ago.

The combination of language and music is compelling, and Byron
has empowered himself to walk proudly in his community. He was
asked to teach classes in Uchinaguchi. He was invited to write a regular column introducing the language in an Okinawan daily newspaper. And Byron campaigns actively for preservation of the language.

> "When a language is lost a whole culture is lost! In a culture is
> dance, songs, pottery, clothing, architecture, food. Our language and
> culture have been lost through assimilation to Japanese and Western
> standards. Young people can't speak the language any more and think
> Okinawan is a dialect. I argue all the time that it is a language; even
> UNESCO has declared it a language. I think it is natural that elemen-
> tary, junior, high school kids learn Okinawan."

Byron's proficiency in Okinawan and passion to help others appreciate its beauty and tragedy has taken him to other countries. He has

been invited to teach intensive classes at Duisburg-Essen University in Germany and the University of Hawaii. He cleverly integrates Okinawan history and politics in his classes and humorously imitates tourists who come to Okinawa only interested in diving in the aqua blue sea and tasting its tropical delights, ignorant about its noble and tragic history and indifferent to the military bases. Teaching about Okinawa to Okinawans and others further strengthens Byron's identity.

Another Epiphany

I was curious about Byron's love life, and recalled a saying: "Tell me who you love and I'll tell you who you are." I suspected that Byron would only be open to an Uchinanchu partner. I know that I wanted a partner who was Japanese, but was that desire simply because I was Japanese, or was I trying to fill a gap in my life and make myself more Japanese? Did I think I would be more accepted as Japanese by having a Japanese woman by my side? Would a white woman at my side have whitened me? Similarly, did Obama's choice of Michelle Robinson answer his complex needs as a self-identified black man who had been raised in a white family without a black father? Does Michelle make him more black?

The choices of partners of multiracial people are often related to our racial identity. We may become attracted to romantic partners from a particular racial background as an expression of our allegiance to a community. Conscious and unconscious dating and mating decisions reveal something racially significant about one's identity and shifts in identity. It is not hard to imagine why I was attracted only to blondes through high school, then only to Asians, and then fantasized that another mixed Asian would be ideal.

I was sure that Byron wanted an Uchinanchu partner, and so was he. But he had yet another discovery when he encountered Yoko. Despite their mutual attraction and attachment, she clearly did not fit into Byron's plans because she is from Yamagata, a part of northern Japan. As a self-proclaimed but constantly challenged Uchinanchu, he figured he needed to marry one to show his true colors. When he told Yoko he could not marry her because she was Yamatunchu (mainland Japanese), she confronted him with his own prejudice: "How can you complain of discrimination and yet practice it yourself?" It was an epiphany for Byron. They married in 2003 and now Yoko is his partner and greatest supporter. He looked into the heart of prejudice and saw that he himself, who had suffered so much from it, had practiced it against others. It was a source of transformation and healing, for as he accepted himself, his otherness—accepted himself as both victim and victimizer—he also became forgiving of others in many ways. Finding someone who accepted him as he was enabled him to accept himself and go forth as himself, expressing his identity in his native language.

Our life stories now merge in an interesting way, Byron's as an Amerikakei Uchinanchu, mine as an Amerikakei Nihonjin (American Japanese). When we first met, Byron saw mostly differences. He assumed that my life had been easy. It seemed to have had everything that he had missed and longed for—a loving father, a life in America, English. It is true that I have been blessed with many gifts, including those obvious ones. But each gift comes with a price. English was gained; Japanese was lost. Byron was shocked when I told him that my golden life in America included childhood bullying for being a Jap and the pain of my father's alcoholism. At first Byron dismissed my complaints of not being seen as Japanese and said, "It's totally different for you. You can respond in English. And you can go home to America any time you want. I can't."

He is right, I have a far different reality with more choices. I can play the foreigner for people and satisfy their desire to interact with a *gaijin* by responding to them in fluent English. And if I can't stand it any more, I can always return to the United States. Unlike Byron, who would have to find a way to do so, I even have the legal right to live there any time I want.

But Byron has come to understand that I also find it troubling to constantly be seen as a foreigner, to be reminded that what people see in my face is not what is inside me. I am lucky to have two nations, two homes, but to leave one home for the other is done only with regrets and subsequent longings.

I continue to visit Byron on my frequent trips to Okinawa, as we bond over our mutual belief that our lifework is intimately connected to our heritage and experiences. He is the most dramatic example I know of an "American Okinawan" who views his life in ways that offer visions of action instead of victimhood. He puts his life on stage every day, visible on television and radio, at weddings, events, and on the street. From his first words, he presents himself unabashedly as a *shima haafu* who did not know his father and does not speak English. He has become an accomplished player of the traditional Okinawan sanshin music that evokes the soul of Okinawa and enables him to touch the hearts and raise the spirits of his fellow Okinawans. He has empowered himself by mastering Uchinaguchi. He is a living symbol of an American Okinawan, one who "looks American" but is completely Okinawan to a degree that puts others to shame.

"I found out that I am not American despite having American blood and though I have Japanese nationality, I define myself culturally as Uchinanchu. That can be chosen and it has nothing whatsoever to do with the color of skin. One has to build societies where one can choose one's culture and then all kinds of discrimination based on skin color and so on will be dissolved. Otherwise, you could say that I am not a real Uchinanchu because my father is American. But there are plenty of Yamatunchu and Americans learning to play sanshin. Playing sanshin is not something restricted to Okinawans. That's the key concept, being Okinawan culturally. I don't like the ideas of blood or nation (*minzoku*). If you talk about race, which is stupid anyhow, I am the first one to be excluded from being Uchinanchu. But this notwithstanding, nobody in the world at the age of thirty-seven speaks Uchinaguchi as well as I do."

Including himself as Uchinanchu, Byron now includes others, even those with no Uchinanchu blood.

"I am Uchinanchu due to culture. So is my wife. She is from the Tohoku region, but she speaks Uchinaguchi very well. Culturally she has become Uchinanchu. The two of us, who are not Uchinanchu by blood, are Uchinanchu because we love the culture. We enjoy being Uchinanchu culturally, and for me it's good for self-fulfillment. I hate the term *haafu*, which is used to designate people like me; I always wanted to be someone who is whole."

One Sunday I went with Byron to the Radio Okinawa studio where he does his weekly broadcast from two until five o'clock. I watched as he sat across from Yara Etsuko, with a large, hanging microphone, and I listened to them go back and forth in dizzying fashion, animatedly exchanging remarks. I could not understand a word Byron said, just like some listeners. In the broadcast he speaks only in Okinawan, Etsuko only in Japanese. She understands what he says and relays this to the listeners. This radio program has helped propel Byron's image as a true Okinawan and gained him the admiration of young and old alike.

But is Byron fighting a losing battle? In Germany he is asked, "Will the language die?" Byron laughs at the directness of the question before defiantly holding up his sanshin and declaring, "No, because of this! Music lives on and as long as we have the songs to remind us of the words we will save the language. The consciousness of young people is changing too. Older people wanted to become Japanese, but now, it's good to be Okinawan, and people want to learn their own language." Byron is not always so optimistic and sometimes cries out that Okinawans don't take enough pride in their culture.

My latest visit with Byron in summer 2011 leaves me invigorated, as always. I am moved by the way he fights stigmatization, class prejudice, and racism every day. His presentation of self says to others, "I am not who I appear to be. Don't judge me by this appearance; this face is a façade that fools you, it tells you nothing about who I am inside. Yes, there are Okinawans who look like me! And we are not "half," we are not less, we are whole, just like you. I have lived my entire life here; I want people to understand my feelings. I am no different than them."

Byron's new way of being is not without its frustrations. Every day is a struggle against others' perceptions and assumptions. I watched one day as he was being photographed for a magazine. The big smile on his face vanished instantly when a child walked by and shouted out to him in Japanese English, "Haroh!" His super energy was suddenly gone and it took a few minutes for Byron to smile again and resume his ethnic performance for the camera. But he has learned not to let such treatment get him down. We toured a replica of an old Ryukyuan village, and I observed as Byron greeted a group of elderly women who responded to his facility with the language by remarking how unusual it was that such a young man, and Yamatunchu at that, could speak their tongue. Byron took it in stride, explaining to me that in their world, ethnic difference was not between Okinawan and American, but between Okinawan and Japanese.

In searching for identity, Byron found it in sounds, in music, and that led him to words, to language, and that in turn connected him to others, to a community. In the process of healing himself he finds meaning in the circumstances of his birth, and acceptance of the opportunity this has given him to do something that is not only personal but also communal. He discovers that his personal healing releases healing energy to an entire community. In his transformation he experiences vulnerability in such a way that he moves beyond himself and his own personal needs and connects not only with all parts of himself but also with others. Byron has become a cultural healer, with a felt responsibility to work in ways that bring people in touch with what is valuable, seeing beyond differences to a deeper vision of common humanity.

> "I'm a strange person, but perhaps because of that I can so seriously engage myself in the struggle of going around looking here and there for words that I love. . . . If I hadn't been born with a face like this, I wonder what I would be doing."

My warm relationship with Byron tells me he has another challenge ahead of him. I notice I could be the same age as his father and that Byron has started to study English and even writes a little English in e-mails to me. In calling himself Amerikakei Uchinanchu he openly acknowledges his American part, in a way similar to how I have started to call myself Amerikakei Nihonjin. I feel that he is beginning to embrace his complexity by exploring once more his American roots. Not that it would ever replace being Uchinanchu. But to speak English, to visit the United States, to feel some connection to the father he never knew may be nurturing for Byron. The connection may make him even more whole.

FIVE

Bi Bi Girl

When I was a university student in the early 1980s, I lived for a while in a ramshackle three-story apartment in Cambridge with an assortment of characters. One was Ricardo, a black man with whom I shared the passion of my studies with Dr. Chester Pierce on racial microaggressions. Ricardo clearly understood what Pierce was talking about and related his story of a black friend who approached him tentatively on a Roxbury street corner where he was sitting on the curb. The friend had exclaimed with relief, "Damn, I thought you was some white guy!" I laughed, not because it was funny, but from a feeling of familiarity and camaraderie. When he found out I was a student of psychology, he revealed that his father was Robert Guthrie, the author of *Even the Rat Was White*, a classic in the field that exposed its racial biases. He then told me something that surprised me: he recalled that one of his dad's students had done a dissertation on mixed race Japanese blacks. I was amazed that such a study existed and that it was even possible to do a doctoral dissertation on something that I thought was simply personal. I immediately contacted Dr. Guthrie, who generously offered to send me a copy of Christine Iijima Hall's study on black Japanese.

The discovery of Hall's pioneering work opened exciting possibilities for me as a new graduate student with the realization that I could make biracial identity the subject of my own dissertation. I then found a psychological study of white Japanese by George Kitahara Kich; this was such an exciting find that as soon as I moved to San

Francisco for my clinical internship at the National Asian American Psychology Training Center, I contacted George to discuss his work. Using these two foundational writings as well as studies by historian Paul Spickard and sociologist Michael Thornton, I launched my own study, which a few years later came to fruition.

While I felt that George's original writing on biracial identity development was groundbreaking work of great importance, his later writing on bisexuality seemed irrelevant to my interests and unrelated to me.[1] I recall thinking that the work made a strange connection of biracial and bisexual—it made sense, but I was not curious. I was not ready to go in that direction; I saw it as a distraction from our main issue, which was race. I saw sexuality as a mainstream concern of dominant white folks, and I thought that if we engaged in that dialogue we risked losing our focus and even inviting unwanted attention to our strangeness. A focus on bisexuality also threatened my identity, which was less about being biracial and much more concerned with being Asian. At the time, I was immersed in the dichotomy: either you are Asian or you are not, and I was Asian and determined to prove it. For me, being biracial was simply a form of being Asian, not an existence in the marginal space between the two groups, and I could not see the value in exploring the marginal area of sexuality to promote a biracial Asian agenda.

I now realize that this is what George's writing on bisexuality is all about. Anxiety lay beneath my lack of interest, dismissal of the importance of the issue, and view of it as threatening to negate more important issues. I felt fear regarding bisexuality and was unable to expand my rigid categories of sexuality, though I was trying to do that for race. Had I been more open, I might have learned from self-reflection that this is how others view biraciality—as a threat to their fixed classifications of race.

George explored the margins of sex and race, seeing similarities in biracial and bisexual identity development. He also saw how biracial and bisexual people are oppressed and marginalized by many groups—straights, gays, lesbians, whites, blacks, Asians, and other monoracials. George pointed out that just as monoracial groups have historically positioned biracial people as both idealized and disturbed, bisexuals have been castigated by heterosexuals as well as by gays and lesbians as indecisive, untrustworthy, and irresponsible. Beverly Yuen Thompson has written about what it means to her to be bisexual.

> I am bisexual because I recognize that both women and men have contributed to my life and I want the freedom to choose a partner based on a person's integrity rather than on genitalia. I am firmly located not only in a time when queer people are oppressed but also in a time when a vital queer community has developed that gives me the ability to understand what that identity means. I am one of many people who are bisexual, queer, fence sitters, and switch hitters. I am called queer, dyke, straight. I am comfortable in other people's discomfort. I am loyal to my love for women, I am loyal to my love for men, and I am loyal to my beliefs in feminism and antiheterosexism.[2]

In 2003, I met Wei Ming Dariotis at a conference of the Association of Asian American Studies in San Francisco and had another opportunity to engage in the issue. She had written articles such as "On Growing Up Queer and Hapa" and "On Becoming a Bi Bi Grrrl." By that time, my own identity had evolved from a binary, either/or dichotomous view to one where I felt both/and—firmly planted in different identities and more able to exist in marginal spaces. Secure in the awareness that I am Japanese, Asian, Asian American, I could handle the ambiguity of being Irish and American, though I was not ready to consider the possibility of being white. But I was more open to considering the complexity of a biracial and bisexual identity.

I was first attracted to her name—Wei Ming Dariotis. I often wondered what life would have been like if I had been given a Japanese name. Sometimes I imagined that a real Japanese name would have saved me from the nickname "Ping," which my friends bestowed on me in their attempt to reconcile the dissonance between my face, which labeled me as Oriental, and my name, Steve, which made me seem way too American for them. But what kids would have done with a real Japanese name like Takeshi or Masafumi is easy to imagine.

Wei Ming had a Chinese name but still felt out of place and did not think of herself as Chinese.

> I was raised vegetarian because my (white) father followed a Sikh Master; it was part of his 1960s thing, just like avoiding the draft in Vietnam (which is why I was born in Australia) and marrying his Chinese girlfriend (which is why I was born). So I couldn't eat anything at my stepfather's Chinese family banquets. Through thirteen courses I would sit there asking for, "Another bowl of rice, please?" I may have been the only Chinese person there using a Chinese first name, but it was clear to everyone that, whatever I was, I was not Chinese.[3]

I was also drawn to the circumstances of Wei Ming's upbringing. It seemed that she had the kind of childhood some of us dream about—raised in multicultural San Francisco, surrounded by Chinese family—the ideal place to be Asian. But what if one was an Asian who others thought didn't look Asian? Rather than Asian, one would be something different, something strange, appearing out of place in one's community, even in one's own family. Wei Ming lived on the edge of Chinatown with a first-generation Chinese mother from Hong Kong, a Chinese American stepfather, and their child, her little brother. But instead of making her feel Chinese, it made her feel not-Chinese.

> I didn't look like I fit into the picture. When people saw our family they would think my mom, my stepfather, and my brother fit each other. But who was this other person? "Who was I?"[4]

Wei Ming's family experience, in which she is the one member viewed as not Asian, is very different from that of many other mixed Asians and raises a fundamental paradox. Wei Ming's cultural surroundings were Chinese, yet her salient feature in this environment was being not-Chinese. I, like many Asians raised in white communities in the United States, was surrounded by mainstream culture, yet my salient feature was being not-white. Such circumstances can create a rift between one's actual culture and identity. In my case, besides the influence of my mother and sisters (which, of course, was huge), I was much like my white friends in terms of culture, yet I was labeled "Oriental" and I ambivalently accepted this identity. In Wei Ming's case, by the time she got to college she already thought she knew that she wasn't Chinese, but did not know what she was.

> While I had a good grasp on who I was, "Wei Ming Dariotis," I did not understand the mixed heritage the name implied; I did not know what I was. I did not have any clear sense of my identity as a unitary whole. Instead, my childhood and adolescence were filled with the intense demands other people made on my identities.[5]

A great discovery for Wei Ming was that she did not have to fit herself into her images of authentic Chinese or white Americans. To meet other Chinese Americans like her was liberating. This began when she went to a meeting of a Chinese American student group in college.

> I went, and instead of being surrounded by Chinese Americans who spoke Cantonese and whose grandparents had been held on Angel Island, I was surrounded by East Coast Asian Americans who all knew the same basics I did—how to use chopsticks, and also how, when someone asks you what you are, you say, "American." Suddenly I didn't have anything to prove.[6]

Wei Ming began to see that she did not have to be like the "authentic" Chinatown Chinese Americans she knew from experience and media images. Nor did she need to be like the second- or third-generation East Coast Asian Americans she met who had grown up in white communities. Though she did not consciously wish to pass for "white," knowing that was something she could never really be, she had grown up thinking she was white-ish, a kind of European "ethnic"—Greek, Italian, Spanish, Jewish—the kind of people she was frequently mistaken for being. It wasn't that she wanted to be any of those things so much as just feeling she wasn't Chinese. She had been so caught up in feeling not-Chinese that she couldn't comprehend the possibility of being Chinese-and-something. But in college, she began to see for the first time that she could be Chinese American while maintaining her various European heritages; she could be both. Wei Ming also developed awareness of how her parents had crossed racial boundaries to be together and began to question gender boundaries.

Sexuality

As for many biracial people, race was the salient feature in Wei Ming's youth. Her identity development, however, was complicated by her emerging feelings of being bisexual. Mixed heritage youth may not be shown ways of adopting a mixed, multiple, or flexible identity, and for queer mixed race youth there is silence about how to deal with their emerging feelings of sexuality in adolescence. The struggles may come one after another, with racial concerns beginning in childhood and issues of sexuality surfacing in the teen years.

> "When I spoke on the annual queer alumni panel for my high school one year, I shared my wish that someone had named bisexual and mixed heritage Asian American as possible identities; having these identities would have saved me the constant angst of struggling with how to answer the 'What are you?' question."

Going off to college was a chance for experimentation, and in her first week she joined in a sensitivity training exercise in which participants sat in a circle and told their "coming out" stories.

> I still remember how terrifying it was to say, "My name is Wei Ming and I am a lesbian." We didn't have the choice of saying bisexual . . . at the time I accepted this but now I see it as a negation of the experience of bisexuals.[7]

College was a time of great discovery. The chance to read feminist books, develop feminist consciousness, and seek out feminist organizations fundamentally changed the way to understand herself and the world around her. Wei Ming met people whose politics and sexual orientation were diverse, and the familiar struggle between seeing herself as Asian or Greek reemerged in the experience of agonizing between the choice of gay or straight. Although neither represented her feelings, the messages from both the gay community and dominant straight society were the same: choose. But was it possible to choose? In the same way she knew she was not just Chinese, she knew she was not lesbian.

At this time Wei Ming realized that bisexuality was an option, and the identity that most accurately describes who she is. Her multiracial identity struggles told her that to claim a bisexual identity would be a hardship because others would analyze her through their monosexual template of understanding. She knew that people would be confused by what they perceived to be unnatural or problematic because both her racial and sexual identities would cross lines of separation. But being a mixed race person might help her navigate borders of sexuality; she knew the difficulty of having to explain her race and also enjoyed the benefits of being in more than one group. Bisexuality seemed the natural conclusion.

While sexual identity may seem natural for the individual, it can pose problems for others. In Karen Allman's experience, her lesbianism somehow whitened her in the eyes of others. To them, lesbian means white, and an Asian lesbian was beyond their imagination.

> An Asian American professor, one with whom I had often spoken about our shared experiences with racism on our campus, once told me, "You can pass for white any time." I had to stop myself from immediately running to look at myself in the mirror, and I must confess that I spent a lot of time scrutinizing my appearance in the following weeks. Had my features suddenly shifted, perhaps in the middle of the night, when I was sleeping? She seemed to think that my Asian heritage was something hidden within me, a secret that only she could see, and that racism was something I could choose to experience or not. I wondered if perhaps my lesbianism somehow "whitened" me in her eyes, and I wanted to tell her that lesbians, too, wondered "what" I was, had never heard of Asian lesbians, marveled over my command of English, and wondered if my mother was a "war bride" or a "geisha." How does one negotiate a multiple, situated identity if race, gender, and sexual orientation are taken for granted as so separate and boundaried?[8]

Karen's musing on her face in the mirror reminds me of my own reactions when someone tells me I don't look Asian or Japanese. The statement always jars me, upsets me, and leaves me confused and wanting to sneak off to the bathroom to check my face in the mirror.

The beginning of an essay by Claire Huang Kinsley captures this strange feeling of wondering and not knowing "What do I look like?"

There are many people who will tell you what they think. But sometimes you just don't want to hear it anymore.

To start with, I don't know what I look like.

I'm not complaining. There are plenty of worse fates. But still, how odd—to look at yourself in the mirror, to see the face you know best of any face in the world, and to ask yourself, "What do I look like?" and to not really know.[9]

I tell myself, "I am Asian, therefore I look Asian." So I always think I look Asian. But I know that what is happening is not simply logical and cognitive in the other person or in me. I know that others are dealing with their own issues and that affects their perceptions. And I know that something strange is going on inside me—something deeply emotional. A wound is being reopened, or is it now just an old scar that is being rubbed the wrong way? I didn't want people to notice that I looked different when I was a child. But they did and they told me I didn't look like them. I wanted to look like them but I didn't, and that was the source of a lot of childhood heartache, which also led to solidifying my Asian identity.

Queers and Communities

While any biracial person may experience this focus on racial ambiguity, the complication expressed by the women in this chapter is how the association with sexuality seems to whiten the biracial person in the eyes of the observer. In the eyes of the gay or lesbian activist, the person's Asianness may disappear. A gay biracial Asian friend told me that a non-Asian gay person he worked with confided, "I don't even think of you as Asian, certainly not as a person of color, just as one of us." But among Asians, he hid his homosexuality for fear that he would be ostracized, so he found that either context threatened his identity as a biracial, bisexual person.

Appearance is further complicated by the attribution of sexual "passing" by persons who do not reveal their sexual identity to others. Bisexual individuals who "look straight" may be charged with passing in the dominant society and rejecting their true identity because they won't choose a side, similar to racial passing. Wei Ming asks what privilege of safety her apparent heterosexuality afforded her, while also challenging the assumption of passing.

> What would it mean for me to "pass" as white or heterosexual? What parts of myself would I be "passing by?" . . . But I won't try to "pass" because I know who and what I am. To "pass" would be to lose myself.[10]

But if we can pass—and some try to—what does this mean for our racial status? Wei Ming raises the uncomfortable topic of white privilege and acknowledges that some hapas have it, due to their physical appearance or family background. She states that mixed heritage Asians may have different experiences of racism or privilege and asks if hapas "count" as full Asian Americans.

Where does this leave the biracial, bisexual person? Where does he or she find a home or allies? Not in the dominant society if he "looks queer," "acts queer," or speaks out for queer rights. Not in gay and lesbian communities if he or she dates people of the opposite sex. And not in Asian American communities, where a bisexual person occupies an even more tenuous position than other mixed individuals. Wei Ming writes of the predicament of those of partial European ancestry.

> The logic of ethnic nationalism often disparages homosexuality as much as heterosexual dating outside the ethnic group—particularly "dating white." In as much as homosexuality is also often seen as a "White disease," queer mixed heritage youth of partial European ancestry are often perceived as traitors to the group identity.[11]

Many activists fight discrimination by making a clear demarcation between ally and enemy. In the same way that biracial people who do not choose the minority side may be placed with the enemy, bisexuals who do not choose can become the enemy. The great danger is in buying into the binary opposition of race and sexuality, the either/or dichotomizing that leads to "us" versus "them" consciousness and a rationalization for violence and oppression. Ideas of sexual and racial purity lead only to division, disempowerment, and exclusion, while inclusion of those who cross borders, who declare that they are both/ and, who refuse to be limited and contained in rigid categories, is a way of fighting against discrimination. Recognition and acceptance of identities and ways of being that cross borders of sexuality will alleviate the alienation that bisexuals face in the gay and lesbian community as well as in the straight world.

Bisexuals may question their own orientation, some agonizing over which box to check, feeling that the heterosexual lifestyle confines them—questioning that if they are not heterosexual, then they must, as women, be lesbian, yet knowing that they cannot be lesbian if they are attracted to men. They may find hope in discovering a bisexual identity. They may also discover that the problem is in the system, the structure, and not with them. The problem is that the rules of the game do not fit the reality, leaving one falling through the cracks of the binary opposition paradigm of identity. Rather than be forced to commit to one identity over another, it is the definitions that have to change so that those who have been marginalized out of the "box" can be included. Multiracial bisexual people draw courage from camaraderie, knowing that they are not alone in a world that tries to deny their existence and knowing that merely by existing they challenge stereotypes and the status quo.

Don't Worry, Be Hapa?

Another area in which Wei Ming has emerged as a distinct voice is in the promotion and then the abandonment of the term *hapa* for mixed race Asian people. She was part of a generation for whom the word became a self-identifying label. Originally a Hawaiian word, *hapa* means part or mixed and was first used as *hapa haole*, meaning part Hawaiian and part white. In Hawaii it came to mean other mixtures, including Asian and white, and was later used on the mainland, beginning in the Japanese American community in California in the 1980s. The Hapa Issues Forum was started in 1992 as a response to the exclusion of multiethnic members from the Japanese American community at a time when questioning of multiethnic people's right to participate was also common in pan-Asian communities. The organization, which disbanded in 2007, encouraged understanding and inclusivity in Asian American communities, provided a space for people to feel comfortable about their identity, and did political advocacy work. The term *hapa* remains popular as a recognizable group label and term of self-identification, and symbolizes community for increasing numbers of the 2.1 million Asian or Pacific Islander Americans, 16.8 percent of the population, who identified with multiple heritages in the 2000 Census.[12]

Living in Japan, I viewed the increasing use of *hapa* from a distance, although I did join a Tokyo-based group called the Hapa Club. My familiarity with the word dates to the mid 1980s when Lane Hirabayashi declared it a term of self-definition (see chapter 3). His assertion was prompted by its controversial meaning and use, since some Japanese Americans were opposed to what they deemed a term with negative connotations as used in Hawaii.

After using *hapa* for fifteen years, in 2007 Wei Ming wrote her essay "Hapa: The Word of Power," in which she explained why she would no longer use it. In a show of solidarity with fellow activists, Wei Ming decided that there was too much irony and hypocrisy in the use of the word by Asian Americans, that it was even a colonizing violence in which she had participated, and she declared that it was time to recognize that the use of the word *hapa* by herself and other Asian Americans caused some people pain. She first described how much the term meant to her.

> When I learned the word "Hapa" I felt as though a whole new world had opened up to me. Before this, when anybody asked me, "What are you?" I had to answer, "Chinese Greek Swedish English Scottish German Pennsylvania Dutch." This was a list of my ancestry. It is my heritage. However, this list is not my identity. Heritage does not equal identity. "Hapa" gave me such an identity. Instead of worrying, "Where am I going to find another Chinese Greek Swedish English Scottish German Pennsylvania Dutch American?" I realized I already had a Hapa community
>
> The word "Hapa" made me something more than just a half Chinese or a fake Filipino. . . . The word "Hapa" has given us a space

of our own, a place where we can be us, without having to explain ourselves. Anyone entering the space created by the word accepts our identity. . . . The word "Hapa" makes my community visible, that is its power. . . . It provides a sense of community and identity in one simple word.[13]

Wei Ming then explained the dilemma of applying the term to anyone of mixed Asian or mixed Pacific Islander heritage when it implies Native Hawaiian mixed heritage. She framed the issue in terms of the relative power of Asian Americans in this context.

This is not merely a question of trying to hold on to a word that, like many words encountered in the English language, has been adopted, assimilated, or appropriated. This is a question of power. Who has the power or right to use language? Native Hawaiians, in addition to all of the other ways that their sovereignty has been abrogated, lost for many years the right to their own language through oppressive English-language education.

Given this history and given the contemporary social and political reality (and realty—as in real estate) of Hawaiian, the appropriation of this one word has a significance deeper than many Asian Americans are willing to recognize. To have this symbolic word used by Asians, particularly by Japanese Americans, as though it is their own, seems to symbolically mirror the way Native Hawaiian land was first taken by European Americans, and is now owned by European Americans, Japanese and Japanese Americans and other Asian American ethnic groups that numerically and economically dominate Native Hawaiians in their own land.

A word used to give power to one community, while taking power away from another, is not a word I can use in good conscience. I will not use "Hapa" any more in my academic writings as a shorthand for Asian Americans of mixed heritage.[14]

Wei Ming predicted that it would be hard to abandon the use of *hapa*, though she also noted how the Hapa Issues Forum has folded and the Hapa Clubs that had started on so many college campuses in the late 1990s and early 2000s have mostly abandoned this term in favor of more general mixed heritage inclusion. I do not know how many people who once used *hapa* have been reluctantly swayed by Wei Ming's position or by the arguments of Native Hawaiians condemning its use by others. At a spring 2011 conference on Critical Mixed Race Studies, I did not see or hear the word. Of course, this could be because Wei Ming was one of the organizers of the conference; it does show that she has not only responsibility but also some power to influence the use or disuse of the word. I know that others, like mixed race scholar Paul Spickard, believe it can be used with respect.

> Hawai'i is a place where a lot of people are mixed, and not just with Haoles and Hawaiians. There are people who are Japanese and Chinese, Korean and Filipino, Portuguese and Black and Samoan, and a lot of other things too. By the 1970s, *hapa* was being used by everybody in Hawai'i to refer to anyone who was mixed. Then Asians from the continental United States visited relatives in Hawai'i and brought the word back home with them. And they started applying it to anybody who was mixed and part Asian.
>
> I sympathize with resentments some Hawaiians may have at their word being appropriated by Asian Americans. But that is the nature of language. It morphs and moves. It is not anyone's property. . . . The Hawaiian origins of the word *hapa* are worthy of respect. The people in this book use the term respectfully. That is all anyone can ask.[15]

Wei Ming does not suggest a replacement word but asks that we find a name we can all love calling ourselves and that also causes no one else pain. She offers the possibility of reshaping the word rather than destroying it, and I wonder whether we can use it with an inclusive meaning, not as "our" term signifying mixed Asian, but with a broader understanding that acknowledges where it came from by including mixed Native Hawaiians in its definition.

I think that the Hawaiians who raised the issue and the support of Wei Ming and others have helped to educate us about the power of words, their complex origins, and how our usage can be erroneous or even offensive. It is ironic how the once colonized (Asians) are accused of being the colonizers, the oppressed becoming like their oppressors. The anger that some Native Hawaiians feel at what they perceive as ignorant misappropriation of language is understandable. Placing the use of *hapa* in the context of colonization and oppression is an important education for those who do not know history and are shocked to learn that *hapa* is not a new term meaning only "half Asian."

Understanding the evolution of the term reminds us that language evolves and words take on new connotations or denotations. Many of these linguistic alterations happen as a result of colonialism, though some are simply the borrowing of concepts. University of Hawaii professor at the Kamakakuokalani Center for Hawaiian Studies Jonathan Kay Kamakawiwoʻole Osorio offers a view of the word as a gift.

> Incorporating this word in order to recontextualize ethnicity in California in ways that make intermarriage less threatening, more acceptable—I don't find that upsetting at all. I think that makes sense. But I would hope that [non-Hawaiians] would understand that it came from a culture and history where intermarriage was seen as a natural thing. . . . I think that it's another one of those words that Hawaiʻi, through its own historical experience, can sort of "gift" to American society. Gift, theft—those are sometimes really interlocked words.[16]

I personally don't use it much, partly because I have lived in Japan so long and therefore don't identify with it, but I can understand why it is so attractive, perhaps like the term *haafu* in Japan. I also do not use either *hapa* or *haafu* much because neither expresses my identity completely. I am interested in creating a separate, distinct space with others who identify as mixed race, but I persist in my efforts to include others and be included within existing groups. While I might explain myself as *haafu* or hapa for convenience, I do not want to be marginalized as different, but included by expanding the boundaries of traditional categories like Japanese, Japanese American, or Asian American.

If I were to use *hapa*, I would do so with an understanding that it is a gift from Native Hawaiians, indigenous people who have a rich culture and history that has endured more than two centuries of outside intruders seizing their land, destroying their health, exploiting their culture, and taking their language. If I were to use it for myself,

I would respect its origins and use by others. I would use it in an inclusive way—after all, it means a person of mixed ancestries, and that is what I am.

Community Healer

Wei Ming's work continues on the biracial, bisexual frontiers as a community healer, serving as a voice of conscience calling out for inclusion of Asian Americans in the dominant society, and biracials and bisexuals in Asian American communities. She reminds Asian Americans that they are not only excluded but can also exclude others, like biracials, gays, lesbians, and bisexuals. She challenges Asian Americans to be aware of their own racism, their power and privilege, and to understand how the oppressed can also be the oppressor. This work requires self-reflection and courage, forcing Wei Ming to look within herself and use herself as an agent of personal and social change. Over time, she has realized that her agency can be nuanced and need not only take an active form such as protest on the street. Being in a particular place at a particular time, simply making others aware of her difference, can be another.

Wei Ming knows that her difference consists of more than just race. Her activism in Asian American communities involves bringing queer issues to the fore as well. She knows that by reminding people that it is possible to love men and to love women, that bisexuality is legitimate, she can have a profound effect on others' lives. She does not limit this openness to her circle of friends; she has come out to her students as well. Once, a gay student thanked her, letting her know that he had never felt as safe as he did in her classroom. She has since made it a priority to make her classroom a space of safety and understanding for students, no matter their race, sex, or sexual orientation.

Wei Ming challenges the boundaries of groups, asserting that being queer does not make one less Asian American, nor does being Asian American make one less queer. She questions the lines of authenticity, inclusion, and exclusion that dilute power and calls for acceptance of diversity among Asian and Asian Pacific Americans as a way of empowerment. She envisions a wider concept of community that includes embracing the issues brought to our attention by women, queers, South Asians, mixed Asians, or others. She encourages us to not be divided, to connect with multiple, overlapping communities of people and to make the circle bigger and bigger. "Identity is a fluid and fluctuating quality that depends as much on sharing stories with others as on discrete identifiers. Thus, I find my identity is never just about me, it is most importantly about my connection to others."

SIX

I Am Your Illusion,
Your Reality, Your Future

It is easy to imagine Rudy as a hip-hop artist. When he tells me that he was part of a group called Aztec Tribe that released several albums from 1991 to 2003, I can picture a young Rudy Guevarra "rockin' the mic." He says he always loved hip-hop, and when he first heard Kid Frost's record *La Raza* in 1990, he knew he wanted to get involved as an artist. To hear a Chicano rap on a record with music that was also culturally familiar resonated with him. Rudy had already written poems and experimented with hip-hop at house parties, but it was this record that inspired him to become an artist himself and with his friends make music that represented who they were as a multiethnic Chicano rap group—and put their city, San Diego, on the map.

Young Rudy was also involved in gangs. He got into it with his cousins, rebelling against his strict father and finding a different kind of "family" that allowed him to express his anger and frustrations, even violently at times. He dropped out of community college in 1990 and spent five and a half years making music, running the streets, and getting into trouble.

> "I could be who I wanted and do what I wanted without any consequence (or so I thought). I found fighting and getting into trouble liberating and exciting. I felt immortal, especially when I escaped incidents that could have left me dead. I am definitely not proud of the things I have done in the past and wish I could take back many things,

but it was a road I decided to take and in the process I grew to understand who I was and eventually, how I did not want to end up."

Rudy learned through his experiences about himself and how he
wanted to live his life. Though he rebelled against his father, he also
learned from him. It would take some years for Rudy to work through
his youthful issues, but his parents served throughout this period as
guides, teaching him by example in how they lived their lives.

"Although my father was strict with me, I always remembered his
words (though I pretended not to listen) about having an education
and not doing hard manual labor like him. My father worked as a
mechanic when I was growing up so I remembered seeing him working on cars at home after he got out of work and on weekends. He
was always working on cars. I remember one day looking at his hands
all greasy and bloody. He showed them to me and said, "You can do
better than this with your life."

Rudy's words bring back memories of my father trudging home
from work after a hard day of manual labor, carrying his lunch box.
He came home late one day from the hospital with his pinkie heavily
bandaged and splinted. It had been crushed by a rock so badly that it
was permanently set without a joint. Over the years, he would show
it to me sometimes when he was drinking heavily and say, "You better
make something of yourself so you don't end up like your old man,
digging ditches." But it took me a long time to figure out whether my
success and achievements made him feel better as a father or worse
about what he viewed as his own failure to achieve anything in his life.
Rudy's mother, like mine, was a simpler role model.

"My mother also worked very hard and always came home from
her job at an industrial laundromat exhausted, but still finding the
time and energy to cook and take care of us. Watching them made
an impression on me that would later resurface and have me question
the time and potential I was wasting hanging out in the streets."

My mother was also a silent saint, working to the point of exhaustion, a superwoman who would work all day and come home and
have dinner on the table for three hungry kids. I remember complain-

ing once when I was a graduate student about how tired I was. My mom laughed and said, "I'm tired for past thirty years!" I never complained again about my hard life of reading and writing. Like Rudy's, my parents were always there as a reminder of why I should value my life, take it in my hands, and do something with it. But changing our lives is not easy, and it may take a shock to wake us up. For Rudy, it was confrontation with death.

"My father would oftentimes get on my case for hanging around with the homeboys and running the streets but I didn't listen to him. I also remember my mother crying a lot because of the things I was doing. It wasn't until I started seeing a lot of my friends get killed in gang and/or drug violence that I started to question my path. That, coupled with the music thing being more and more discouraging and not what I expected it to be made me realize that I needed to change my life and go in a different direction.

"It was at my friend's funeral that I had a major epiphany. Looking at my fallen friend lying in his casket and asking myself, Do you want to be the next one lying in a box with your family all around you mourning your death and wasted life? It was a realization that hit me with a force I cannot express. The images of my parents, their sacrifices and hard work, my father's hands, my mother's exhaustion and tears, the teachers who told me I had potential, all of the bad things I had done, were overwhelming, like a ton of bricks collapsing over me. At that moment I said to myself, enough, and I walked away from it all. I told my cousins and some of my closest friends who were still involved that I was leaving to go back to school and pursue my education, and they respected my decision. Some other friends were not so understanding and talked bad about me, but in the end, I needed to make a change that would be positive and live a life that I, as well as my family and community, could be proud of."

Rudy's poignant story of his painful awakening hits me hard as the parent of two teenage boys. As a father I want to protect them from making mistakes but I know I can't. They want to experience things themselves. I worry about how they will make sense of the times in their lives that others and they themselves will see as "wasted." I wonder how they will find meaning even in activities that we regard as "mistakes." Will they find a way to use life's painful lessons? Will they live without regret for their "failures"? Rudy understands my concerns and explains how he has found a way to accept all that has happened in his life.

"Although my life was not normal in terms of going straight through college after high school, I am thankful for my experiences. Those experiences shaped who I was as a man and how I wanted to keep growing as a human being. When I decided to go back to school I came with a life lived and some experiences that were not those most of my peers shared at the university, which added to the diversity most schools claim they want to include. When I was in discussions about race, racism, violence, police brutality, and particular socioeconomic conditions, I could express an opinion that was not shaped from just reading a bunch of books, but a lived experience. I challenged many assumptions and made people rethink who my communities were and how our lives were shaped by issues such as race, class, gender, and all of the other isms we deal with."

When Rudy walked away from his gang life and cut back on his activities as a hip-hop artist, he decided to put his focus and energy into going back to school and making something of himself through education. He recalled teachers who had seen the good in him and encouraged him. He was able to see the contribution he could make in an educational setting from the lessons he had learned through his tough experiences.

"I always had teachers who saw potential in me, but told me that I had to get my act together; that I was a smart kid, but making bad choices. My high school teachers, Mrs. Edler in particular, said I would be a good teacher if I ever decided to be one. So I thought about those conversations, the fact that my parents worked really hard for us to have better opportunities so I didn't want to waste any more time, my intellect, or others' faith in me."

In 1995, at twenty-three, Rudy returned to school like a hurricane and swept through Southwestern Community College, then transferred to the University of San Diego in 1997, graduating in 2000. From there, he went straight to graduate school at the University of California at Santa Barbara. By 2002 he had a master's degree and by 2007 he had a PhD in history. What motivated him so strongly?

"I had a newfound passion for becoming a professor and teaching others. I found teaching was very similar to performing and that I could engage in positive interactions with others, sharing knowledge and life experiences, especially with my students. I also wanted to make my family and all those who saw potential in me proud. I wanted to do it for myself too, so that I could finally do some good in the world and show others that there is another way to live, to be a man, and to make a positive impact in people's lives, especially our youth, who like me were oftentimes lost and misguided. I wanted to be a role model, a mentor, and someone the youth from the communities I grew up in could relate to and work with. My motivation through college was my family and seeing all of the sacrifices my parents went through for us. My mother was also sick at the time (she had a brain tumor) so in between helping take care of her and going to school, I wanted to make her proud of me. I was worried she would not live to see me graduate but by the grace of our Creator, she lived to see me graduate from college and get my PhD."

Rudy was also motivated by his desire to tell a story that had not been told. He realized when he was a college student that he had heard many wonderful stories in his family. He found a new appreciation for his rich multicultural background, Mexican and Filipino, and how these came together in people like him, Mexipino. He had mentors along the way, like Michael Gonzalez, who first helped him to understand how he could tell this story from a historical perspective and to see that life as a professor could be rewarding and meaningful.

"When I was an undergraduate I knew that I wanted to tell our story as Mexipinos in San Diego. As a child I grew up loving to hear the oral histories of our family, so I guess I always had it in me to be not only our family historian but someone who could tell all of our stories collectively and what it meant to be Mexipino in a multicultural family and community. I was always the kid at the table listening to family stories, intrigued and wanting to know more. It was important for me to tell this story because there were so many of us who were the products of multiple generations of Mexicans and Filipinos intermarrying and having multiethnic Mexipino children. Since no one really told this story yet, I felt compelled to do it, as someone who also came from these communities."

Rudy started to enthusiastically study about mixed race and felt at first that he had found something that addressed his experience. But he quickly realized that there was little written about Asian–Latin American connections, finding few voices of Asian Latinos and Latinas. Those he did find were enough to help him start thinking about how his experience contributed to this collective narrative in Asian American studies and Chicana/o studies, and about what was missing from much of the literature on mixed race peoples of the United States. Most of what he read about other mixed race people did not adequately describe the Mexipina/o experience.

"When I started reading about mixed families and mixed people, I felt like something was missing. There were stories of great conflict due to vast cultural differences between the two sides of the family. But my story was different, because there were deep similarities and connections between the Mexican and Filipino sides of my family. I thought that if I could tell the story it would be an important experience to talk about, a minority/minority experience, a more complex look at race and ethnicity, a working-class story."

A Mexipino Life

So Rudy began his study. Since he loves food, his thoughts first turned to warm memories of childhood meals. Rudy fondly recalls watching his grandfather tend the guava tree he grew for Rudy's mother while singing along to the Mexican rancheros that blared from his tiny radio on a rusty table tray in the backyard. When Rudy's mother called them in for lunch, his *abuelito* would start whistling while Linda Ronstadt's album *Canciones de mi Padre* echoed from the house. They both knew that they would be eating *caldo de res con arroz* (beef soup with rice). Watching his grandfather eat was a celebration of singing, laughing, and smiles. His mother would be warming up tortillas, filling the house with her love and delightful aromas of *comida mexicana* (Mexican food). Rudy also remembers his other grandfather (*tata*) coming by to visit every month from his home in San Francisco.

"I would stand in the kitchen and watch him and my mother cook Filipino delicacies, such as chicken adobo (vinegar marinated meat with rice), *pansit* (noodles), and *lumpia* (egg rolls). He would have us in tears laughing at his jokes, while the smell of soy sauce and vinegar permeated the entire house. From them I learned to cook both Filipino and Mexican food by watching, listening, and partaking in the joyous occasions that we got to spend with each other as a family. I loved this experience. I had the best that both cultures could offer: food, family, and memories. Many of our family functions centered on these experiences. We often ate Filipino food while listening to Mexican music, bathing ourselves in the multicultural experience that was for me the essence of being a multiethnic Mexipino. Growing up in a multicultural household was normal to me."

While his multicultural household was normal to Rudy, he thought he was unique, the only one who had this experience of being both Mexican and Filipino. But later in life he realized that there were many others like him.

"Oftentimes my Mexican and Filipino friends did not know that I was both, because my physical features looked more Mexican to them (whatever that meant). When I let them know that I was also Filipino, I got the look over, then the eventual 'Yeah, now I can tell by your eyes,' as if that were the only way I could be recognized as Filipino. I found out over the years that I was not the only one who had this distinct experience, meeting others who were also Mexipino. Not only did I meet those who shared in my multiethnic background, but I also met others who had relatives who shared in this identity. Oftentimes I heard, 'Yeah, my *tía* (aunt) is married to a Filipino.'

"We laughed at the fact that we had similar stories of eating both Mexican and Filipino food at dinner and other family functions, as well as the smells that came out of our kitchens. I had one friend who often joked that he was the only guy in his barrio who ate burritos and *bagoong* (fermented salted fish paste). Another friend told me that his favorite thing to eat during Christmas was *pancit* and tamales. These were fond memories that we all shared, which strengthened our identity as we spoke more about our families and our lives. In sharing these stories we would also exchange labels that we identified with, such as Mexipino. Other terms we identified with included Filicano, Chilipino, Flipsican, Jalapino, Chicapino, Flippin' Mexican, and fish taco, among others. We laughed at the terms we called ourselves, all the while sharing in a sense of pride that we had a language that described our distinct experience. We were a small but growing group within two separate communities that reflected our multiethnic history."

Rudy discovered that his experience was not unique, but he still felt that it was largely unknown or misunderstood. He turned to poetry to try to explain his feelings as a Mexipino, writing "Clueless" when he was thirty-one.

Clueless

What's it like to be me, you ask?
    Better yet,
        What are you?
So many times I hear this phrase
    From those who don't know what I am
But for those who think they have a clue
    You assume,
        That I'm what you perceive me to be
But it's not what I see in my reflection
    It's not what I see when I look at my mother,
                      My father
I'm the product, the offspring,
    The creation of two worlds
        Now into one beating heart,
            One soul with a desire to be seen
Don't look at my goatee,
    My baggy jeans,
        My short combed back hair,
            Or even my head when I rock a pelón

My skin color can be deceiving
    Unless you've painted my picture for me
I'm not the brown unknown,
        But a Filipino dragon flying high up in the clouds
            I'm the ancient serpent of pre-Columbian
                cultures,
                Living among the warriors of the inner cities
                    and yuppies of the suburbs
I am your illusion, your reality, your future
Mestizo you call me,
        But what the hell is that?
                Does that include all of me?
                    My Asian, Indian, African, and Spanish roots?
Can you see my multidimensional character?
        The complexity of my being, my existence
            Which thrives on the ignorance of the masses
I am the Filipino you once despised, the one you hated,
        The Mexican you abhorred, ignore, and continue to attack
                    But wait . . . What if I was both?
Could you deal with the double reality of my presence?
What am I you say?
        What's it like to be me
            A multiethnic individual of the twenty-first century
                A creation of two similar cultures, yet very
                    different histories
I am a Mexipino
Mexican by birth, by land, by blood
        Filipino in the same right and with the utmost pride
        I may not be your typical Pinoy,
                Your typical Chicano,
                        But I am one among the many
                            So deal with it.
I may be foreign to you,
        Exotic, even threatening
                But so many times I can be invisible too
My illusion masks my inner thoughts but not what I see
        And it sure as hell won't cloud my sanity
                I know who I am

See my genetic, cultural, social, and political identity
Is often in question but it's all the same to me
I'm the multiple Mestizo
If you can call me such a thing
From the shores of the Philippines my ancestors call
Sending messages from Cavite, Pangasinan
Land of my forefathers
Lest I not forget
Blending in the whirlwinds of the Americas
Touching down unnoticed, dancing
In Michoacán
Purépero my grandfather says
Lest I not forget
Let the voices of my ancestors carry me
Into the cradle of my country
America . . .
But what am I you ask?
What's it like to be me?
If you don't already know
Then I can't help you
Because I already gave you
The clue that passed you by.[1]

Rudy refers to himself as a "multiple Mestizo," knowing that the meaning is elusive. *Mestizo* refers to people whose roots are mixed; it describes both Mexicans and Filipinos. The descendant of mestizas and mestizos, Rudy himself is unmistakably mestizo. Still, he questions what it means to be mestizo, because to many people it is Spanish and Indian. Rudy's diverse and complex mestizo story is a part of those narratives systematically excluded from Western humanist representations of the world. His story challenges the "West-Rest" dichotomy and its attendant forms of dehumanization. Rudy's mestizo is Asian, indigenous, African, and Spanish, his heritage traced through a father of Filipino descent born in the United States and a mother from Mexico. He is a fourth-generation Mexipino. His great-grandfather on his paternal side came to San Diego in 1924 from the Philippines and his great-grandmother is from Baja California, Mexico. His maternal family came from Michoacán, Mexico. Even early in life, Rudy knew that he was both.

> "As a kid I was told to be proud to be Mexican, to be Filipino. When asked to choose one, I would say 'both,' draw my little box. I wasn't gonna reject father or mother, my personal journey, who my family is, who my community is."

While marriages between Asians and Americans often seem to transcend vast divides, the Filipinos and Mexicans who married came together naturally and seemed so similar. It made sense that Filipino men would marry Mexican women—since both Mexico and the Philippines were colonized by Spain, they shared a similar culture, Catholic religion, and to some degree language. This was the historical connection that Mexicans and Filipinos came to share in the twentieth century in places like San Diego. Their shared Spanish colonial past gave them similar cultural practices, such as the Filipina debuts that are similar to Mexican *quinceañeras*, coming of age parties for young women. Both groups celebrate religious and community fiestas, the practice of *compadrazgo*, or godparenthood, and have strong ties to immediate and extended family. These experiences reinforced familial and kinship ties as Filipinos and Mexicans intermarried and baptized each other's children, providing intimate connections between communities and producing several generations of Mexipinas and Mexipinos in San Diego, including Rudy's family. Although there is a greater influx now of Filipinas to the United States, intermarriage continues, with Mexican and Chicano men and Filipina women also marrying. These bonds continue to have a lasting impact on both communities, with Mexipinas/os serving as bridges between communities.

> "Looking back at the city's Mexican and Filipino communities, as well as my own family history, has given me a greater understanding about myself and the distinct experience I share with other Mexipinos. As a distinct group within two separate overlapping communities, we are the bridge that reinforces the already close historical bonds between Mexicans and Filipinos. We are proof that multiplicity is a good thing."

Rudy is careful not to romanticize the relationship, pointing out that there is historically both economic and social competition between Mexicans and Filipinos that made this relationship complex at times. Sometimes Mexipinos feel that they have to prove themselves to both Mexicans and Filipinos that they are "Mexican enough" or "Filipino enough." Their physical appearance comes into question at times, as does their ability to speak either language. Though there are times when they feel fully embraced by both communities, sometimes they have to perform their ethnicity in order to be accepted. Having Spanish surnames and brown complexions complicates identity issues for Mexipinos, for often they are perceived as Chicano or Latino. Some feel they have the best of both worlds, while others struggle with an ambiguous identity.

At the University of San Diego, for example, Rudy felt that he was treated with indifference as a Filipino by the Filipino Ugnayan Student Organization (FUSO) and felt racialized more as a Chicano. As a result, he joined the Movimiento Estudiantil Chicano de Aztlán (MEChA) but not FUSO. Although he was accepted as Chicano, he still made it a point to tell his peers in MEChA that he was also Filipino, and he questioned any attempts by them to exclude or marginalize anyone who did not fit what they thought a Chicana/o was supposed to be or look like. As someone who identified as both, Rudy felt he had to educate others in both his communities that there are those who are multiethnic, who belong in those communities and spaces, and who can identify with both.

The way Rudy was treated in college may reflect changing demographics and social relations in the communities from the time he was a kid. Historically they occupied the same level in the social and racial hierarchy, but today Rudy sees some Filipinos disassociating themselves from Mexicans and other Latinos, with whom they are often confused because of similar appearance and Spanish surnames.

> "In order to make a distinction, especially with regard to their politics on immigration, I have heard Filipinos comment, 'We are not like them (Mexicans). We came here the right way' (i.e., legally). That is problematic because there are a lot of undocumented Filipinos or TNTs (*tago ng tagos*), yet it is something that is not spoken of because

there are those in our communities that want to make it seem like it's not a Filipino problem, just a Mexican or Latino one.

"Education and intelligence is another example. Because Filipinos are lumped together with Asians, they are also considered the 'model minority,' a term that is very problematic and one that neglects the diversity of experiences within the Asian American and Pacific Islander communities, and also within the Filipino community. There are a lot of Filipinos who are highly educated and come from a privileged social class, especially those who immigrated after 1965. The communities I grew up in, however, were pre-1965 and we did not have a lot of doctors, lawyers, or engineers. We had mechanics, janitors, service workers, military, and other blue-collar workers. These communities still exist today and have a lot in common with groups like Mexicans or Chicanos, African Americans, and other Pacific Islanders who live and work in these same communities. I know just as many Mexicans and Chicanos, Chicanas, who are also highly educated and whose families believe in education, so it's not always a matter of realities, so much as how stereotypes influence our perceptions of each other. Education is a matter of access or rather (in)access, and communities that come from lower socioeconomic conditions have more barriers to those resources, especially when you intersect race to that formula. Because both Filipinos and Chicanos are responding to a U.S. racial hierarchy, oftentimes they can fall victim to reinforcing those hierarchies, believing in and perpetuating stereotypes about each other. But a lot of my friends and colleagues, as well as others in the Filipino and Chicano communities, see our issues with immigration, race, and so on as collective issues around which we try to build coalitions with other communities of color who have a shared experience with oppression and marginalization in all its forms."

Rudy challenges each community to expand its borders and overcome its internalized oppression and colonization. Even though Mexicans and Filipinos are mestizos, that does not mean there is no racism in their communities.

"Colorism is an issue in both my communities like in most other communities of color. Those who are lighter skinned are considered by some to be more 'beautiful' and if you are darker in complexion

you are called names like *negro, prieto* (dark), . . . even the 'n-word.'
There is this obsession with getting 'too dark' and being in the sun
too long. Even having physical features that were related to being
more African American or indigenous was seen as less attractive than
the European features, which always bothered me. To see the power
that colorism has in our communities, all you have to do is look at
The Filipino Channel or Latino telenovelas to see who are the main
actors as heroes and heroines, and who are the servants or the antago-
nists. I would see women in our communities also straightening their
hair, using skin lighteners, wearing colored contact lenses, even dye-
ing their hair blond to find a sense of attractiveness that they didn't
see in themselves. I now know and can articulate the gender, racial,
and class issues that create this in our communities, but even when
I did not have the formal education or vocabulary to express this, I
knew something was not right about it."

Asia and Latin America

Mexipinos are part of a largely unknown population with both Asian
and Latin American roots. Yet in the 2000 U.S. Census, 119,829 "His-
panics" identified themselves as also Asian and 249,000 "Asian Americans" also identified with Latinas and Latinos and "other races."[2] These
Asian Latinas and Latinos reflect various types of *mestizaje* (racial and
cultural blending) and include immigrants or border crossers from
Latin American countries who were originally Asian immigrants to
those countries or descendants of those immigrants. Their appearance
can be explained by several trends, including steady migrations from
Asian and Latin American countries; the physical proximity and increased interaction of ethnic groups in large cities and farming communities; and the progressive rates at which multigenerational Asians
and Latinos marry across racial lines. Like Rudy's paternal ancestors,
many of the Asian immigrants from Latin America and the Caribbean
were already racially mixed, due to the heavily male Asian migration
to those multiracial regions.

Asian Latinos and Latino Asians have a rich history and diversity,
including communities of Punjabi Mexicans in the first half of the

twentieth century along the cotton belt of the U.S.-Mexico border from Texas to the Imperial Valley of California. There were also Chinese Mexican families. But the majority of Asian Latinas and Latinos are recent immigrants from Latin America and the Caribbean, representing a new link between the two largest immigrant groups in the United States—Asian and Latin American. Most visible are Cuban Chinese who joined other Cubans in fleeing Cuba for the United States after Fidel Castro took power in 1959, many reestablishing restaurants and other businesses in Miami, New York, New Jersey, and, more recently, Los Angeles.

One could be cynical and say that the Latin American connection with Asia goes back to Columbus—sailing for India, getting lost, finding himself in Cuba, yet convinced he was in Japan. Was this an early form of what Edward Said called "Orientalism"—the constellation of false assumptions about the world to the "East" that fueled the prejudice and discrimination of the "West's" colonial and imperial ambitions?

The first Asian–Latin American connection that I learned of was also disturbing—the U.S. government's incarceration of more than two thousand Japanese Latin Americans during World War II, seized mostly from Peru but also from eleven other countries in Central and South America. I became more cynical about my government when I read how the United States tried to get rid of them at the end of the war, accusing them of being "illegal aliens." Almost all went to Japan because the Latin American countries refused to take most of them back, though a few hundred remained in the United States and built new lives in the face of enormous challenges and hardships.

Those who went to Japan were few in number compared to the Latin Americans who came when I lived there in the 1990s. Hundreds of thousands of people came from Latin America to work in the land of their ancestors—a land their ancestors had once left in search of new lives in the Americas. Though Japan needed them for labor, the government wanted them to go back when jobs dried up in the collapsing economy—and when the new migrants' celebrations of *Carnaval* showed the Japanese that culture is not passed through "Japanese blood." Many stayed, and there are permanent communities of Latin Americans in Japan today.

Professor Guevarra

Rudy's focus is on the United States, but he is increasingly looking west toward the Pacific in his work, with his next project a study of Latino migration to Hawaii. Rudy has also built a community of friends in Hawaii over the last ten years. They have become his family, and Hawaii a second home to him. I wonder whether his movement across the Pacific will stop at Hawaii or eventually take him all the way to the Philippines. Although he had both cultures growing up, he seems to have had more Mexican than Filipino, so perhaps his movement toward the Pacific is a deep calling for balance by nurturing his Filipino islander side. Rudy is a dedicated teacher and community healer, and I believe that this movement is not simply personal but bears meaning for others.

Rudy continues to challenge narrow definitions and build bridges between communities. In his position today as a professor at Arizona State University, Rudy has opportunities to educate others about the ways in which they discriminate, whether they are aware of doing it or not. When he was invited in 2006 by the Filipino Ugnayan Student Organization to give a talk, he spoke on what it means to be Filipina/o and how we define this term, given issues such as mixed race identity, colorism, language, and other factors. After his talk he was able to speak to the organization's leadership and share his own experience of how he felt marginalized from FUSO when he wanted to be a part of it when he was at the University of San Diego.

> "I wanted them to be aware and mindful that there are those of us who are down with our communities and want to be a part of them, regardless of how we are racialized. In other words, allow for many types of Filipino experiences to be part of the collective. This goes for my Chicano and Latino brothers and sisters and other communities who have these same issues. As a historian and ethnic studies scholar who teaches on the Filipino and Chicano experience, I always make it a point to help students see how complex our identities and communities are. I always hope that they walk away with a new understanding of these identities and that they can share them with their families and communities."

Rudy has taught Chicana/o, Pacific Islander, and Asian American studies, and is now a professor in Asian Pacific American studies. Does this mean he has a greater affiliation with Asians and Pacific Islanders? No, he says it just happens to be where he got a job, although that is also because the field of Asian American studies has been at the forefront of research on mixed ethnicities and comparative-relational studies. Rudy uses his classes to expand borders. On the first day of a new semester in his Asian Pacific American studies class, he greets the students with "Welcome to Chicano Studies 101!" It is Rudy's playful way of easing tension and inviting them to think about borders, as well as directly addressing any questions that might exist in their minds about who he is in relation to his subject.

"I feel that living in two cultures helps us to understand how particular communities perceive the world and interact, and just how complex these experiences are. I believe that being there to show you support your communities and want to be part of coalition building, as an embodiment of particular communities coming together, enables these processes to occur. You are someone that hopefully both cultures and communities can relate to and trust so long as your intentions are noble."

Rudy is not simply a bland college professor, but retains some of his youthful flair, seeking self-expression in various ways. A few years back, he wanted to create a clothing line that would acknowledge and celebrate experiences of multiracial, multiethnic people, so he started Multiracial Apparel, offering t-shirts, sweatshirts, and the like featuring sayings such as "Beautifully blended," "Mexipino," "AfroChicano," "Hapa," and "What are you?" Rudy also expresses his multiethnicity on his body, showing one of his tattoos on his Facebook profile and selectively revealing the rest.

"I ended up getting tattoos all over my upper body and down my right leg. The left side of my body is indigenous Filipino tattoos done by Filipino tattoo artists, which symbolize my family and culture. The right side was done by a Tahitian artist who did indigenous Mexican designs to represent my Mexican family and culture. They come together in my chest to represent their blending into who I am as a Mexipino. I did not get all of these tattoos until a few years ago. I plan on getting more. Although I did get one tattoo when I was in my early twenties with my nickname on my back (my cousin did the tattoo), I did not want to get any more until I was ready for them. As I began to learn more about who I was culturally, I wanted to continue to wait on my tattoos until I found something that spoke to who I was as a multiethnic Mexipino. I am glad I waited because I got the tattoos I always imagined and met the people at the right time who were meant to do them. I have faith in our Creator that these things happen in such a way, so whether the tattoos come in a dream, through conversations with your artist-practitioner, and careful thought, they shape themselves to what you are meant to carry, which connects you to your family, your culture, your ancestors."

I wonder about the meaning in Rudy's tattoos. I recall a woman I knew in Japan, fathered by a white American she never knew, who dreamed often about her face that stigmatized her as racially different. Mayumi's face symbolized her psyche, expressing her deepest self. Mayumi and many others are conspicuous in their surroundings—their two sides are so apparently different. For me, my physical difference from others has often drawn great attention and instilled self-consciousness. It seems clear to others, and sometimes to me, that my long sharp nose is Irish, my oval face Japanese, my fair skin Irish, my dark hair Japanese, my hazel eyes a mix of Irish blue and Japanese black. Maybe in Rudy's Mexipino world the two sides are so similar that they require markings on his body that express them. In Rudy's brown body, black hair, brown eyes, is it apparent what is Filipino and what is Mexican? If not, his tattooed body now clearly shows both.

Mestiza Consciousness

In trying to understand Rudy's identity and experiences, I am drawn to Gloria Anzaldua's writings on borderlands. She asks, "What does the mestizo or mestiza have to offer the world?" and proclaims a mestiza consciousness that bears meaning for all of us. To me, Rudy embodies this kind of consciousness.

This assembly is not one where severed or separated pieces merely come together. Nor is it a balancing of opposing powers. In attempting to work out a synthesis, the self has added a third element which is greater than the sum of its severed parts. That third element is a new consciousness—a mestiza consciousness—and though it is a source of intense pain, its energy comes from continual creative motion that keeps breaking down the unitary aspect of each new paradigm.[3]

Anzaldua's mestiza consciousness offers a vision to help us overcome our separateness and divisions and to heal ourselves from what most deeply threatens us. It promotes the recognition of commonality within the context of difference, questioning what it means to classify people with simple words like "white" and "people of color" that sometimes bear little meaning. This kind of consciousness challenges popular notions of identity, seeing its complexity and focusing on inclusion rather than the divisive politics of exclusion based on traditional categories that diminish our humanness.

Mestiza consciousness tries to make boundaries more pliant and categories such as race and gender more permeable and flexible. It is synergistic, moving beyond separate and easy identifications, across classifications among different groups that legislate and restrict identities. While mestiza consciousness does not deny differences, for differences are usually inequalities and disparities, it does not use differences to separate us from others. In rethinking the borders of race, gender, and identity, it resists creating new binaries out of frustration and resentment, a sense of tribalism, or entitlement. Individuals with mestiza consciousness identify with groups and social positions not limited to ethnic, racial, religious, class, gender, or national classification; they self-define not by what they exclude, but define who they are by what they include.

In Rudy's mestiza consciousness he is a multiethnic bridge connecting multiple communities far beyond their own borders. He is Chicano; he is Filipino; he is Mexipino, offering a new way in which to see our multiethnic communities and the world around us. He envisions the process of coalition building between all communities taking place when we notice our centers of connectedness and understand how we share in the same struggle for social and economic justice.

SEVEN

Grits and Sushi

Grits and Sushi. I know grits and I know sushi, but Grits and Sushi? That is the name of Mitzi's blog. She admits she really wanted to call it Grits and Goya, but "'sushi' had a little more of a ring and was more accessible." Mitzi was born and raised in Texas, something she once tried to deny; the reference to grits exemplifies her southernness. The cornmeal mush brings in her African American father and a heritage that has given her many trials, as it is manifest in various cultural contexts. *Goya* expresses her Okinawan roots, her mother's heritage, historically distinct and painfully marginalized—the bitter melon symbolizes the invisibility and disempowered status of Okinawa. Mitzi did not use it in her blog's name, as a concession to Okinawa's invisibility. Sushi, however, evokes a symbol of Japan that is understandable, even loved by Americans. It is quintessentially Japanese, and Mitzi's use of the word expresses how Okinawans, and Mitzi herself, are both *a part of* and *apart from* Japan.

Mitzi brings all these elements together in her blog because this is who she is; she seeks to create a "communal space" for folks interested in similar issues. Growing up in the U.S. South the daughter of an Okinawan woman and an African American father, Mitzi had to explore many different types of identities: those given to her by others, those she made up to make sense of her daily life, and identities that would make sense to others, depending on their own cultural context.

What does it mean to a child to be "mixed" in a way that others find confusing? How does a child make sense of others' stares, labels, and emotions? How does a child learn from others who she is, who she is not, and who she should be?

Mitzi learned early in life who she was from her parents and others around her. Sometimes children are immersed in culture and it doesn't need to be taught. Mitzi's father never sat down to "teach" her about being black; she says she was surrounded by blackness and lived it, growing up in all-black neighborhoods in Houston and attending predominantly black and Latino schools.

Mitzi actually learned a few things about Southern black culture from her mother, who inadvertently began to speak a mix of Okinawan and Southern U.S. English, incorporating expressions such as "fixin' to" and "ya'll" into her vocabulary. Her fluid combination of grammar, syntax, and multilingual colloquialisms was especially noticeable when she was mad, like when she screamed at the kids to clean up their rooms: "AGIGIBIYO! [Oh Lord!] This room is so dirty. You are a GIRL so you have to be neat. Kusai [stinky] dirty room. Ya'll have to clean NOW."[1]

Without a natural environment to immerse her children in her culture, Mitzi's mother also fiercely held on to her original heritage and taught them, like many women displaced from their homelands who fight isolation and feelings of powerlessness by teaching their children about their native culture. Women who married Americans, like Mitzi's mom or my mom, struggled between making their children Americans and making them Japanese or Okinawan. Often outwardly they had to satisfy the demands of their husbands' insisting that their children were American. But inside the home and in their intimate relations they could make their children Japanese or Okinawan, sometimes surreptitiously. Having Japanese or Okinawan children gave them company in their isolation and separation from family, community, and country. Mitzi's mother learned how to be the wife of an African American man without giving up her own Okinawan culture.

> My siblings and I would stay at my grandmother's house once in a while (she cooked the best collard greens), and when my mom came to pick us up she'd teach her how to cook a Southern meal for my father. Our meals were an indicator of how much my mom held on to her traditions. My father made his requests for chicken, steak, or okra and my mom learned to cook these things. But we always had

Japanese rice on the side with nori [dried seaweed] and tofu and fishcake with these really noisome beans that are supposed to be good for you.[2]

Though she herself was blending cultures, Mitzi's mother distinguished sharply between cultures when she taught the kids how to act, differentiating between Okinawan and American behaviors and values. One was good and one was bad. And naturally, her way, the Okinawan way, was good and the way the children should act. The other way, the American way, was bad—and overwhelming in its negative influence, needing to be constantly controlled and subdued.

When we disobeyed my mother's rules or screamed, we were being too "American." If I ever left the house with rollers in my hair, my mom would say I shouldn't do American things. *"Agijibiyo* . . . where you learn this from? You are Okinawan too. *Damedesuyo* [don't do that]. Don't talk so much like Americans; listen first." My mother always told us: never be too direct, never accept gifts from people on the first offer, and always be humble and modest. Those were cultural traits and values that I inevitably inherited (and cherish) being raised by a Japanese mother.[3]

Why did Mitzi's mother insist, "You are Okinawan too"? Perhaps she was just trying to provide balance, as society told her kids that they were black. Maybe she just wanted company, to be more than a group of one. Parents can also work out their feelings about their partner and themselves by projecting qualities onto their children. My mother also taught us that Japanese and Irish were different, and you knew who were smarter and who were lazier. Fortunately, my father agreed—so there were no arguments, only jokes about the Irish. Mitzi's mother believed that positive and negative qualities came from genes or blood, so because Americans and Okinawans were different, mixed kids would have some of each.

I don't know why but I think Okinawans have a different blood— we don't act like Americans. Um. What about us, mama? Oh, you have mixed blood, so that's why sometimes you are good and sometimes bad.[4]

Mitzi's mother's teaching about being Okinawan shows how identity can become a battleground for loyalty when each parent insists that the child belongs to his or her ethnic group. The child may be pulled back and forth between parents and extended family members, each wanting the child to claim affiliation. Or conversely, children may be pushed away to the other side, rejected for being too much like the other parent, the other group.

The ethnic mixture in the child is framed in different ways. The child might be told she has the "best of both worlds." Some parents encourage their children to accept who they are as a mixture, rather than choose one side over the other or reject any part of themselves and their family. Today, more parents insist on their child's right and need to identify with all parts of their heritage. But it wasn't so long ago that parents taught children like Mitzi that they should just accept being black because "society won't see you as mixed or Japanese but black." The "one-drop rule" dictated that any amount of black blood made a person black. But times are changing, and I wonder why Obama is not the forty-fourth white president as well as the first black president.

Every black Asian I have interviewed says that black communities are more accepting of multiracial people than any other community. Among those individuals who wish to accept all the parts of their heritage with equal weight, however, some feel that they are excluded. If you identify as other than black you can be criticized for wanting to escape from that designation and climb the social ladder by claiming to be something else, whether Indian, Japanese, or passing as white. When Tiger Woods explained to Oprah in 1997 that he identified as "Cablinasian" (Caucasian, black, Indian, Asian) rather than black, he set off a storm of controversy. Critical comments came from those who denounced what they saw as a denial of being black, while multiracial advocates argued that Tiger was positively affirming all of his ancestries and finding wholeness by embracing all of his parts.

Identification with a parent's ethnic group can also be a matter of loyalty. Mitzi's mother was the target of jokes and derogatory comments after she had her first child with an African American man. She learned to walk hand in hand with her children while being stared at and hearing people talk. Mitzi saw her mother rejected by relatives in her father's family too, and perhaps keenly felt her mom's isolation and wanted to align with her for mutual protection.

> It was my mother who told us that we would be discriminated against because of our color, and it was my Japanese mother to whom we ran when we were called niggers at the public swimming pool in Houston. To say to this woman, "Mom, we are just black," would be a disrespectful slap in the face. The woman who raised us and cried for years from her family's coldness and rejection because of her decision to marry interracially cried when my father's sister wouldn't let her be a part of the family picture because she was a "Jap"; this woman, who happens to be my mother, will never hear "Mom, I'm just black" from my mouth, because I'm not, and no person, society, or government will force me to say that and deny my reality and my being, no matter how offensive I am to their country or how much of a nuisance I am to their cause. I am Blackanese.[5]

I personally identified as Japanese because as a child this identity was thrust upon me by others, but Mitzi's affirmation of her Japanese and Okinawan heritage flew in the face of American society's labeling of her as black.

> Our bodies, our presence, our reality are a nuisance to some because we defy a definite and demarcated set of boundaries. We confuse those who try to organize ethnic groups by highlighting these boundaries because they don't know how to include us or exclude us. We are Blackanese, Hapa, Eurasian, Multiracial.[6]

We are "offensive" and a "nuisance." Offensive because we raise disturbing thoughts of interracial sex? Offensive because our very bodies destroy the neat boundaries cherished by so many people trying to control and order their world into boxes of white, black, and yellow? A nuisance because we threaten the rigid racial categories and authority of established interest groups and those heavily invested in maintaining distinctions and barriers to membership? Mitzi's multiracial identity was attacked by those threatened by it.

> Nigga-chink, black-Jap, black-Japanese mutt. The neighborhood kids, friends, and adults labeled my siblings and me with these terms

especially after they recognized that my mother was completely intent on making us learn about Okinawan culture. On New Year's Day, we had black-eyed peas and mochi. We cleaned the house to start the year fresh and clean. "Don't laugh with your mouth too wide and show your teeth too much," my mom would always tell us. "Be like a woman." I had not realized that I covered my mouth each time I laughed until someone pointed it out to me in my freshman year in college.[7]

When Mitzi was in high school, an exchange student from Brazil told her that she did not need to identify as black when "you're so much better." Her identity was nurtured, conversely, by meeting others who introduced her to new possibilities of identities beyond monoracial labels. In college she found cultural anthropology, a field that is about identity and how identities shift, to be a great tool to help learn about the world and explore her own identity.

As I began to travel and see how race played out across the world, I started to have more clarity in how race is shaped by so many other factors. . . . I began to really listen to how articulations of race and blackness could maneuver and shift in various spaces—neoliberal, rural, militarized. . . . That work propelled me into my own identity work even further, with new tools on how to ask better questions.[8]

Mitzi also explored the Asian American world on campus and began to write.

"On Being Blackanese"—I first wrote this essay back in my undergrad years at Duke for a friend who was the editor of a cool little zine called "The Raging Buddha." It was a publication for progressive Asian-Americans on campus. I had never felt totally included in the Asian American community on campus but that request to write something for them shifted my identity at that time in more ways than they ever realized. I saw an Asian American community that was radical, inclusive and wanting to learn the best ways to embrace me as a blackanese woman—by first understanding where I saw myself. It moved me to think about my identity with much angst and joy.[9]

Blackanese

Mitzi met other black Japanese—whom she also called Blackanese—such as Tatsu Yamato, the son of a Japanese father and African American mother. Hair was once a big thing for Tatsu. There's "good hair" and "bad hair," and you don't always get the kind of hair you would want. Tatsu's hair subjected him to ostracizing comments from black kids when he was growing up in Seattle. He now cuts his hair short, but there was a time in his youth that he wished for longer hair.

> I just looked at pictures of my hair when I was a baby and thought that if I let my hair grow out long enough it could be healthy and non-kinky, shiny, black, beautiful flowing locks. I wanted to look like some cool-ass samurai dude, his hair blowing in wisps in front of his face. Weird racial identity games were going on in my head. Secretly, I hoped that my hair would tell me which way to swing and more secretly, I hoped it would swing toward the brown-black straightness of my father's Japanese head. However, as my hair grew out, it seemed pretty obvious to others that such was not going to be the case. . . .
>
> Yeah, so see, I wanted people to just know—to feel uneasy as I walked around with my brown skin beneath a head of flowing samurai hair, messing with their conceptions of race. I wouldn't say anything. I'd just be one bold, beautiful statement of defiance against America's whack color game. Or maybe I just wanted to escape my blackness.[10]

Tatsu's musings about wanting to look like a samurai touch me because I too have wanted that. Unlike Tatsu's, my hair is just a little wavy so I have no problem with growing it long. But wanting to look like a samurai raises a similar question: am I just wanting to escape my whiteness?

Like our hair, faces, and clothes, our names also signal to others who we are. Tatsu Yamato—could there be a more Japanese-sounding name? Did his parents imagine what happens when the bearer of that name is perceived to be black? Tatsu's name has been a source of tension. In Japan, he would write it in kanji characters, but others would write it in katakana, indicating that it was a foreigner's name. He suspected they changed it so that he did not "trick" anyone into thinking he was "really" Japanese before meeting in person. Were they reminding Tatsu that regardless of what he might think, he was not really Japanese? But to Tatsu and to other Americans, his name is a constant reminder that he is Japanese.

Back to Japan

Before going to Japan, Tatsu had been warned by Americans that Japanese are prejudiced toward blacks and have rigid stereotypes, having absorbed Western racism. Magazine articles told him Japanese could be more prejudiced than whites, and scholarly work on Japanese perceptions of blacks warned that there is a long history of bias against blackness. Some prejudice is class-based, with the upper classes favoring their own whiteness, which they preserved by not having to work in the fields. Tatsu read that black Japanese since the Occupation have had a hard time—and little choice but to go into the entertainment industry. He read accusations that even the patron saint of Amerasians, Sawada Miki, held racial stereotypes that their African blood made black Amerasians especially endowed with athletic and musical ability.

But Tatsu had reasons to go to Japan and find out for himself. What he found was a deep and mysterious connection that kept him in Japan for eight years and moved him to seriously consider living there forever. Although he went with great expectations of what he would find, he was surprised at how well he was received. He came close to setting down permanent roots in the place where he lived in rural Japan and eventually separated from the country only with tremendous difficulty. Before leaving he wrote to Mitzi: "I don't know how long this is gonna last, so you'd better get your butt out here before your blackness goes out of style."

Despite Tatsu's reassurance that her blackness would be in style, Mitzi still wondered how she would be treated—"exotified"? ignored? disdained? She too had heard stories of Japanese racism toward blacks in the dismal literature that never failed to mention racist statements by Japanese government officials in the late 1980s and early 1990s.

Before going, Mitzi recalled childhood memories and how they had affected her life. She knew that skin color mattered in Japan. She had heard enough from her mother and from friends who had experienced direct forms of racism to know that blacks have been treated badly in Japan. Mitzi wanted to go to Okinawa, where her family was from, and where mixed race kids have been caught in a tough situation complicated by the tense climate created by an extended occupation and subsequent colonial-like status. Amerasians have been vulnerable to being targeted by Okinawans' anger and frustration toward their occupiers from Washington and Tokyo. Being black and Okinawan, although Mitzi had been raised in the United States in a totally different context, still she knew that she would be affected by Japanese and Okinawan attitudes about skin color.

In my family we too were aware of Japanese attitudes toward skin color. One sister, Margie, had almost pinkish fair skin and the other, Jo, much browner skin. I once heard my Japanese grandmother tell my mother, "Too bad Jo doesn't have skin like Margie." Mom got mad, and was always annoyed when my grandmother scolded her for letting Jo play in the sun.

Mitzi's mother also kept her inside to make her more Japanese.

I was never allowed to play outside until the sun went down or else she warned me, "I would become more like my father's color" and therefore less Japanese. Perhaps many of her fears came from the uneasy times she spent with my older sister living in Korea, Thailand, and Japan in the 1960s and 1970s. She was constantly the object of harassment for having a "sambo baby" and was called the nastiest names for betraying the nation with her sex. She was immediately associated with military domination, with prostitution, with misplaced allegiances.[11]

Mitzi had heard her mother's stories of how she left Japan to shield her children from abuse, having lived through volatile times of virulent antimilitary sentiment and prejudice directed at the women and children of the Americans.

My mother had told me many stories about why she refused to enroll my sister in a Japanese school and they all seemed to stem from the belief that it would be detrimental to her daughter's self-esteem. She would rather leave Japan than have my sister suffer from the kind of name-calling she received outside of school hours. My cousins who are half Okinawan and half white American had similar stories of buses passing them by and stories of bullying in school and how even later, signs on certain dance clubs in Koza City would not only say, "no Americans" or "no GIs" but also "no hâfu" allowed. The undercover Japanese have the potential to be the most threatening because our allegiances are hard to place.[12]

But Mitzi was drawn to Japan to search for her roots. She ended up going as a JET (Japan Exchange and Teaching Programme) teacher, an assistant English instructor. She requested Okinawa as her first choice but was sent to Sado Island, off the west coast of Honshu. There Mitzi witnessed changing images of blackness; she did not doubt that the kinds of prejudice and discrimination she read about still exist, but she questioned the stereotypes that Japanese are racists who accept blackness only through consumption of popular images. She wondered how accounts about racist Japanese benefit those who promote them by "mystifying their own xenophobia." Through her experiences, Mitzi learned about everyday practices and the ways that blackness is negotiated. She found herself unexpectedly included in inner circles. She wondered if this was happening because she was *haafu*, half Japanese, or was it possibly because she was black?

> When working in Sado Island, a fellow colleague from the United States, who had been in Japan for much longer than I, was a bit shocked when I told her that I was being asked to cut the persimmons and help serve tea in the mornings. She exclaimed, "I don't know any other *gaijin* (foreigner) teacher that's been asked to help out like that, regardless of how demeaning that may be as a woman and a newcomer. It means you're being pulled into a more *uchi* (insider) role and that the other teachers trust you."[13]

Tatsu's and Mitzi's experiences are not exceptional. My sister-in-law Ann is a native of Kenya, who met my wife's younger brother Taiji when they were graduate students in anthropology at the University of Nairobi. They have lived in Tokyo for nearly twenty years and she has become part of the family. While she admits the excessive rules sometimes bother her, she mostly describes her experience in Japan as positive. When we are together in public I have not noticed any signs of discrimination, hostility, or neglect. On the contrary, I have seen Ann treated extremely well by Japanese. At a sports day event at my son's school, I marveled as several people approached her out of the blue in a friendly and outgoing manner that I have never received. She has a steady stream of students at her private English language school.

Ann describes many experiences of being drawn in and embraced by Japanese. Perhaps some of those Japanese are friendly to all foreigners. But I wonder whether others find white foreigners to be intimidating and strange and feel more comfortable with Ann, allowing her into certain intimate spaces. While Japanese who feel the opposite may be numerous, Ann's experience is that many people see her as approachable and engage with her easily. Could this be because of her nonwhiteness, that they view her as occupying some space in the world as a black African woman, which they long for?

Having grown up as a majority person in Kenya, Ann may be insensitive to racial microaggressions, which may occur more than I know. But my friend Howard Irvin, who grew up in pre–civil rights Virginia, loves Japan and vacations there nearly every summer. I wonder what it is that he likes so much about it. Though he is sensitive to race relations and microaggressions, he has not felt offended. I suspect that the language barrier, the experience of not knowing what people are saying and not picking up the nonverbal cues, may be insulating. Perhaps Howard finds release in no longer being a black man in a white man's world. It is a whole new context. Is he exotic? Are Japanese eager to show their nonchalance in accepting a black man as a visitor or even as a neighbor? In any case, he likes what he finds. He doesn't like seeing Africans selling hip-hop goods by pretending to be from Los Angeles, but he has no problem with Japanese people:

> "Japanese aren't obsessed with skin color in the same way as Americans. Of course, I'm sure there is discrimination and racism, but it seems more about 'you're Japanese or you're not.' I don't feel that being 'a big black guy' is held against me. If I choose to live in Japan I can go anywhere in the country and never walk in fear of a hate crime against me or being pulled over for 'driving while black.'"

Mitzi's experiences were not all wonderful. Like Tatsu, she did not encounter full acceptance as Japanese. Perhaps if they had, Tatsu and Mitzi would still be there. Mitzi was often made to feel that she was not Japanese, but did not see this as being because of blackness as much as "halfness," her incomplete, impure Japaneseness.

> I had a feeling at times that I was on the border of disappointing everyone for not knowing better and on the edge of forgiveness because my blood has betrayed me from ever really becoming Japanese. However, never did the issue of me being half black ever come into those feelings of non-belonging I may have felt, neither was that ever raised or insinuated in any context. I do not take my experiences to be universal but I think there is still a hole in academic literature in regards to this issue.[14]

Mitzi's experiences may not be universal. Like Howard's, they may be favorable partly because she was there temporarily and therefore perceived to be a guest. What if they were permanent residents? What problems might occur in marriage, in employment? What about the treatment of their children? Would racism then raise its ugly head?

Mitzi believes that racism in Japan does not reduce blacks to mere victims, but that they still have agency. She believes this to be true not just from her personal experience, but also from the growing collection of narratives of blacks who have had positive experiences as tourists, temporary workers, or permanent residents. She insists that their experiences cannot be dismissed as anomalies to the academic images of blacks as objects of consumption, asserting that there is no universal "black experience." Her coauthor Aina Hunter warns:

> Racial essentialism fails to account for the many different variations on . . . "the black experience" . . . of a black British model in Shibuya, an illegal immigrant from Ghana, an American banking executive in Tokyo, an American GI stationed in Yokohama, and an English teacher in rural Japan. . . . Could [they] ever share a similar "black experience"?[15]

But is Japan really any different today? What does Jero's popularity tell us? In 2008 he emerged as a rising star in a most unexpected way, creating harmony and dissonance by singing the traditional form of

Japanese blues called *enka* in hip-hop clothing. He appears to be black, but his Japanese sounds smooth. His recording company wanted him to dress in kimono but Jero said no, that would not be him. Is this a bold move to sing enka in hip-hop clothes, refusing to bow to tradition, asserting himself as he is? Or is it resignation to the way people would look at him, as if it were incongruence to see a black man in Japanese clothes?

Jero is not technically *haafu* as he is "one-fourth" Japanese. He is the next generation of mixed ancestry people who broaden the meaning of *haafu*. Is he authentically Japanese? I think of my own nieces, also one-fourth Japanese, and wonder. I guess it depends on the person. Because his grandparents were divorced and his mother was also divorced, Jero ended up being raised largely by a Japanese immigrant with her mixed ancestry daughter, and grew up hearing and studying Japanese.

Crystal Kay is another popular performer who offers a smooth racial mixture—her face, skin, and hair familiar, yet strange. Her blend of Japanese and English brings both affinity and authenticity. Yet, despite spending her whole life in Japan, she describes herself as Korean (her mother's ancestry) and American (her father's) rather than Japanese. What does this tell us about acceptance and rejection of mixed people as Japanese? Is Jero that good, or just a curiosity? Does the popularity of Jero and Crystal Kay mean that Japanese are no longer prejudiced toward black people? That depends, of course, on which Japanese you are talking about—and which black people. Those like Tatsu or Mitzi who write about their experiences are highly educated, and a great number of them are Americans; they encounter good treatment partly because of their social capital. Other black Japanese are not so fortunate.

In my research on mixed ancestry people in Japan I found race and class differences to be significant factors in their experiences. One young man told me that the black mixed experience is totally different from the white mixed experience, claiming he fought every day as a child. I realized that his experiences as a kid raised by a single mother and in public school were far different from those of Blackanese in international schools or those in schools on the military bases, often raised in two-parent homes. In Okinawa, some children are identified as *shima haafu*, locals who grew up without their fathers and can't speak English.

Besides class, another difference in black experiences is contextual. Mitzi's mother's home of Okinawa has the highest concentration of so-called Amerasians, or *haafu*, because of the large American military presence there. The racial dynamics and political climate are unique in a place where the United States occupied, colonized, kept political control for twenty-seven years after the end of World War II, and even today maintains extensive military bases. Some claim that Okinawans, as dark minorities themselves, feel affinity with blacks and black Amerasians. But they are still caught in the complex politics of Okinawan nationalism, Japanese state interests, and American hegemony.

Mitzi knew Okinawa through her mother's imaginative reconstruction.

> The Okinawa I imagined in my head as a child was full of homes with sweet, well behaved children who followed their mother's every order. I know because my mother told me every time we misbehaved. Or played us that song Tinsagu Nu Hana. (*What does that song mean, mama? It means obey your mama! Like all Okinawan kids do.*) . . .
>
> The Okinawa I imagined was also scarred. I imagined my mother as a child walking through a war torn place, over the dead bodies she saw during the bloody battle of Okinawa in WWII. I recreated the nightmares she might have had. (*I never forget, those dead bodies.*) . . .
>
> Yes, the Okinawa I imagined was a blend of diasporic memories, militarized memories, my mother's own idiosyncratic ideas (some personal, others cultural) about race, gender, blood . . . and my southern lens which had formed to see those same things in other ways.[16]

I noticed that Mitzi sometimes refers to her mother as Japanese while her mother calls Mitzi Okinawan. This distinction is rich with meaning about identity, as is her mother's use of not only Japanese but also Okinawan language amidst her English. For Mitzi, the careful choice of terms is a question of audience and context.

> "As a child I would say my mom was Japanese because I didn't quite understand how Okinawans were different from Japanese mainlanders. It was not especially clear to me until I went to Japanese Saturday school (in high school) and my Japanese language teachers would correct the words in my skits because they couldn't understand what I thought was actually Japanese. When I would show my mom, she'd

just laugh and say, 'of course your teachers don't know what this is, it's Okinawan!'

"Now it's a question of audience. For my Internet audience, I think most people don't understand how Okinawa has historically, politically, and culturally been positioned between the United States and Japan so I will first start with grits and sushi . . . for instance, or I'm black-Japanese . . . and then after drawing people in will challenge that naming. I start with the outwardly familiar to draw in interested parties and then educate once I've got their attention. At least that's what I hope I'm doing. It's a very strategic and conscious decision on my part how I will name, dename, rename, and challenge certain concepts. It's all about context, projection, audience, and recontextualization. To a lesser degree, it's also how I fluctuate between the terms *black* and *African American*. It's a conscious choice. My mom also sometimes uses Japanese and if she's talking to someone who is totally ignorant, for instance, and she knows if she says, 'I'm Okinawan,' it might as well be Timbuktu. They might not be able to map it mentally so in those instances, she decides what the hell—I'll go with Japan on this one. If I say 'I'm Blackinawan,' I guarantee you that most people will think it's an actual ethnic group instead of me playing with the ways we are racially cataloged. At least with *Blackanese*, most folks can grasp that. . . . It's a way to engage with the familiar and then I later say, I'm really black and Okinawan."

When Mitzi eventually did return to Okinawa, her aunt took her to the family tomb to pay homage to their ancestors and discuss the duties that must be performed to honor them at the tomb and home. Another relative took her to a spot where they could peek over onto military property and see an Okinawan family tomb. They noted the irony that family members cannot freely perform their rituals because they need special permission each time to go on base. While Americans move freely all over, Okinawans are restricted from many parts of their own island.

Mitzi still has work to do in Okinawa. She wants to explore how the racial meanings of blackness vary by space—in the militarized zones, urban centers, and rural villages. She has already helped create a rupture in the prevailing theories, which have argued that imaginings of blackness are wholly imported from the United States and that mirrored racial ordering exists transnationally. She has challenged how current discourse positions Japanese as having fixed notions of blackness. There are deep-seated prejudices and discrimination, but there are also evolving images of blackness, and benevolent treatment as well. Essentializing blackness and black experiences is dangerous if we are to understand the complexity of the lived experiences of people in Japan.

Back in the USA

Mitzi returned to the United States, married, and had two children, another generation of mixed Asian Americans. Her life is now further complicated by her children's racial appearance. In a reversal of her mother's situation in which the children are darker than the mother, raising assumptions about the woman as one who bears the children of a black man, Mitzi is darker than her children, raising different assumptions about who she is in relation to the children. Mitzi married a light-skinned Cuban man; their two children have remarkably light complexions, showing the incredible variety of the next generation of mixed Asians, genetically one-quarter or three-quarters Asian. Her children are "one quarter Japanese," light enough to be mistaken for someone else's kids. Mitzi asks, "Are these mongrelized bodies or the embodiments of the wonders of hybridity?"

"I was in a post office, in a pretty mixed neighborhood in Oakland. I was putting a box together. My son was in a stroller next to me, very light skinned. A woman approached us and said, "Are you allowed to do personal errands while you're on duty?" And I was kind of looking at her like, what is she talking about, . . . because it was such a weird question. Then I realized she thought I was the nanny, and she was totally policing our proximity, our union. And when I told her "This is my son," she backed away, upset—not at herself, more at the situation, our being together in that space. She didn't apologize, just walked away."

Her interracial family is policed by others who appear somehow upset by the nature of the family, particularly disturbed by the relation between Mitzi and her children. Now Mitzi is thinking about changing her last name to her husband's because she may need to prove they are her kids. She has her own experiences and is gathering stories of multiracial families that illuminate this dark area where strangers exert their privilege to insert themselves as saviors for white children seemingly threatened by black kidnappers.

She also maintains her blog, Grits and Sushi, hoping to move it to a space beyond the "boring/exotified 'I'm mixed and I'm proud' stance" with a blend of her musings on race, family, Okinawa, militarization, transnationalisms, blackness, and the South. She wants to show how she sees "race moving across these different contexts, to jot down the patterns I've noticed and try to make sense of the changes and how those meanings affect people who are in or between Okinawa and the United States either physically or emotionally."

Mitzi is engaged in other forms of cultural healing activities. For the 2010 Critical Mixed Race Studies conference in Chicago, she brought a group together including transnational adoptees and Yumi Wilson, another Blackanese with her own healing story of searching for roots in Japan (see epilogue). Mitzi was also involved in the Lessons of the Battle of Okinawa exhibit at the National Japanese American Historical Society in January 2011. She hopes that such an exhibit provides ways of remembering that, though painful, nurture healing from the traumas of war, even sixty-five years later. She was deeply moved to see the conversations between her and her mother on display. Mitzi has been receiving her mother's story about that sorrowful time for many years, in hopes that she can help close the gap between parents who have experienced such extreme horror and their American children and grandchildren, for whom such experiences are beyond their imagination. She wants to help younger generations learn how to listen to war stories as a healing gift.

In February 2011, Mitzi organized an event in Berkeley with fellow Blackanese Eriko Ikehara, an Okinawa native, that they called "Blackness in Flux in Okinawa." They brought together academic presentations and artistic performances by black Japanese who shared their poetry, art, and other creative works that speak to blackness in flux in their own lives. She presented again in Berkeley with Eriko on Okinawa in April of the same year at the Hapa Japan conference. Now she is on her way back to Okinawa, this time with her whole family, including her mother, for a longer stay of nearly a year that promises to be transformative for the whole family.

In her blog, Mitzi wrote that the Lessons of the Battle of Okinawa event ended with dance.

> For those of you readers who don't know about Okinawa or Oki-
> nawan dances for that matter, this is the music that moves nearly
> every able-bodied Okinawan to jump up and start moving (and also,
> I admit I'm being a bit essentialist, but we really can't help but do
> that particular whistle when it's really calling us. It's in our blood).[17]

I notice that when speaking about Okinawans, Mitzi says "we" and "us," and even uses the expression that it is in "our blood." I feel her connecting with all her parts and engaging in activities that bring others together to also connect with themselves and others—the university and community, artists and academics, blacks and Japanese, Okinawans and Japanese, whites and blacks, Latins and Asians— healing the hurts of human suffering caused by the illusion of our separation.

EIGHT

I Cut across Borders
as If They Have No Meaning

I admit that I was a little surprised when I opened the door. After all, he had said his name was Marshall Bennett; he was interested in Japan and my work with minorities, could we meet? And yes, I judged by his voice on the phone that he was a white guy, that's just the way he sounded. But when he appeared at my doorstep he looked like your typical Asian guy. So why was his name Marshall Bennett? I couldn't help but wonder. It annoys me, angers me at times, when people make assumptions based on my name or appearance, and I advise others about the importance of not doing this because of how offensive it can be. But good Lord, I do it myself!

It brought me way back to a time many years ago when my co-worker Pat and I were exchanging stories of our job interviews at a day-care center. Pat was a light-skinned black woman, and in her application she had informed the hiring committee that she was African American. She went to the school for an interview and knocked on the door. The friendly smile on the face of the woman who opened the door immediately vanished when she saw Pat. With a look of complete bewilderment she blurted out, "But . . . you're supposed to be black!" Although we laughed about it, I felt bad for Pat but was glad that it hadn't happened to me. I suppose I looked Asian enough to the woman interviewer. Another mixed Asian friend apparently had not satisfied her interviewer, who later confided to her, "We were hoping you looked more Asian."

Since I myself have an appearance that sometimes fools people, and I know a lot of other people like me, I stifle my curiosity about someone's background and wait to see whether the person decides to tell me or not. It was not long into our conversation that Marshall mentioned that he was a "Jewish adopted Korean," or maybe he called himself "an adopted Korean American Jew." He didn't dwell on it, but talked about his work researching minorities in Japan. Why Japan, I wondered, and not Korea? It reminded me of a friend who returned to Asia after a long hiatus, not through her native Japan but through Korea. Were they both going to places close to where they really wanted to return, but much less threatening? Or were they simply going to where the opportunities appeared, not knowing at the time that it was one step in the direction of home?

Marshall had first gone to Japan for nine months in 2000 and returned there in 2003 for two years. During his second stay, he found himself mesmerized by the Korean drama *Winter Sonata*, which became so wildly popular on Japanese television that it was hailed as a major step in improving Korean-Japanese relations. Marshall was fascinated by the plot, in which the main character, Kang Joon-sang, gets struck by a truck, loses his memory, and starts a new life in the United States with a new identity. When his former Korean lover reconnects with him, Joon-sang gradually discovers his true past and the love he had with her. In his writing, Marshall compares himself to the character Joon-sang, who assumes a new identity as Min-yeong Lee.

> *Winter Sonata* seemed to be a reflection of my dislocation and confronted the guise of my identity. Perhaps it is an indication of the metamorphosis for the person I really am to be.
>
> In trying to convey his identity to Yu-jin, Min-yeong hesitatingly says, "Boku wa hen (I'm strange)." I cannot find any other line that so depicts my moments of confusion. I'm Korean, but I was raised in the United States. I'm Korean, but I don't speak it, and will talk to my Korean family in Japanese. My American family can speak English, but neither Korean nor Japanese. My life in translation realizes its complexity when I turn off the dubbing and cannot understand the entire story. Life in mono.[1]

Marshall watched the show with Japanese audio and subtitles, because he cannot fully comprehend Korean.

> Japanese was my second Asian language. . . . At the time I never thought of it in those terms, and I am not sure if I really wanted to. However, when I change the audio from Japanese to Korean, I am always surprised by the alteration of my perception of the characters. They seem to undergo a magical transformation. It is almost as if I have discovered who they really are. At the same time, if it were not for the Japanese dubbing and subtitles, I would not be able to understand their thoughts.[2]

Why would Marshall not want to acknowledge at that time that Japanese was his second Asian language? Was he not ready to go all the way back to his roots? Was he reluctant to awaken long dormant longings, to resurrect the dreams and unleash the locked-in secrets of his first language? What might he discover if he went all the way back?

Born Again Asian

Marshall points out with irony that when he eventually found his birth family he could only communicate with them in Japanese. He never imagined when he started to study Japanese in high school in Australia eight years before that it would help him to communicate with his Korean family, but studying Japanese was the beginning of his discovery of his past. Perhaps it was a subconscious inclination that his many travels during university finally led him to Japan and a decision that fortuitously allowed him to study in Korea for five months. He was in the midst of an incredible journey of self-discovery, a time of recapturing long-lost memories and regaining a culture he had been separated from for most of his life.

Marshall says that his journey really started in college, where he first encountered a diverse group of other Asian and non-Asian students, opening up a whole new world of stimulation, discovery, and confusion. He realized how complex his life really was and struggled to find connections to his past and between the various worlds of his present. Over the course of his college years, conversations with friends and travel abroad forced him to confront difficult questions: Am I not white? How Asian am I? Why do people always say that I don't look like a typical Korean? Why did my birth parents put me up for adoption? How would my life be different if I wasn't adopted? If I seek out my birth family, how will my adoptive family feel?

These questions seem taboo to some adoptees who come from home environments where questioning is discouraged, sometimes in extreme fashion. One transnational adoptee told me, "Whenever I tried to ask questions or raise my doubts, my parents shut me up by saying, 'You should be happy we adopted you! If we hadn't you would be working in a brothel.'"

The birth family search is an intensely emotional and potentially traumatic issue for everyone involved. I am more familiar with the search for an absent American father by Amerasians raised in Asia by their mothers. The child often longs for the connection, while fearing the possible rejection by the father. The search becomes more complicated for the child when the mother feels threatened by the potential bond with the father, dreading separation and loss.

Marshall's mother showed understanding; she had proposed the idea to Marshall, who at the time was still unaware of the possibilities before him. His close friends offered help and support by encouraging him to connect with his Korean self.

> "My Mom told me that she was okay with me searching for my birth family. . . . Only at the end of my search did I realize that she was scared to lose me. After all, I am her only child. Although I was not fully aware of the implications of what I was doing, I said that I was all right with the idea of meeting my birth family.
>
> "In my search and journey of learning about my past, I was helped by others along the way. My roommate and best friend, who I considered much wiser than me, once told me that when he looks at me he cannot help but think that I am Asian. Although it was just a passing comment, the impact . . . was powerful and it took me a while to realize its meaning. I had not really understood what it meant to be Asian for fourteen years; at the time I was nineteen. I first started to associate with Asians by going to the Chinese

American Students Association group, because that's who my Asian friends were at the time. To be honest, in the beginning I learned a lot about Asian American culture from this circle. I know that this route seems unusual, as the logical choice would have been to join the Korean American club, but I think there are many paths to understanding one's identity. . . . I did meet a classmate who was herself a Korean adoptee and who had already met her birth family after high school. She helped me to understand the sort of experiences I would confront. She experienced many emotional difficulties in coming to grips with her identity as a result of meeting them. Even though a couple years had already passed since she met them, I realized even at that time that her sadness, anger, and frustrations stemmed from an identity crisis. As she was a good friend, I learned a lot from our conversations, her mistakes, and what I could anticipate.

"Personally, I think adoptees need to have a certain amount of maturity and stability in knowing who they are before embarking on their search because the process of reuniting and the subsequent aftershocks (for some) can be so traumatic. I remember reading a book about adopted Koreans (*Birth Is More than Once*) and how many develop fantasies about who their parents are and become disappointed when reality does not meet expectations. I told myself before I met my birth family that it doesn't matter who they are or what their background is because I will accept them as they are. This really helped me in coping with all of the unexpected challenges in meeting and learning about my birth family and past."

When an opportunity appeared, and without considerable thought or planning, Marshall went to Japan for his junior year. It was his first time in an Asian country since his adoption. He lived with a Japanese host family, an experience that awoke memories and long-suppressed longings. He felt a strange familiarity with them that made him reflect on the life with his Korean family that he had missed by being adopted.

"In college I went to Japan and stayed with a host family. I felt a mixture of feelings about my past and who I was at the time. I especially felt regret for what I had missed. To not be in contact with your birth culture for fourteen years of your childhood is time that can never be made up. Being with a Japanese host family made me realize what it would have been like to be raised by an Asian family and how different my life was with my American family."

Great awakenings are filled with moments of immeasurable joy at one's newfound discoveries, the expanded family and community, the revived connections, along with the moments of deep regret for the life missed, the losses one has suffered, the years of separation and missed opportunities. Marshall knew that he could never be the same and wondered how he could integrate his new self into the self he had once known. He reveled in the richness of his discoveries.

"Quite simply, I fell in love with Asia. I embraced it metaphorically and so began my sonata of rediscovering the love I had lost. . . . It was only then that I allowed affinity to become destiny and let this opportune moment draw me to search for my Korean birth family. I was shocked that not only part of my family was still alive, but that I had two older brothers. I was speechless. Furthermore, out of synchronistic coincidence, the year I started Japanese lessons in Australia was the same year that my oldest Korean brother moved to Japan. What's even more unbelievable is that one of my cousins married a nice Japanese woman and both reside with my aunt in Korea. Because of all this, I have family members to talk to and who can act as Korean-to-Japanese translators when I visit."

On his odyssey back home Marshall was crushed to find that both his parents had died young, perhaps because of the harsh lives they had led as impoverished farmers. He did find his aunt, his mother's older sister, who gives him the closest feeling of connection to his mother. He felt his aunt's regret and shame that her little sister had to give up her third child for adoption. But Marshall could understand why when he saw the poor conditions in which they lived, eking out a living by struggling on a farm in Gwang-ju. Marshall also connected with his older brothers. They are still drawn to each other, perhaps with a feeling that all they have is each other. But he feels his oldest brother's jealousy and resentment that Marshall escaped from a grueling life and was raised in luxury in the United

States, enjoying unimaginable material comforts and education. His brother calls him *erai*, a great person, a word Marshall would never associate with himself, but understands how he would appear that way to his brother, a man denied educational, economic, and social status. Marshall began to notice that even his clothes, brand name products ordinary in his circles, were signs of affluence to his brother.

After returning from his first trip back to Korea, Marshall attempted to capture some of his feelings in "Colors."

She looked back with familiar eyes;
wearing colors that made sense to me.
As if the gaze was an echo
to an invitation never responded to
or a friend given no longitude.

She beckons with a hope
unfamiliarized to myself of years past,
past process of disenchantment;
what happened back then?

Is there anything magical left
of this nostalgic trance;
a stoic heart embroidered on bark
or the fluidity of age marked it dark.

She whispers promises of rescues
against the follies of years of latter me.
It tormented beyond concussion;
my conscience rejects causes of recollection.

And I ask is this safe; may solid colors
promise prescribed balance?
Familiarized backgrounds of a forgotten
age; incurable malnutrition
at this late stage?

As veins reach for an earth to make a
home, she suggests a wind of respect;
can't you call this home?

On two backgrounds
I've forgotten where I am;
my responding gaze asks for a chance;
can we dance two, to engrave balance
for romance?[3]

Marshall was reclaiming a surrendered identity—one given up, disowned, or denied in the face of loss. His search was for belonging and community, recovery of ethnicity, and discovery of authenticity. He embraced self and purpose, turning that which torments into what connects one to all of life. What once was seen as a curse was felt as a gift and with it a responsibility to use that gift. His identity, always there, was being liberated, actualized, and becoming a bridge from past to future.

White Boy in America

No longer indulging in the innocence and naïveté of his narrative of being an ordinary white American boy, Marshall had to learn to place his life in a larger picture of a giant wave of child migration that is inextricably related to global geopolitical events. He is one of an estimated two hundred thousand children from South Korea who have been adopted into families in North America, Europe, and Australia since the end of the Korean War. More than half have come to the United States. At first these transnational adoptions were an emergency measure to find homes mostly for Amerasian mixed race children born in the aftermath of the war, but the practice became an institutionalized way of dealing with poor and illegitimate children. At the time Marshall was adopted in 1983, it was a common practice that was beginning to draw international attention and negative media coverage—especially during the 1988 Seoul Olympics—that associated South Korea's economic ascendancy with the export of orphan children. As a result, adoptions were gradually curtailed and by the mid 1990s the largest number of Asian adoptees in America were from China. These adoptions too are connected to policies and practices in the home country, as nearly all adoptions from China are girls; the one-child policy of family planning leads to the relinquishment of daughters because of the strong cultural preference for boys to carry on family lineage.

Like most American transnational adoptees of his generation, Marshall was raised as simply a part of the family. It was accepted belief and common practice that the best way to enhance adoptees' adjustment to their new country was to raise them as if they were just like any other American kid. While his parents were cognizant of his background, they may not have been aware of the different approaches to raising such children. They certainly did not mean to deny his cultural background, but because of Marshall's apparently good adaptation to frequent moves and living in white communities, his parents did not consider how his background could have been instilled while he was growing up.

"My parents did not know much about the details of my background even though they did their best to answer any questions I had. It was just a matter of them not being aware of the option to mention Korean culture or offer language classes while I was growing up. I know that I say this with hindsight, however, as I was in many ways unaware and in denial about my cultural background, so I am not sure if I would have even accepted such opportunities to learn about my past. I don't blame them for the way they raised me. With maturity I have learned that all parents make mistakes in raising their kids and at the end, . . . I like to think that they did the best that they could."

Marshall was expected to regard himself as simply a member of his family, a part of his new community, and a citizen of his new country. His was a color-blind upbringing, commonly thought to be best for the adjustment of the child to his new life. His parents did not do or say anything to help him understand himself as Asian. Would it have been desirable for his Jewish parents to have taught him about Korea? Would he have been receptive? Perhaps the best that parents can do is offer—and if the child shows interest, to follow through, and if the child does not show interest, to be accepting of that too.

To Marshall, his life seemed normal. He had come to his Jewish parents when he was five years old, young enough to retain only snapshot memories of his life in Korea. Living among white people, he came to think of himself as white too. It wasn't that he wanted to deny being Korean, he just had no idea what it meant. Viewing the drama *Winter Sonata* following his college years brought on deep reflection on his early life as he saw himself reflected in the main character.

> My own gradual loss of my memory as In-chae Chun, my Korean name, began when I was almost five years old and was adopted by an American family. As I came to learn the English language and American culture, the only recollections of Korea I retained were flashes, like still shots from dreams, and the black-and-white photos of me at the orphanage. Ten years later, like Min-yeong Lee, I too, believed that I was American.
>
> Yet, the perception of myself was further complicated by believing that I was white, a common plight that many second generation Asian Americans find themselves in when they are growing up. In *Winter Sonata*, the camera focuses on Min-yeong's puzzle of a painting with a missing piece. As a young teenager I tried to compare myself to pop-idols such as *Beverly Hills 90210* stars . . . Luke Perry and Jamie Walters. This was like trying to fit a puzzle piece to the wrong jigsaw puzzle.[4]

Such conflicts are common for many Asian Americans, whether mixed race, adopted, or simply growing up isolated as Asian in America. Marshall thought he was white because that is all he saw around him. He was so unaware of his difference that he kept looking at his six-foot-tall father and wondering, "How come I'm not getting taller?" But there was more going on inside Marshall than he realized at the time. He confesses that when he finally had the chance to meet Asian girls he had no interest in them. "I only liked white girls," he admits with some embarrassment, acknowledging another consequence of his upbringing.

A familiar label for transnational Asian adoptees, though it has variations, is "Fake Asian." People tell them they look Asian, but don't know anything about the culture. Some people say, "You're not a real Asian, you don't sound Asian." Others might tell an Asian woman, "You sound like a white girl!" One adoptee told me how she empowered herself unexpectedly by mastering Spanish, which gained her acceptance in Latino communities and Latin American countries she visited. She was pleasantly surprised that people accepted her because she could speak Spanish, and so she in turn identified with them. She later worked among African Americans for years and their acceptance prompted her to identify with them too. But she realized that she identified with everything but Asian, and sought to liberate herself from her "Asian Phobia"—her fear of anything that reminded her of her heritage, because she didn't know anything about it—by educating herself about her own and other Asian cultures in deliberate acts of empowerment.

I remember a woman from the Philippines who teased me by challenging my identity: "I thought you were Japanese, but you're American!" As a self-identified Asian who was raised among whites in America, I asked myself, am I faking it, if a "real Asian" can tell that I am really American? I questioned how authentic I was in declaring an Asian identity. Such challenges not only created doubts in me, but also drove me to engage in activities that would empower me. I strove to make myself into an Asian that everyone would recognize and respect. Like Marshall, this journey was directed by a strong and insistent urge to return to Asia.

The Adoption Controversy

The once standard manner of not actively teaching children about their ethnic origins has been challenged for years by those concerned with the possible negative consequences of adoptions that cross racial or national boundaries. Black social workers raised the issue in the 1970s, protesting the adoption of black children by white parents who they claimed were unqualified to raise the children with a strong black identity. Along with Native American activists and organizations, they argued that transracial adoption was a form of cultural genocide, prompting adoption agencies to stop the practice until the 1990s when federal legislation was passed to promote it once again.

In recent years, adopted Asian Americans have spoken out against the potential danger of international adoption. Despite what he saw as his good fortune in being adopted, Charlie McCue expressed a belief that the conflicts of name, race, and culture make transracial adoptions generally not a good idea.

> I realize that my life here is much better than what it would have been in Korea. I realize that I was adopted into a very, very loving family. I totally love my family and I realize how fortunate I am. But fundamentally I still believe you're robbed of something. You're put in this environment and situation where usually your parents don't understand anything about you culturally, and so you're forced to live your life as this white person when you know that's not you. It creates a lot of self-loathing in people. I really believe that Asian babies need to grow up in Asian households.[5]

In *The Language of Blood*, Jane Jeong Trenka tells the story of her life growing up in a conservative Christian home in northern Minnesota after being adopted from Korea. She writes of the frustration when questions arose for her but went unanswered in her new home. Her desire to meet her birth mother was threatening to her adoptive parents and the eventual search created a rift with them that has been hard to bridge. Trenka is not against transnational adoption, but feels that adoptive parents need to provide a lot more for their kids: "I think if you have a child who is of a different ethnic group—and I am pretty militant on this—you need to move to where there are others."[6]

More moderate views are expressed by other writers, such as Katy Robinson, author of *A Single Square Picture*.

> I would tell parents that the process or journey doesn't end when they bring home the child of their dreams. No matter how much they feel like the child is "theirs," a transracial adoptee has a history, culture and identity that preceded the adoption, and it is important for adoptive parents to recognize this without feeling threatened. The best that parents can do is to try and incorporate their child's culture into the natural fabric of family life and encourage the child to explore his or her past when the need arises.[7]

Lee Corbett, adopted from Korea by a white Southern family, voices a balanced view: "It's preferable to have a child raised in their same ethnicity but also preferable for a child to be adopted rather than be in an orphanage or foster care."[8]

While the views of these adoptees are diverse, they all call for a greater degree of effort by adoption agencies and adoptive parents to view transnational adoption in a more complex framework that includes political power dynamics. Although views on adoption tend to highlight altruistic or humanistic reasons, there is an uneasy link between wealth, power, and privilege on the one hand and race, ethnicity, and culture on the other. International adoption is now a lucrative enterprise, leading to the involvement of organized crime in illegal adoptions as well as those who entice poor women to place their children in adoption. Early general practices of adoption were not always in the best interests of adoptees, and the situation today is even more complicated. We need to not only understand the circumstances in the country of origin but also try to do more to allow families to keep their children, while we recognize that international adoption from Asia will continue to be a viable way in which Americans can create or expand families and hopefully give children a better life.

Balancing and Blending Identities

Coming to terms with what it means to be adopted transnationally and transracially, Marshall also faced the ambiguity of his past, including the lack of information about his birth circumstances and disconnection from his birth family, culture, and nation. In their new countries, most adoptees from Korea, like Marshall, were raised with little exposure to people from their birth country or other adoptees. As adults, through flows of communication, media, and travel, they come into increasing contact with each other, Korean culture, and the South Korean state. Since the 1990s, as infants continue to leave Korea for adoption to the West, a growing number of adult adoptees have returned to seek their cultural and biological origins. Some have chosen to live in South Korea as repatriates in order to reconnect with their lost birth culture and heritage, and thus make sense of the transnational adoption paradox in their lives.

Marshall has spent some time in South Korea, but has mostly felt a need to bring things together in the United States. He became a graduate student at Stanford in East Asian studies, in what became an opportunity to embrace an identity as Asian American. He engaged in activities to integrate the largely foreign student population of Asian graduate students into the mostly U.S.-born Asian American undergraduate population. His own experience and perspective as Asian born, his American socialization, and his lived experience in Asia all helped him to have the vision and motivation to try to unite these usually separate groups of students. In 2010, Marshall received an award from the Asian American Activities Center at Stanford for his contributions to student life, an achievement that he cherished as an indication of how far he had come in his life from being the color-blind white boy to being recognized in this way as Asian American.

Marshall is also renewing his ties with Judaism, his religion from childhood, which he describes as a deep cultural bond. But being acknowledged as a Jew may pose even more problems than being seen as Asian. In the eyes of others, Marshall is the "right race" as Asian, but the "wrong race" as a Jew. In a recent visit to a synagogue, an elderly woman usher approached Marshall as he entered and coldly informed him, "This is a religious service." He snapped back at her, "Thank you. And not all Jews are white!" Another woman usher standing nearby practically fell over from the force of Marshall's charge. His Jewishness is always contested and must be defended and explained. The Star of David hangs naturally from his neck, though he was self-conscious of that when he met his aunt in Korea and noticed the crucifix around hers.

Marshall says that his life still feels compartmentalized, internally and externally. He has made connections, but blending them is a challenge. Friends are all separated into different worlds. There are the Asian friends, the Asian American friends, the adoptee friends, the Jewish friends, all separate. In each of these worlds he may still have a feeling of being "the only one." In those moments, when he is isolated or hurt, to whom can he turn who would understand? The obvious group is Korean adoptees, and Marshall has made efforts to connect and reach out and bring others together through a website and blog on Facebook called Adopted Korean Jews United.

I did not realize it at first, but I am aware now that including Marshall's story in this book, in which all the other stories focus on people whose biological parents are of different ethnicities, may be seen as yet another way of emphasizing his marginality. My intention was the opposite, to make connections between his experience as a transracial, transnational adoptee and the experience of mixed race people. I wanted to move beyond accepted racial boundaries in our thinking and show that many people have similar experiences of mixed roots. My hope was to be inclusive by showing that Marshall's parents too were mixed—two biological Asian parents and two adoptive white American parents.

I view Marshall's development as a healing process of transitions toward meaning, balance, wholeness, and connectedness. There is a profound change in his worldview, a transformation that brings with it new ways of experiencing the self embedded in and expressive of community. In his healing process he is developing a synergistic view that values the coming together of cultures—their interrelations and apparently dissonant combinations—and the creation of an often unexpected, new, and greater whole from the disparate, seemingly conflicting parts, a more effective total resource. He sees himself limiting his identity when he tries to fit it into the norms of any group, and expanding his identity when he tries to express it more fully in its complex and rich form.

Marshall's emerging hybrid identity is Jewish, white, American, Asian, international adoptee, and possibly more. He is "cutting across borders" and defining himself according to the salient features in his life rather than trying to force himself into existing identity paradigms. He is inspired to share his personal journeys and to increase public awareness, educating within and outside the adoption community and Asian American community. He is one of a number of Korean Jews and others who are organizing worldwide to give voice to their concerns, forming social and political organizations to strengthen identities, build social bonds and support networks, and establish legitimacy within Asian American and adoption communities. His activities are a way of finding his own voice and helping others to find theirs. Together, Asians from different homelands are creating a third space, in which they have voice and agency, advocate on their own behalf, and identify as both Asian and adopted, rather than being forced to choose between these identities and cultural groups. This third space takes Marshall beyond the spaces imposed by biology or ethnicity to places where he feels a tenuous sense of home.

> "I think one of the hardest things for me to balance is my connection with Japan and how the culture and language have served as a conduit for understanding my Asian background. After all, I use Japanese to communicate with my Korean family, and beyond my academic studies of Japan the culture has helped me understand other Asian cultures, including Korea. It's awkward when I sometimes apologize to a Korean for my Japanese being much better than my Korean language skills. At the same time, though, I cannot think of or regard myself as Japanese as I am aware of the rigid boundaries in how Japanese define themselves. I know that this sounds weird, but regardless I cannot help but feel a connection with the country and its culture. As a result, while I was born Korean, my path in understanding my Asian heritage doesn't always make me feel Korean. This is compounded by the fact that when I meet native Koreans and Korean Americans, many of them doubt my lineage . . . because of the way I appear. Only when I tell them my Korean name do they then believe me. Many native Asians think that I am Japanese, Chinese, or half-white and half-Asian. It's hard to fit in sometimes, and it's difficult having to defend my affiliation in so many cultural circles because it makes it hard to feel comfortable."

Marshall is developing a new vision of what it might mean to live and work in this third space as a foreign diplomat.

> "I am pursuing the Foreign Service because it seems to be the best career for me to apply my life experiences and academic background. Since my undergraduate career I have been passionate about facilitating cross-cultural communications. This is due to the fact that I have had to deal with intercultural challenges for most of my life. I have had to learn to juggle my Asian American, adopted Korean

American, and Jewish backgrounds. Because of such experiences, I feel like my whole life has prepared me for such a role. Thus, I want to also help others through the process of negotiating differences. I know what it's like to feel lost, and I think when people find themselves in this situation a little friendly guidance along the way can make a big difference in turning the confusion into as much of a positive experience as possible."

In his personal statement to graduate schools Marshall wrote:

The process of reconnecting with my Korean heritage and understanding the cultures that constitute my identity has influenced my aspirations to become a diplomat and facilitate dialogue between the United States and other state representatives. Because of my cultural background, I am an example of how globalization has created identities that can no longer be defined by one nationality or culture. Navigating racial, ethnic, and national differences has been integral to my personal and professional identity formation. I believe I have finally found a career in which I can apply my passion in facilitating cross-cultural communications and witness the impact of my efforts at a grassroots and international level. In achieving my dream of becoming and serving as a career diplomat, I hope to participate in the actual cross-cultural communications involved in public diplomacy itself. Whether in Asia or other regions, my objective is to let others know that despite cultural, economic, and ideological rifts, we have choices in how to negotiate differences. Because of my diverse background, I feel called upon and uniquely positioned to help facilitate understanding in the international community. In promoting U.S. foreign policy, we need individuals who can serve as intermediaries and representatives of the United States' diversity, and I believe I am well suited for such a role as a diplomat.

At thirty-two, Marshall moved east in the summer of 2011 to attend Georgetown University's School of Foreign Service. He moves beyond the personal by placing his life in a broader social context, believing that he has been given the opportunity to unite different worlds. He sees his struggle as transcendence, requiring the ability to move beyond boundaries and limitations imposed by self, others, or systems.

Marshall is connecting not only with all parts of himself but also with others and a realm beyond himself, with a felt responsibility to work in ways that bring people together despite their differences, fully realizing their common humanity. Marshall expresses how he views his life in "Wisps."

I cut across borders
as if they have no meaning

I gaze upon Asians—
mesmerized acceptance,
reflective white

A long time ago
I called for home
Now I am not sure
what that is?

I cried for someone
to console with . . .
I laughed at myself
for trying to be accepted

I use culture
for my convenience;
Apply pressure
when it is not there.

Use my mirror as a reflection
mesmerized acceptance,
What is there?

I drive a couple of miles,
to see what else is out there

I hold fast
to what remains,
Who knows how long
I will be here . . .

I cut across borders
as if they have no meaning.

I asked myself
for a reason;
I know it's out there
Somewhere

Finger hold a ledge,

It's better
than what's down there.

A long time ago
I called for home
Now I am not sure
where that is?

I asked myself a question
they're everywhere . . .

Remember my reflection
Apply pressure
when it is not there

Take time
to answer them,
they're somewhere

I consoled my crying;
I want to know
why am I here

I gaze upon myself—
You'll see
why I am here

A long time ago
I called for home
Now I know
that I'm here[9]

NINE

Victims No More

Flying through the Japanese countryside, comfortable in our lush seats on the air-conditioned bullet train bound for Tokyo, Norah and I chatted about our adventure. We had spent the day high in the mountains at a manganese mine where Korean laborers dug for ore to fuel the Japanese military machine from the late 1930s until the end of World War II. Norah's mother and my colleague, Soo im Lee, had led a group of scholars and activists on an excursion to view the mine and better understand the efforts of people to save it and the on-site historical museum, a memorial to the men who labored there.

That morning we had assembled at Osaka Station and boarded vans that traversed the city streets and suburban sprawl and finally went up winding riverside roads deep into the hills that at some point became mountains. We arrived at last at the museum and were greeted by Lee Yog sik and his mother and were escorted straight to the mine, where we donned hard hats and followed Lee inside. The heat and humidity of the summer day quickly faded as we moved deeper and deeper inside the narrow tunnels, descending into darkness. The dampness, at first refreshing, soon became chilling.

Lee told us that a man might hammer all day lying in a cramped space and only make a few centimeters' headway. "He might have to be in this position," he said, pointing to the life-size doll placed there. I tried to imagine a day in the mine but shuddered at the thought. My life of ease did not allow my imagination to go that far; my limited empathy compelled me to divert my thoughts to the reality that I do not have to do that, I am free to keep walking toward the exit. I lingered a bit to see what I could learn from being there about the trials of others, but eventually emerged into the sunlight. The looks on the other visitors' faces told me that they too were glad to be out of the mine.

We assembled in the small museum of the history of the mine and listened to Lee explain how laborers were brought from Korea. Lee is the son of a man who worked in this manganese mine, extracting an essential ingredient for iron and steel production that the Japanese military needed for weapons. Lee tells us that we should not forget what happened and that children must know this history so that we don't repeat mistakes. I agree, but when he explains that the workers were forced to come here from Korea I wonder whether Lee is overgeneralizing. Historians report that Japan began labor mobilization in 1938 and conscripted labor in 1939, but that most of those forcibly brought to Japan chose to repatriate after the war. Some laborers who remained in Japan had come from Korea earlier in the colonial period as Japanese nationals. That migration had not been forced at the point of a gun; Japanese colonization and agricultural policy in Korea had disrupted Korean society and displaced millions of people, many of whom came to Japan to escape unbearable conditions in their homeland.

Perspectives such as Lee's are inevitable as victims deal with their trauma. I have visited Hiroshima many times to honor those who suffered in that horrible tragedy and I have seen how the Peace Memorial Museum presents the atrocity in a light that places Japan as a victim, rather than in a wider context of a Pacific war that included military aggression. Must such horror be portrayed simplistically to give a clear message? In Okinawa, the Himeyuri Peace Museum honors the high school girls who valiantly nursed the wounded until their own deaths. My visit there reinforced my image of the tragedy of their sacrifice and suffering. But I was surprised when my friend pointed out that the message was confusing because the girls could be seen not simply as victims, since they were enthusiastic supporters of the Japanese emperor and the war itself. Would knowing this make us less sympathetic and reduce the impact of the message that war is hell? Is it therefore acceptable to simplify the story or must the story be told in its full complexity in the name of truth? Is it too painful to say that Okinawans were not pure victims of Japanese militarism, or that the Pacific war was not simply a story of Japanese victimized by American aggression?

Japanese politicians have been chastised for claiming that colonization brought great advancements to Korea, glossing over, or completely denying, the oppression. The traumas of colonization are too great to allow unreserved recognition of related advances. The issue of victimization is immense for Koreans and Korean residents in Japan. Several of my Korean students at Tokyo University admitted that they were in Japan not just to learn from the Japanese but to take that learning and beat them.

Such antagonistic sentiments are seen among some other people of Korean ancestry living in Japan as well. I am curious about Norah's family, knowing that they came before the start of the war. I learn that Norah's grandfather, Lee Chon soon, came from Korea in 1929 when he was four years old. His father was already in Japan as a migrant worker when his mother bribed a fisherman to bring her and her son to Shimonoseki.

They were both Japanese nationals because Japan had extended Japanese nationality to the colonized people of Korea, making them part of an expanding multiethnic empire. Hundreds of thousands of people migrated to Japan in search of a better life, learning Japanese and adopting Japanese names, the language and names of their colonizers. Lee Chon soon became Takeo Masao; he attended school, learned to read and write Japanese, and was able to acquire jobs that paid higher wages than his first-generation father could earn. Lee recalls, "In Japan, I experienced more of a systematic discrimination such as being paid lower wages than my Japanese workmates. This may sound shameful, but I thought that if I could pass as a Japanese in Japan, daily life would be a lot easier for me than in Korea."[1]

Takeo's views on Japan were also influenced by the kindness he and his mother received from a doctor in Wakayama who rented a shack to them when they could find no other place to live. This made an indelible impression on Takeo, who always taught his children that Japan is not a completely discriminatory society—there are good Japanese too. He taught his children to use their own eyes to see individuals rather than prejudge people by their ethnicity.

His view was also influenced by his experience when he was ordered by his parents to return to Korea by himself at war's end to determine whether the family should resettle there. After being raised in Japan, the nineteen-year-old had difficulties adjusting to his new life in Korea. He disliked life in the countryside. Koreans discriminated against him, calling him Japanese due to his heavily accented Korean. He realized that his identity made him an outsider in both societies. On one hand, he was not accepted in Korean society because in many ways he was culturally Japanese. On the other hand, he remained an "alien" in Japan because he was ethnically Korean.

Lee Soo im was the eldest of three children, born in Japan in 1953 as a Korean national. She grew up as Takeo Reiko, a name meant to identify her as Japanese and hide her Korean ancestry. This changed dramatically at the time of her high school graduation. Teachers were being advised by the Ministry of Education to be aware of the needs of their minority students, so instructors at her school had called in all twenty of the Korean girls to encourage them to come out publicly. Her teacher confronted her with the words, "You should force yourself to come out!" Angered, she answered "Why? Can you take responsibility for what will happen to my life?" Her teacher conceded, "I don't blame you if you don't want to do it."

But she kept thinking about it, and the night before the graduation ceremony she decided to do it. The school had prepared two diplomas for each of the Korean girls, one in each name, but Reiko was the only one to choose the one with her Korean name—Soo im. She was so scared she almost fainted as they came closer to her turn. Finally, when her name was called she shouted "Hai!" and went up on stage to receive her diploma. She noticed kids whispering and she thought, "Oh no, now I have lost all my friends." After the ceremony her friends surrounded her and one stunned her by saying, "We didn't know your parents divorced!"

"What are you talking about?" Soo im asked.
"That's why your name changed, right?"

"No, I'm Korean," she replied.
Everyone froze.
Finally one girl broke the silence, "Oh, really."
Then another one said, "Let's go shopping."
They never talked about it.

To the U.S. and Back

After graduating from college, Soo im tried to get a job in Japan but found no opportunities as a Korean. The San Francisco Peace Treaty in 1952 had left her parents without Japanese nationality and the *jus sanguinis* nationality law made Soo im Korean although born in Japan. She realized that if she was Japanese she would have a chance for employment, so she decided to naturalize. She was not given an application form, however, when she told officials that she wanted to naturalize as an individual, not as a family. The officials insisted it should be a family application. But her father refused to go along with her, shouting, "Over my dead body! You do whatever you like, but I do not want to be Japanese!" So she left Japan, angry not only with Japanese, but also with her father for his stubborn disregard for the effect of his refusal on her life.

Soo im eventually went to UCLA for graduate study, where she met many immigrants who were studying to be TESOL teachers. Her Jewish roommate's similar form of "invisibility" impressed her. Soo im also learned how overt racism in the United States is part of everyday life for the many minorities who are visually distinguishable. She hated being Korean at the time, but being forced to use the name Soo im Lee in the United States (since Takeo Reiko was an alias) gradually changed her. Soo im met Koreans and Japanese who were kind to her and accepted her as one of them, and started to feel it was okay to be bicultural, to relate to both groups. It is not unusual for Koreans born in Japan who come to the United States to feel socially and culturally most comfortable in the company of, and most accepted by, Japanese. In contrast, they discover they have little in common with "real" Koreans and are less welcomed in their communities. Accepting this experience is a step toward liberation from the obsession with being Korean in Japan.

After studying in California Soo im went to Boston, where she met and married a foreign student from the Middle East and gave birth to a daughter. She was amazed that her baby could be an American simply because the child was born in the United States. This was in stark contrast to Japanese nationality, which at the time was not granted unless the father was a Japanese national, even if the child was born in Japan. Although no one in the family had Japanese nationality, Soo im decided to raise Norah in Japan and returned there in 1980. At first the family tried to raise their child like an ordinary Japanese girl. They soon discovered that Norah's experiences were colored by her physical appearance, which set her apart from her peers. At twenty, Norah spoke of her diverse educational experiences.

"My parents put me in a Japanese preschool. But this is a bitter memory for me.

"Once when I was playing in the sandbox, a boy came up to me and suddenly said: 'You can't play here!'

"I asked him 'Why not?'

"'Your eyes are a weird color!'

"That moment was the first time I was made aware that I was a *gaijin* (foreigner) among Japanese. Though I was a strong-willed child I couldn't answer him back, and just cried. From then on that child bullied me and I was helpless to stop the sadness and hurt. I tried as best I could to act in ways that I wouldn't be noticed and I developed an inferiority complex about being different.

"When my parents noticed this change in me they sent me to an international school in Kobe. I still remember clearly the first day I entered the school. There were blond children, kids with blue eyes, children with brown skin, Japanese kids who couldn't speak Japanese so well, kids from thirty countries! Being among these students in an environment that appreciated differences, I was released from my inferiority complex of being a foreigner. I started to develop confidence in myself and felt comfortable with my differences. I know that not all biracial children in Japan are provided with the opportunity to be sent to international schools, given the high tuition cost. I was very fortunate and it worked out well in my case."

Being accepted by others at her new school allowed Norah to accept herself and eventually enabled her to accept others, changing her attitudes toward Japanese society that she felt had rejected her. Later, going to an American university further changed her views on the value of diversity.

> "American educational environments highly value uniqueness and the system enhances a person's individuality and accepts diverse ways of thinking. In an American university, the diversity of students and their individuality enhance the great energy of the campus, providing mutual stimulation for all. In this kind of educational environment being different from others is not a disadvantage; instead I was taught that it was an advantage."

Norah's separation from Japan enhanced her appreciation of Japanese culture. Her experience in the United States also gave her ideas about how to make Japanese society better. She pursued East Asian studies with a deep interest in Japanese history and a belief in the crucial role of Japan in international society.

> "I was able to see the beauty of Japanese society and culture objectively once I separated from it. Things I took for granted living there, like formal manners, appreciation for subtleties, empathy for others . . . beautiful things Western society can learn from. . . . I hope the Japanese sense of virtue and dignity aren't lost and that I don't lose these values either. But I also feel it is necessary for Japanese society to develop by having a stronger value of coexistence and equally integrating Japanese and foreigners. Dreaming of that kind of Japanese society encourages me in my studies in the United States."

Norah turned her disadvantage into a gift, seeing how it enabled her to develop her identity and appreciate cultural differences.

> "To me as a person who has felt inferiority at being not Japanese, I now feel pride in being able to appreciate and accept different cultures and ways of thinking. Because I was a foreigner I could develop a clear understanding of my identity earlier than most Japanese youth. I think this is a key concept for Japanese educators in the future. It would be great if they can give youth stimulating lessons about the importance of creativity, originality, and uniqueness through education. This is my dream."

Nationality

Norah knew that she was not Japanese, not just because another child
had told her so but because of her realization that legally she was not
Japanese but American. Soo im told Norah that she herself was not Japanese and neither was Norah's father.

> "In our small family there were three different nationalities, like a
> mini–United Nations. . . . It wasn't easy being a foreign family in this
> Japanese society rooted so deeply in the ideology of a monoethnic
> nation."

Three people—father, mother, and child—and three nationalities.
What does such a family tell us about the meaning of nationality? Is it
personal or just legalistic if each member of the family can be different in this way? Does it show a new individuality that permeates even
the nuclear family where each member is a unique and autonomous
person? Is this the new transnational family? And why do the father,
mother, and daughter all have different nationalities anyway? Do
nationality laws unite or divide families?

Now that she was raising her child in Japan, Soo im was determined more than ever to naturalize. Again, the officials claimed that
fathers are the *koshu*, or family head, so Soo im was told that her
husband and child also needed to naturalize. The concept of a three-
nationality family was too far outside the Japanese legal concept of a
family. Eventually, Soo im warned that she would charge them with a
human rights violation, and she prevailed. In 2000 she filed an application and a year later in 2001 she was informed she was Japanese and
no longer a foreigner, ending a long battle that first started in 1974.
Soo im naturalized on her own terms, with her own name. For years,
officials advised applicants to choose a Japanese name, providing examples in a handbook with names like Kaneda or Shimizu. This was
all extra-legal guidance that pressured applicants to assimilate, imply-
ing that becoming Japanese required stripping oneself of a previous
identity. Most naturalizers took their *tsumei* (legal alias) or "passing"
name. Today, however, many officials follow the letter of the law and

advise that any name is acceptable. Norah's mother naturalized as Lee Soo im, her *honmyo*, or original name.

Naturalization has been a major issue in Korean communities in Japan, as it raises the difficult question, can a Korean be Japanese? The question is necessary because the nationality law forces people to submit to procedures of naturalization to become Japanese citizens. It seems different from my personal question, can an American be Japanese? Or more specifically, can a Japanese American be Japanese?

I too naturalized. But how was this different from Soo im's naturalization?

"You had an easier time," Soo im told me, insisting that she had to naturalize because of discrimination, while I did not. Her claim that I had certain advantages is no doubt true. But which advantages were most important? My Japanese mother? My whiteness? My American nationality? My Japanese wife? My Japanese children? My position as professor in the elite Tokyo University? My status as a national government employee? I was probably favored for all of these reasons, racial and national, conveying the power and privilege as an American with whiteness as well as "Japanese blood," however tainted it might be.

But how disadvantaged was Soo im? Judging by the statistics showing thousands of naturalizations each year by Koreans, the process is not too difficult any more for most applicants. Soo im encountered opposition mainly because other members of her family, first her father, then her husband, would not naturalize.

In 1996 I attended a meeting in Kawasaki of a group called the Association for the Return of Our Ethnic Names. Members had all naturalized with Japanese names. Pressured by officials to do so, they were now going through legal procedures to have their names changed to their Korean names. I was drawn to their battles and to their stance on terminology and wondered what it signified for their identities. They referred to themselves with the cumbersome term *Nihon kokuseki o motsu Kankokujin* (Koreans with Japanese nationality). They did not refer to themselves as Nihonjin (Japanese). Their reluctance to refer to themselves as Japanese shows their own insistence on equating ethnicity with nationality. I asked whether it is not possible to be a Kankokukei

Nihonjin but they told me they cannot use the word *Nihonjin*. I wonder whether this is because of their own opposition or their expected
rejection by the mainstream should they attempt to claim membership.

I often wonder how long we remain "different" because others see
us and treat us differently, and how much we continue to perpetuate
our own difference. If the majority consents to be color-blind, we can
say, "Okay, it's about time." Or we can say, "Not so fast, we're not
ready yet. When there is real equality we can consent to becoming
invisible. Until then, we can't be invisible, we need to be different."

If I raise this question I encounter reactions that tell me that I don't
understand the situation. Trying to be deliberately provocative, I asked
an Okinawan writer once whether Okinawans were not Nihonjin,
meaning Japanese citizens, knowing that the term *Nihonjin* to her
meant an ethnic group. My question prompted an emotional response
from some people in the audience who tried to convince me that it was
not the minority's problem but the rejection by the majority that made
it impossible for Okinawans to say they are Japanese. But I believe that
there is agency in acknowledging that one is Nihonjin, a Japanese citizen, with the meaning of Japanese just that, divorced completely from
meanings of ethnicity. I am out of touch with reality, I am told. Until
the majority changes its use of the word, minorities cannot change
theirs. I feel that we do not need to accept the identities ascribed by
dominants and can assert identities denied by others.

Soo im has become a voice of assertion of Koriakei Nihonjin (Korean Japanese) identity. She believes that the path she has chosen—
naturalizing and becoming a Japanese national—is one way Koreans
can empower themselves. She felt that as a Korean national she could
demand equal rights but the state could deny them. As a Japanese
national she feels more power to insist on equality. By calling herself
Koriakei Nihonjin, Soo im shatters stereotypes and forges new images
and representations of who the Japanese are.

I wonder whether Norah now sees her mother any differently.
How would she describe her? Is she still a Korean resident in Japan
(Zainichi Kankokujin), or Korean Japanese (Kankokukei Nihonjin)?
Labels are clumsy. *Zainichi Kankokujin* literally means a Republic of
Korea national in Japan. When a Zainichi is in the United States, is

she still Zainichi? Is her mother still Zainichi even though she is a Japanese citizen? Why not describe her as Japanese, rather than Korean? Is she more Korean than Japanese because she has Korean "blood"? Does ethnicity trump nationality?

"Even after her naturalization, I still identify my mother as Zainichi Kankokujin. I have to admit that my definition is quite expansive and usually includes those who naturalize. Her name, Soo im Lee, also explains her ethnic roots. I might tell people that she has *Nihon kokuseki* (Japanese citizenship). In English, I usually say she is Japanese with Korean ethnic roots. In the context of conversing with other Koreans, however, I tend to bring out the Korean first by saying, 'My mother is Korean but she was born and raised in Japan' or I just use the Korean term, 'Jae-il Kyopo.'"

I have taken a path similar to Soo im's, naturalizing as Shigematsu Stephen, though the official told me I could choose any name at all. Playfully, I asked him whether Tokugawa would be okay, and he smiled and assured me it would. Out of curiosity, I asked if Koreans were told the same thing, and he insisted that they were. He suggested that Murphy would be an apt choice. I assumed he thought that since I looked like a gaijin, complete assimilation would be impossible, and my name might as well match my appearance. Or he may have just been deferring to an American. I considered the possibility, which would allow me to proclaim that even someone with the name of Murphy could be Japanese, but I decided that this would be too much of a stretch for majority Japanese to accept and that my Japanese identity would simply be denied. So I took the name Shigematsu, my mother's family name, to make it easier to assert myself as Japanese. I believe that we can construct new images of who is Japanese, making this identity broader and more inclusive. I refer to myself as an Amerikakei Nihonjin (American Japanese), challenging others to imagine a Japanese of mixed ancestry, not in a separate and distinct category of *haafu*, but as a variety of Japanese.

The irony of Soo im's situation is that when she was Korean, everyone thought she was Japanese, as she was known as Takeo Reiko. Now that she is Japanese, everyone thinks she is Korean, because she is known as Lee Soo im. People tell her that if her name is Lee, she cannot be Japanese. She has to insist she is Japanese, but she has been accused of calling others Nihonjin when she is being critical, in a way that sounds like she is distinguishing herself from them. A colleague challenged her on this by saying, "You are criticizing Nihonjin, but you are Nihonjin too!" This surprised Soo im, who retorted, "I don't think I'm the same kind of Nihonjin as you are."

This exchange shows the difficulty of separating the word *Nihonjin*, meaning Japanese, from its ethnic connotations when using the reference *Nihon kokumin*, or national of Japan. Soo im's use of the term *Koriakei Nihonjin* is her way of asserting ethnicity and citizenship, declaring that Japan is a country for diverse people. It is certainly not a denial of her Korean ancestry, for she sees the reclaiming of suppressed or marginalized identities as a crucial step toward freedom. But Soo im feels there is a danger of placing herself completely within the category of "ethnic minority," as completely distinct from the majority. A hyphenated identity is a way of saying she is not just Korean, and unlike most naturalizers who pass as majority, she is also saying she is not just Japanese. Perhaps Soo im is a *fujun* (impure) Zainichi Kankokujin and also a *fujun* Nihonjin.

As Soo im embraces a complex identity, I too resist defining myself just as American—and others' attempts to box me into this category, which I feel that left unchallenged would validate existing stereotypes about the homogeneity and purity of the majority and allow others to define themselves as "purely Japanese." I accept being American and also place myself inside "their" box, as an impure Japanese. I challenge others to see the diversity within themselves and the connections with those they imagine to be outside their group. My identity is based in internal diversity, a sense of living in the borderlands.

Multiple Identities and Homes

After studying in the United States for six years, Norah took a journey to Korea in August 2004. She had always wanted to study abroad, and Korea was the obvious choice. At first everything felt new and exciting. She felt foreign, and there were so many things she did not know, especially about contemporary culture and society. But as she gradually acquired the language she felt more at home, more Korean. She was surprised to realize how much she already knew. People treated her like a foreigner and explained everything to her, but she already knew about things like ancestral worship and foods, because she grew up with them. When her mother came to visit her, Norah was able to translate for her and introduce her to Korea.

In Korea, she lived with a Korean American girl. They often exchanged experiences. The roommate felt sorry for her, asking "How can you stand being stared at?" But Norah felt immune to their stares, being used to it from her upbringing in Japan, though it was much more extreme in Korea. Koreans couldn't label her easily, so were curious, or just thought she was an exotic foreigner. Her roommate didn't like Korea because many people expected her to behave like a Korean female, and when she didn't, they got upset. But there were not the same expectations for Norah. Koreans would think, "Oh she's from America, you can't blame her." And when she acted Korean, they were surprised and delighted.

Norah now had another culture to integrate into her complex identity. I wonder how she brings her diverse ethnic parts together into a whole.

"American is a legal identity. I didn't particularly feel American when I moved to the United States for college but after living in the U.S. for nearly a decade, I'm probably a bit more American now. My U.S. citizenship has become increasingly important as part of my identity. My citizenship has helped me access scholarship opportunities that noncitizens are not eligible for and it provides me with the option of permanently residing in the United States without any problems.

"Japanese is a cultural identity. Japan is my home. I grew up speaking the Osaka dialect, eating Japanese food, watching Japanese cartoons, listening to Japanese music while attending an international school. It's where I spent the first eighteen years of my life.

"Korean is an ethnic identity. I still think of myself as partially Korean even though my mother is now a Japanese citizen. Living in Seoul has definitely helped me learn more about Korea.

"My father's Middle Eastern background is also part of my ethnic identity; it's where half of my family is from. I hope to go there someday and learn more about the language, history, and culture. Unfortunately, I had very little exposure to the culture so it's definitely the least developed part of my identity but it's equally important. My last name, which I intend to keep after marriage, will forever reveal my roots."

Although her Middle Eastern heritage remains distant, Norah did visit her grandparents in Turkey in the winter of 2011. Her grandfather lamented over how little his only grandchild knew of her ancestry, that she had never visited and couldn't speak his native language, and he blamed Norah's father for neglecting his duties. They could not tell the grandfather that Norah was engaged to an American, fearing his great disappointment.

Norah's upbringing and research interests bring her back to Japan and into the Zainichi Korean world. She also dreams of researching Middle Eastern immigrants to California as a way of connecting to that part of her ancestry. Her identity attempts to embrace all of these influences.

"I identify myself with my father's heritage, my mother's heritage, and as an American citizen who has grown up in Japan. I embrace all of them in various degrees and ways, and I'd hate to pick just one. It's overwhelming as a self-introduction but people who care will get it. But of course in certain contexts, I'm forced to pick one. For instance, 'American' is what I put to identify myself in all official documents. I sometimes say I'm American simply because that is my legal identity and it's hard for people to challenge it. Perhaps the category of 'American' seems to encompass all kinds of people so I don't feel much discomfort identifying myself as such. My sense of belonging to the United States has also changed since I first moved here. I definitely feel more comfortable saying 'I'm American' compared to eleven years ago although in many ways I'm still not. I'm definitely a Bostonian though. Born in Boston, educated in Boston, Samuel Adams is one of my favorite beers and I'm a Red Sox fan."

There are many terms that just don't seem to fit, and I ask Norah whether she identifies with "Asian American," "Korean American," or "Japanese American."

"Not really. I think my experience and upbringing were totally different from people who identify as such since I didn't grow up in the United States."

"Do you ever say you are Japanese, or Nihonjin?"

"I can say, Osakajin (Osaka native) with full confidence but I never say that I'm Japanese in Japanese or English. But people assume I'm half Japanese all the time. Some Japanese people tell me, *Nihonjin yori nihonjin desu ne* (You are more Japanese than the Japanese)—in terms of aura, behavior, and attitude—which is interesting because they are acknowledging my cultural literacy but asserting that I'm not Japanese by saying *Nihonjin yori*."

How often have I been told the same. The words *Nihonjin* and "Japanese" are usually reserved for those who are strictly defined by race, culture, nationality, and purity of blood. Norah and I fall outside of this definition. Yet we fulfill most of the requirements so well that others are moved to include us within their circle. Norah challenges the borders of ethnicity and nationality and what we think of as culture. She is not Japanese in any of the traditional ways, including ethnicity, nationality, and physical appearance, or "purity." Yet, Japanese may be her most basic culture. So her very being challenges these limits in the minds of others as to who is a Japanese.

I wonder how Norah navigates different social contexts. Does she present herself as Japanese in a Japanese context? Does she then become more Korean in a Korean context, more American in an American context? Is such switching a sign of flexibility, versatility, and multiple cultural identities or is it a sign of a lack of an authentic self, a lack of a consistent and stable identity? Is she a chameleon, changing colors to fit her environment, or does Norah live with a sense of balance, as she is many things and she brings them all together into a whole? Is Norah *haafu*, even though she does not have any "Japanese blood"?

I believe it is important to expand the boundaries of the nation by redefining the Japanese by citizenship, rather than ethnicity. People like me or Soo im, regarded as non-Japanese in various ways, must be recognized as Japanese rather than marginalized as foreigners who should be extended tolerance in a multicultural society. Because we are citizens, we are Japanese. I do not say that Zainichi Koreans are Japanese as well, knowing that this is a volatile issue that each individual must decide. Soo im does not advocate that all Zainichi Koreans should naturalize, but does see this as a way she has chosen to obtain rights.

The controversy reminds me of the case of Chong Hyang Gyun, a Republic of Korea national employed by the Tokyo metropolitan government, who charged discrimination when her application for a managerial position was denied. She and others argue for a citizenship as denizens, with the same rights without legal citizenship. Her older brother Tei Taikin (formerly Chung Daekyun) has written candidly and poignantly why he was opposed to his own sister's lawsuit. Tei is an influential writer who contributes to forging a new view of Korean and Japanese nationality and the consequences for Koreans in Japan. He has narrated his own journey back to Japanese nationality through naturalization. Tei was a Japanese national of Chosen (Korean) status when born in Iwate prefecture in 1948; a Chosenjin (national of Korea as defined when Japan effectively abandoned its sovereignty over the country) from 1952; a Kankokujin (Republic of Korea national) a few years later when his father formally declared allegiance to the ROK; and a Japanese since 2004 when he naturalized. Tei relates that his mother was born in the prefectural interior of Japan (Naichi). When she married his father and moved to his register in Korea she lost her Japanese nationality when everyone in Korean registers lost Japanese nationality in 1952. In 1985 she naturalized and once again became Japanese. But she and Tei's older brother (who had not naturalized) have passed away, and his sister has not naturalized. Families thus continue to be split by nationality and identity issues.[2]

Multigenerational Healing

Although divisions in families continue, healing can occur around nationality and ethnicity on individual, family, and community levels. In Norah's family, each generation has cause for bitterness toward Japan that heavily influenced their feelings about being or not being Japanese. In healing their personal wounds and confronting their personal dilemmas, family members also influenced each other to overcome crippling feelings of victimization that were barriers to forgiveness and development. The message that Soo im's parents gave her early in life—to judge people by their character, not their ethnicity—made an indelible impression on the young girl. Her engagement with "others" in marriage and her ability to see the "other" in herself, her own "Japaneseness," empowered her to embrace a multiethnic identity as Korean and Japanese. Norah was in turn greatly affected by her elders' openness to embrace even more diverse parts and synergize them into a whole being of multiple identities.

The multigenerational influence also went in the opposite direction, with the young influencing the elders. While Norah's early experience of being labeled as a gaijin was hurtful, it set her on a new path in an international school and American university education that opened up her world. Her childhood experiences of difference also started Norah on a journey of accepting herself and becoming whole by connecting to all of her ancestries.

How did observing the development of such a child affect her mother? Perhaps it helped Soo im decide that she could be something more than solely Korean; she could also be Japanese, and this did not threaten her Korean identity. She could be Japanese on her own terms, equal yet different, a Japanese who was also Korean, modeling for others a way to embrace a wider identity, not needing to choose one or the other but daring to bring them together.

Even more complicated were the experiences of Norah's grandparents, who were born as Japanese nationals but were forced to give up that status and become foreigners in Japan. I wonder how such a child and grandchild affected Norah's grandparents. Did watching their daughter fiercely maintain her Korean ethnicity while demanding equal rights—even daring to call herself Japanese—convince them that they might do the same? Did observing their granddaughter synthesize her diverse roots give them thoughts of new possibilities?

Soo im was not the last person in the family to naturalize. In an amazing move, her parents naturalized in 2009 when her father was eighty-four and her mother seventy-six. Her father explained that he had paid enough taxes and contributed to society long enough without the right to vote. He also admitted that he naturalized because he did not want to die bitter and angry at Japanese for denying his rights. In 2010 he voted in an election for the first time. Norah went with him on election day. "He seemed happy," she says. But the split in the family remained, as the other daughter joined but the son refused to go along with the others and remains a Korean national. As in Tei's family, nationality, ethnicity, and identity still divide family members.

Still, this is a story of hope and inspiration. Norah's grandparents had lived their lives maintaining the distinction between Japanese and Koreans socially, and for much of their lives in legal terms as well. Though offered the opportunity to become Japanese, they refused, opposed to what they perceived as the loss of their ethnicity as the price to pay. Even later, when the government offered to let them become Japanese and still keep the symbols of their Korean identity—their names—they refused to budge. They wanted to show that they had pride as Koreans and that Japanese society was still discriminatory.

What moved Norah's grandparents to change so late in life? Did they experience growth through an acceptance of the realities of who one is, one's situation and circumstances? Were they helped by seeing in Soo im the possibility of creatively constructing a healthy and sustainable personal identity as Korean Japanese? Did they recognize the illusion of separation in Norah and her face, where the coming together of peoples is so visually striking? Did they see the delusion of separating "self" and "other," and overcome bitter resentment at the denial of their rights, to finally embrace their power and agency?

Perhaps they sensed that as victims we are stuck in our development, denying ourselves growth and maturity by clinging to the past. Blaming someone for our misfortune may relieve some anxiety but ultimately is self-defeating and does not allow us to rise above the situation and move on with our healing. Buddhism teaches that if we haven't forgiven, we keep creating an identity around our pain and that is what is reborn, that is what suffers. We need compassion, loving kindness, sympathetic joy, and equanimity to avoid resentments and hatred, to understand suffering in the world—our own and others'.

TEN

American Girl in Asia

I used to hate it when someone asked if I spoke Japanese. "No," I'd reply, with some irritation. "My mother is Japanese American, third generation. My father's family came over from England in the 1600s. I'm American. I speak English."[1]

Akemi Johnson begins her essay with this reflection on how she once wanted people to understand that she is American. As a child in the United States, I too did not want to be perceived as any different from other kids, although I didn't have the quick and ready response that Akemi had. I was born in Japan, my mother was Japanese, and my father was the son of immigrants. I guess I wasn't so sure that I was American and didn't think that the person asking would believe me if I claimed to be a fellow American.

I might have wondered why a Yonsei hapa has the name Akemi—a name that implies Japan and Japanese connections. *Yonsei* indicates a fourth-generation descendent, so it was her great-grandparents who came from Japan. Hapa kids from my generation, born in Japan or in the United States, weren't named Akemi—Angela or Agnes maybe, but not Akemi. Our parents were sure to declare we were American. They needed to tell themselves, their children, and others that we were not Japanese but American. Clearly the parents of Yonsei no longer have this need to protect their children with names that tell others

"I am American—not Japanese!" Instead, Akemi's parents announced a connection that is generations removed from the old country.

I went to school in America in the 1960s as Stephen Murphy. New teachers read my name and smiled when they looked at my face. Kids were puzzled and frustrated by my name. I was branded "Oriental" in their eyes; I needed a name that fit, so that is how I got my nickname "Ping Pong," or "Ping" for short.

Akemi was given a name that declares her difference and labels her as Japanese; she is several generations more removed from Japan than I am, thirty years younger, and she grew up in the 1990s in California, in the San Francisco Bay Area, a place that I idealize as a multicultural wonderland. She comes from a marriage between Americans—one of whom has Asian ancestry. In Akemi's generation there are many more people of mixed Asian ancestry; their numbers have increased to the point that they are nearly 20 percent of the Asian American population, and this number is still growing. Nowhere is this trend more evident than among Japanese Americans, where the number of those of mixed ancestry has expanded with each generation to the point that in Akemi's generation it is now common to be hapa.

"Over and over I say that what I am is half. I am half and people understand, filing me away."[2] Half. That is a weird concept. How can anyone be half anything? Hapa are still not always regarded as authentic Japanese Americans; some members of the community feel that hapa should not be allowed to compete in community beauty pageants in which the queen is a representative of Japanese Americans. But even these purists grudgingly concede that the numbers of hapa are overwhelming and they must be included, so qualification requirements establish a certain percentage of Japanese ancestry. By "blood quantum" Akemi is "half Japanese." The math is simple. Her mother is 100 percent and her father is 0 percent; add and divide by two and the answer is 50 percent. But is there any meaning in classifying a person as 50 percent? Are human identities quantifiable?

I wonder what it was like for Akemi growing up when and where she did, north of San Francisco. After high school she moved to New England for college before setting off for extended stays in mainland Japan, Cambodia, Okinawa, and Hawaii. What was she searching for? She is a writer; I turn to her essays to help me understand her experiences.

> When I was growing up in Marin County, what did I risk, being associated with Japan? On the most basic level, I risked being different from my predominantly white peers. I risked having people compliment me on my English, or view me as an Asian stereotype—demure, exotic, good at math. These were risks I sensed but couldn't articulate; I just knew I didn't want to take them.[3]

Years after her time as a student, Akemi had a chance meeting in Okinawa with Shin Mune, a Japanese American from Northern California. He confided to her about how much he and other Nisei had been affected by their traumatic experiences, including wartime incarceration. Listening to his reminiscences led Akemi to reflect on her own journey.

> When Shin was in third grade, right after the war, there were two other Japanese American students in his class—a girl and a boy who hated each other. Shin thought it was because when you've been locked up together and are freed, all you want to do is separate. Shin himself had white friends, white girlfriends. He wished he could be white.
>
> I never articulated it, even to myself, but at times I wished that too. I grew up in an area that was predominantly Caucasian, and I hated being different. I hated my first name—no one could pronounce it, and it immediately stamped me as Other, as Foreign. I screamed at my parents: "Why did you give me this name?" After high school, I moved across the country for college, and then spent five years bouncing around the United States and Asia. It took me ten years to come back to California to stay.[4]

What's in a name? Names carry associations, images, and baggage. For family names there are social traditions and legal restrictions that limit choices; for first names there is more freedom to choose. It seems to me that most parents don't imagine the ramifications of their choice of names for their children. Would parents knowingly give a child a name that causes resentment for eighteen years? Should parents give names that remind kids of who they are? And how would parents know who their children are just after they are born? Should parents give names that proclaim a connection that no longer exists, or does the name make that connection? Can names be a way of connecting to a past that nurtures and supports a developing identity?

Parents in my generation thought they would save us from names like Akemi. But classmates saw through our attempts to appear to be American and gave us nicknames that they thought more accurately described us. As we grew older and shed these childhood nicknames, some hapa happily grew into ethnic invisibility with their American names. But those of us who wanted to assert our identities as Asian became uncomfortable with our names that labeled us as different from our Asian peers. Many of us claimed names already given, such as middle names, or took family names of our mothers.

I asked my grandmother to give me a name, and so became Hiroshi. Then I decided that wasn't good enough—to be authentically Asian one needed a family name too. So I took my mother's family name, Shigematsu, and added it to my father's family name. It's long and cumbersome and doesn't fit into computerized name boxes, so I get letters addressed to "Murphy-Shigemat." I've been called greedy for having such a name and I've endured countless inconveniences and comments about it, but it makes me happy because it describes who I am, which is what a name should do.

Feelings about our names can change. A new environment in which one's name is seen differently and even positively by others brings on self-reflection and acceptance. Akemi's move across the country to a liberal college campus brought new experiences and new discoveries.

> But, try as I might (claiming, even, that I didn't like rice), I couldn't escape my association with Japan. While my features might have let me slip into a range of demographics, my first name might as well have been tattooed in kanji across my forehead. I spent eighteen years resenting my parents for giving me a name that labeled me as Japanese. Then in college a more diverse environment and ethnic studies courses enabled me to examine these attitudes and find words for everything I'd only felt. Sophomore year, I signed up for beginning Japanese.[5]

What Are You?

At lunch my friend introduces me to someone who lives in her building. He puts his sandwich on the table and sits down before the introductions are over. There is small talk, then suddenly The Question is at our lunch table, thrown in among stray sprouts and sweating cups of soda.

"What are you?" this person asks, casually. (It is most often asked casually, but sometimes it is a forced casual. His casual is genuine; this is a good question and he is eager for the answer.)

"Half Japanese," I say (I sell out), and he starts to chew again, satisfied.

"That's what I would have guessed," he says, proudly. "Hearing your name and looking at your features, that's what I would have guessed. I always thought that was so interesting, you know, Asian freckles. Your eyes and then your hair and then your freckles."

He is studying my face and he himself is less than five feet tall, with a type of disability that has given him short, stubby half arms and a waddling gait.

I refrain from mentioning that this is interesting, too.[6]

"What are you?" This seemingly innocent question provokes such complex reactions that a whole book was written on it, filled with comments by mixed race people.[7] I think it can be a microaggression that some people encounter on a regular basis. I often wonder why I can't just take it in stride and answer nicely, satisfying the interrogator with a simple response. Why do I battle and hesitate, sizing up the person, making assumptions, ascribing motives, carefully judging my retort? Why do I consider turning the question back to the questioner: "Why do you ask?" "Is it any of your business?" Or the killer response, "What are *you*?"

Black Hair

I am eleven or twelve and visiting my paternal relatives in Illinois. It is a hot, sticky, humid day and the trees shriek with cicadas as my cousin Anna and I sit outside in the backyard of our grandmother's house,

coloring. Anna is eight months older than I am and so we are supposed to be friends. . . .

But now we are getting older and it is harder to be friends when
we see each other during my family's annual visit to the Midwest.
Now we are coloring and talking and Anna says casually, "Did you
know that no Americans have black hair? Isn't that weird?" I think
her eyes have trailed from my mother, moving inside the house, to
me, and up to my hairline. At that moment I do not know what
to say and days later, on the airplane home, before we even leave the
runway, I scribble a six-page letter to my cousin. With a churning
fury inside of me that I do not know quite how to deal with I write
that she is wrong—Americans can have black hair, I am American,
my mom is American, everyone's family immigrated to this country
at one point so if we are talking only about the "true" Americans
that must be the Native Americans and guess what, they have
black hair.

I send the letter and she is sorry. It was something her friend's
mom told her, she writes. She is ignorant and stupid. I write that it
is okay and we try to be friends again. . . . Things are never the same.
For years my grandmother speaks of "burying the axe" and I grow ir-
ritated. I brush her off and say of course I have, obviously I have. But
I do not know if this is true.[8]

I was five years old and my sister's friends were visiting our house.
Suddenly I noticed they were staring at the photo of my Japanese
grandparents on top of the book shelf and whispering and giggling.
One girl, a white girl named Kathy, shrieked, "They look weird!" My
dear grandparents.

Brown Hair

Last year at New Year's an embroidered decoration hanging on
the wall of my great-grandmother's house shocked me. All of my
mother's family was there that day—great-aunts and uncles, cousins
and second cousins, grandparents. It was what we did every year at
this time, gathered here and ate teriyaki chicken and potato salad
and brown sushi and elaborate jello molds, canned fruit suspended

in bright orange gelatin. Black beans for good luck. I was there and I was standing in the living room when I saw it, or resaw it, for it had hung there for many years. It was a wall hanging that my mother's cousin had made, sewn together out of bits of fabric. In it she depicted all of the great-grandchildren, seven of us, standing in descending order. I was first, labeled eight years old. My sister was five and my brother was eight months and what shocked me was our hair.

Our hair in this wall hanging was light brown and big; mine pouffed higher than a Dallas cheerleader's. Our hair was in such sharp contrast to the other kids'—straight and black and modest—I wondered how I could have not noticed it before. Now that I did I stood frozen for a moment, watching the others move and talk, appraising the hue of their hair in this light, hoping they wouldn't see mine.[9]

My U.S. driver's license says my hair is black. Compared to the blonds, redheads, and chestnut heads around me it sure seems black. My Japanese driver's license says my hair is brown. Amidst the sea of black heads my brown highlights shine.

Sansei Mom

My mother was raised a Christian but has gravitated toward Buddhism as she grows older. She does not feel like a Christian anymore, perhaps because it is a religion that her parents adopted out of fear and exile, that was pounded into their hearts in a dusty horse stall that was their home and prison during World War II. Now my grandmother has a picture of a grinning face hanging in her house, underneath: Smile, God loves you. She makes meatloaf and mashed potatoes and her name is Mary.[10]

As a child I was sent to Catholic church and Catholic school. It was strange, because my mom and dad didn't go to church with us. It didn't take long for me to notice that my sister and I didn't look like Jesus or Mary or any of the images of the holy people. We didn't look like the priests or nuns either. Now I go to Buddhist temple, a strange mix of Japanese Buddhism and American Christian culture. Sunday morning dharma service, Buddhist hymns, dharma talk, green tea and rice crackers after it's over. I'm not sure I look like Buddha either, but it no longer matters like it once did.

Hapa Beauty

> Girls like us are exotic to Illinois, among other places. We are like geisha—long hair and dark lashes, quiet and mysterious.[11]

When we came from Japan my Irish family had never seen anyone from the Orient, which is how Americans thought of us, as Orientals. What did they see? What associations were in their minds? Geisha girls? Samurai? Bucktoothed evil soldiers? Crazy kamikaze pilots? "Ah so!" Of course, they couldn't tell whether we were Japanese or Chinese, and it didn't seem to matter at all to them.

> It is difficult to know which half of me people see. When he looks at me I want to know what he is thinking, why he is smiling. I worry.[12]

I am always surprised when people comment on my appearance. Sometimes I stop after I say something and wonder what people are thinking. When I talk about Japanese do they think I am American? When I talk about Americans do they think I am Japanese? Or is it the other way around?

> Even before I was born I was beautiful. That was what people said, that was what they told my mother, swollen with pregnancy. I would be beautiful; with my racial mixture there would be no doubt about that. They did not have to elaborate with further description—exotic, unusual, interesting, Asian but not "too Asian," the best of both worlds, Japanese but whiter. To say that I would be beautiful was obvious enough; people's heads were nodding in agreement right off the bat. Yes, yes, mixed race people are always good looking. This is common knowledge. Yes.
>
> I know an Indian American girl who wants a white man to father her children, although ultimately she would like an Indian husband. My kids will look better this way, she says simply, already imagining that they will be beautiful.[13]

Hapa models were once very popular in Japan and other parts of Asia. Agencies that hire only hapa still exist. Hapa were so adulated in some places that governments intervened to blunt their popularity in the name of nationalism. Now in Japan I hear that the best combination is not half and half but three-quarters Japanese and one-quarter white—mostly Japanese, but with a just a hint of exotic foreignness. Is this an expression of growing national and ethnic pride? Confronted with the stark realities of a shrinking population and work force, Japanese society welcomes people from other lands with resignation. Some long for the imagined good old days when Japan was for the Japanese and myths of homogeneity and ideologies of monoethnicity ruled the land. As the newcomers fill jobs and contribute to the society some of their hosts find meaning in the twisted pursuit of scapegoating and targeting these new citizens and resisting their attempts to join the society as equal members.

Asian Friends / White Friends

In college I do not have many white friends. I study race and ethnicity, I learn Japanese. I attend functions for people of color and I feel new things—I feel proud, I feel like a member of the majority, I feel valid, I feel not so special or interesting or unique. I write about racial hierarchy and white privilege and now I am empowered. Now I tell the truth.

At home I lie. At home all of my friends are white and most of them are blonde. One tells me it is interesting that I am "going back to my roots." Some become uncomfortable when I start to tell my truth, because this is new for us, this truth. It is difficult. And so we talk about cars, about hair, about movies and white boys, and we laugh over all these lies.[14]

When my hometown friend Bob came to visit me at college, I was disturbed by how uncomfortable I felt when we went out. He seemed the same, but I had changed. I was worried what my new Asian friends would think if they saw me with him. Would they see the white side of me reflected off my white friend's pale face and blond hair? I wanted them to see me as Asian, but if they knew I had white friends . . . My old friend questioned my new Asianness. "Come on Steve, who are you kidding? You're no more Asian than I am!" he said mockingly. "You're as American as apple pie!" he insisted, inviting me back to our old intimacy with his warm, familiar smile. I smiled back, wondering whether he was right, and decided at that moment not to invite him to visit me again.

American Girl in Asia

In college at Brown, Akemi didn't join the Asian American groups, which seemed to her so ethnic-specific and religious, a lot of them Christian. Later, she found BOMBS (Brown Organization for Multiracial and Biracial Students), and then a hapa group that developed just for Asians. She discovered something important in each and majored in East Asian studies, leading to her first trip to Japan for her junior year in Kyoto, at the end of which she journeyed to Okinawa and visited the AmerAsian School. She went back to Okinawa again five years later on a Fulbright and made the following observations.

> My students at the AmerAsian School in Okinawa (AASO) are trying to learn English. Every Wednesday and Friday morning I volunteer as a teacher for the ESL class. Like most of the AASO students, these kids have Okinawan mothers and American servicemen fathers who may or may not be around. Their native language is Japanese, their home environment is Japanese, they've spent all their years on this island, and likely will live here for many more. But they sit with me struggling through phonics and pronouns, determined—or encouraged by their parents—to learn English.
>
> The AASO is unique in that it enrolls almost exclusively biracial American-Japanese students, and has developed an original bilingual, bicultural, "double" curriculum. Founded in 1998 by five Okinawan mothers, the privately run, K–9 school of eighty students contends that "Amerasian" children have the right to study in both Japanese and English. . . .
>
> Although no official statistics exist, academics estimate that about 250 mixed race American-Japanese children are born every year in

Okinawa, the result of the numerous U.S. military bases here. These children, the AASO argues, are often unsuited for public schools, which offer little language support and allow too much discrimination toward racial minorities.

From my American viewpoint, I can't help but bristle at this segregation. How will Japanese society ever begin to recognize (not to mention accept) its increasing diversity if those who are different are removed from the picture, cloistered at special schools? But I'd be a hypocrite to say these kids shouldn't learn English. Since that course in beginning Japanese, I've taken the equivalent of four years of college Japanese, spent an academic year in Kyoto and more than a year in Okinawa, and earned a bachelor's degree in East Asian studies. Half of the last seven years I've lived in Asia. I've been fortunate enough to create my own bilingual, bicultural curriculum.

But while my efforts involved taking risks, the AASO seems to be about avoiding risks. Viewed in the context of Okinawa, it's not difficult to understand why. The island has a long and conflicted history with the U.S. military bases (and the Japanese government that brought and keeps them here).

The presence of Americans began, of course, with the 1945 Battle of Okinawa, a nightmarish and drawn-out entrance that involved the deaths of as many as 140,000 civilians (more than one-fourth of the population). The prefecture remained occupied by the United States until 1972 and still hosts nearly 75 percent of the U.S. bases in Japan, although Okinawa constitutes only 0.6 percent of the country's landmass.

Every so often the rape of a young girl by a U.S. serviceman ignites international headlines, becoming ammunition for antibase activists and an echo of that original fear: that the invading Americans would run over men with tanks and rape women and girls. The more preferable alternative, many Okinawans were led to believe, was death.

Mixed race American Okinawans are born into this context, and for them the risks of association are greater than those I felt growing up in the States. For someone who looks part white or black or Latino, or has a name like Paola or Shirley or Jack, to not speak English is to risk association with the "island half" stereotype. Tragic, fatherless, the "island half" is the product of an affair between a local, lower-class woman of questionable morals and a young, no-good serviceman with a "love-her-and-leave-her" mentality. Sometimes the stereotype extends to an assumption of rape. If a biracial person speaks English, however, this hints at a different picture: a glamorous, international "half" with loving, married parents and enviable access to the United States.

It's better to be an "American half" than an "Okinawan half," many people have told me. Although some American-Okinawans work to subvert this "island half" stereotype into a positive identity, choosing to master the disappearing Okinawan language over English, more people I've met feel it's important to learn English. This tendency involves not only the bases and Okinawa's past, but also race and class and the global value of English. Japanese society, still operating under "monoethnic myths," often smiles brighter on multiracial Japanese people it can file away as citizens of the world or gaijin.[15]

It is interesting to me that Akemi has spent so much time at the AASO. Interesting because I too have spent considerable time in Okinawa. What were we seeking there, and was it the same thing? Finding stories that established a connection with some of the most dramatic mixed Asian life experiences, did we discover in those stories who we are not and therefore who we are? Thinking about Shin, Akemi reflected once again on her own journey.

> I had run from California, too. A biracial Yonsei . . . I had come to Okinawa . . . to spend a year researching issues surrounding the U.S. military bases. But, like Shin, my real motives were more personal and intertwined with the past, with traumas that had been born many years before.
>
> During World War II, my grandfather and his family were interned at Tule Lake in California, and my grandmother and her family were imprisoned at Arizona's Gila River. Growing up, I never heard them talk about the experience. I learned about the internment camps in grade school, about how tens of thousands of families were uprooted from their homes and forced to live in desolate conditions behind barbed wire, but I never heard my grandparents tell their versions of the story. They referred to that time only as "camp," as if the experience had been as benign and pleasant as summer camp. Later, after they passed away, I spent a lot of time wondering what they hadn't said.[16]

Japanese American at Home in California

My great-uncle is writing about the internment. It is a big step; memories shoved down decades ago fight lukewarm to the surface. For the sake of his children and grandchildren he brings them up and lays them out, crumpled and broken and washed out, but there.

First, the disclaimer, just in case.

"It is hoped that my description of the WWII years would not be interpreted as an indication of extreme anger and hostility to my country."

After Pearl Harbor white neighbors pretended to be officials and tore apart his family's home, searching for "contrabands" and finally settling on his father's fishing poles.

"Having strong feelings about past happenings does not preclude one's love of country."

Signs went up around the neighborhood reading "Open Season on Japs, No Limit."

"The United States, although imperfect, is by far the best country in the world in which to live."

When they were boarded onto the train to be evacuated crowds of people lined the streets to watch. He felt like an animal.

"I appreciate not only the opportunities but also the good life that it has provided my family and me."

The internment camp was surrounded by barbed wire and teenage boys with guns. It was a prison.

"For that I am grateful."

And the rest of my family—grandmother, great-aunts and uncles—hardly says anything at all.[17]

"For the sake of his children and grandchildren he brings them up and lays them out," is a phrase rich with meaning. This revelation of bitter wartime experience has been a major point of contention in the Japanese American community. I recall how a Nisei reacted when I tried to enlist his support for yet another Remembrance Day event commemorating the tragic events that unfolded following the issuance of Executive Order 9066 on February 19, 1942. "Haven't we remembered enough?" he said, half jokingly, but also seriously questioning how much remembering was healthy. I have often wondered about the way that Issei and Nisei bear in silence their suffering and outrage. Isn't this a form of dignity that honors their ancestors and sets an example for their descendants? Perhaps this is the reason for the silence of Akemi's relatives, all except her great-uncle.

But some Nisei are like Akemi's great-uncle and have decided that for their children and grandchildren they should tell their stories. The children and grandchildren themselves, Sansei and Yonsei, have also played a part in encouraging these stories to be brought forth by showing their desire to hear them. Stories require not just a teller but also a listener, and it is only when we have someone to receive our story that we dare to tell it and offer it as a gift.

Japanese like to say *shikata ga nai*, or its colloquial version, *sho ga nai*; this is an expression often uttered by Issei and heard by Nisei. Literally it means "nothing can be done," but I think it means more. My Nisei mentor Kiyo Morimoto, a potato farmer, WWII veteran in the decorated 442nd regimental combat team, and Harvard professor, used to say that this phrase was misinterpreted by those who saw it as an expression of passive resignation to fate. Instead, he saw it as a way of expressing hope. It shows acceptance of an impossible situation— we can't do anything about it, so let's move on. He saw *shikata ga nai* as combining an acceptance of what cannot be done and a resolve to do what can be done. This interpretation is much like the classic Serenity Prayer of Niebuhr, which asks for serenity to accept what we cannot change; courage to change what we can change; and wisdom to know the difference. Like Japanese and Americans, sometimes Buddhism and Christianity come together.

Farewell to Japan

At this point, I'm not motivated to learn any more Japanese. The British woman I know wonders if that's because there's still an element of risk. Maybe so. Maybe in Okinawa I speak English as a way to show I didn't grow up here; maybe I've caught that fear of association with the "island half." Maybe part of me is still uncomfortable claiming a Japanese identity.

But I like to see this lack of motivation in a different, positive light. I like to think that I've learned enough Japanese and spent enough time in Japan to feel satisfied. I've confronted my fears of association—shame, really, of my Japanese ancestry—and won. It's a victory that belongs to my family, too. During that same war that devastated Okinawa, my great-grandparents and grandparents were imprisoned across the Pacific; in the internment camps they learned the grave risks of associating with Japan. By my generation, Yonsei, the climate was safe enough for me to examine that learned shame and reclaim some of our lost cultural identity. It's a multigenerational, cyclical story that seems classically American.

The same kind of story isn't as likely to occur in Japan—yet. For now, the best option for many mixed race Okinawan children might be the AASO. But my hope is that, one day, they will feel comfortable answering either yes or no when faced with the question, "Do you speak English?"[18]

Akemi's Asian journey came to an end when she returned to California in 2009. She moved to Hawaii the following year; that may be as close as she gets to Asia for a while. Not many do what Akemi has done through her journeys to Asia. Writers are often the artistic spokespersons and prophets of identity conflict; they may make a moral decision to endure identity consciousness for the purpose of artistic creation that provides insights and healing for others. Although she may not see herself in this light, Akemi is an exceptional individual who enacts the suppressed drama that many Yonsei are unconscious of but still affected by in their lives, when the traumas of previous generations of ancestors are passed on to them. Akemi's transnational journey of discovery may be her way, as a writer, of living out the stories others will read about.

Perhaps Akemi's discoveries are obvious and inevitable, much like the countless stories we have heard since the days that Alex Haley's *Roots* popularized journeys back to ancestral homelands. On these journeys we may feel the connection and a temporary exhilaration of the mystery of connecting to our roots but we also realize that we do not belong there and are seen by the people there as outsiders. We have to keep searching, and for Akemi this self-discovery was in the United

States as a Japanese American, which is what she was all along but was waiting to discover. For her, the journey there was through Asia to Asian America.

In another sense, Akemi's story is part of a much larger and socially significant phenomenon of returnees to Japanese society. The "return" to Japan for Americans is more commonly done by people of Japanese ancestry in Latin America. The numbers are astounding, far exceeding North Americans like Akemi, with hundreds of thousands "returning" to Japan since a 1990 immigration law made it an easy process for those of Japanese ancestry to migrate and reside in Japan. Their motivation is driven by the forces of a global economy in which the wages paid to a construction worker or hostess in Japan far exceed those earned by white collar workers in Latin America.

What these Japanese Brazilians and Peruvians find in Japan—and what the Japanese find out about them—is an amazing story that is being written as permanent communities form in certain parts of Japan. Conceptions of a Japanese race and perceptions of racial and cultural attributes are being challenged by the encounters between these South Americans and Japanese. Notions of diaspora and the connections between Japanese and those who have emigrated from Japan and settled in other parts of the world are being reconsidered. But an even more challenging question, faced in schools and neighborhoods on a daily basis, is how Japanese society will deal with the issues created by large populations of people who "look Japanese" but don't "act Japanese."

Sansei Mom, Yonsei Daughter

In 1981 Shin testified in the hearings on the constitutionality of the internment, where he heard other former internees say they were wanderers too. They said it was because of their experience in the internment camps. Shin said he couldn't remember the details, but this cause and effect makes sense to me. If the government made you limit all your belongings to two suitcases and imprisoned you behind a barbed wire fence in the desert, when you didn't do anything wrong, one way to cope might be never feeling trapped again, even in your own home. You might not want any material possessions worth losing—or any human relationship worth losing, either. . . .

Shin and I were on similar journeys, despite the forty-five years and two generations that separated us. As a child, I had learned, indirectly, that there was shame associated with being Japanese. I learned this from the silence surrounding my grandparents' time "at camp"; from the way relatives regarded my part-white appearance; from the absence of many Japanese customs, foods, and words at family gatherings. As an adult, I've worked to fill these silences and gaps by learning about the internment, hearing people's stories, and acquiring knowledge of Japan. In college, I studied Japanese, spent a year in Kyoto, and began what would be a long-running research project in Okinawa. I traveled to Hiroshima, where, four generations earlier, my relatives had worked as farmers. The more I learned, the more I felt some deeply ingrained anxiety begin to lift. I began to confront and diminish that inherited shame.

Shin was confronting the shame, too, but Shin had grown up in a different America. He had direct experience of the internment camps, and had dealt with more racism in his life. Although he's made progress in creating a positive ethnic identity, he still seemed haunted, troubled, and restless. His mind and body couldn't stay still.

Perhaps only Japanese Americans of later generations can end the cycle of shame that began with the Issei and Nisei. With exploration, awareness, and reflection, Yonsei and Gosei might break free of those negative memories, building instead a positive Japanese American identity, one that will be passed on to the generations to come.[19]

Feeling the need to connect to her Japanese American roots, Akemi flew back from Japan to go on the Tule Lake pilgrimage for the first time. She naturally thought a lot about her family and what they had been through, including her mother, who was not in the camps. Akemi's mother, Nadine Narita, was born in 1954 in California, long after her parents had been released back into society. Her marriage to Akemi's father, a white man, seemed natural to Akemi because her mom had never placed much emphasis on being Japanese American. But Akemi noticed a surprising change in her mother, who went with her to Tule Lake. When they returned home, Akemi's mother began to examine her parents' records, where she discovered the excruciatingly difficult situation in which her father had been trapped. He was the eldest son and didn't want to leave his family because his father had already been taken, so he didn't want to fight. Shortly after Pearl Harbor the FBI had imprisoned Akemi's grandfather, taking him to Santa Fe, New Mexico. After he became ill he was released to Tule Lake, where he died just a few months later. Akemi's grandfather had been labeled a "resister" for his refusal to serve in the armed forces of the United States on combat duty, wherever ordered, including Japan. But he affirmed his allegiance to the United States and forswore obedience to the Japanese emperor. This incurred the wrath of the infamous "no-no" boys, who pressured him into renouncing his U.S. citizenship; it took until 1958 to reverse this in a class-action suit judgment.

Akemi noted her mother's new, frequent use of the word *Nikkei*, which seemed to symbolize her growing awareness and pride. Did Akemi's own search lead to her mother's? Maybe when it is easier for subsequent generations to explore something, it becomes easier for previous generations who were more scarred by the experience. When Akemi embraced herself as Japanese American, her mother could do so too. Wisdom is seen as passing from elders to youth, but elders can learn from the struggles of youth. Sometimes we find the courage to confront old ghosts once we witness the courage displayed by those who are younger. Their encouragement may help us slay the dragons defending our wounds, thereby allowing wounds to be healed by those who witness and touch them.

ELEVEN

Found in Translation

When I was a young man I decided that I would tell "our" story. I convinced myself that there was a story and that if I did not tell it, it would not be told. "We" were invisible to most people; we didn't exist. To others who did see us, we were strange, exotic. They might try to tell our story, but would they get it right? They would see tragedy, deficiency, and abnormality; they would see beauty, hybridity, and multiplicity—neither perspective our whole story. I thought I could get the story right, and so I began to study and write.

Masa Murotani Fox is a young man who has decided to tell "our" story. A film about us made by someone who was not one of us got him going. At first he thought Regge Life's *Doubles* was great, but then he realized that the director was trying to tell us who we were and what we should call ourselves. Were we really all "doubles," as he called us? And who was he to tell us what label to use? Shouldn't we define our own experiences and call ourselves a name that we choose? So Masa got busy making a film that spoke of his own generation's predicament.

Masa and I both decided to tell "our" stories. But who are "we"? To Masa, "we" were people with stories like his—young, a Japanese mother, American father, born and raised in Japan, family in both countries, bilingual, Japanese school, international school. He produced a documentary film that he called *Found in Translation*, a play on the title of the popular film *Lost in Translation*.

"I had seen Coppola's work and liked it, but then started questioning the story, even the premise, and obviously its depictions of Japan. I felt it unfair that a movie would use Japan merely as an other, an indecipherable, bizarre backdrop to further a story about two American characters who ultimately didn't have any concern for the culture. 'Lost' purposely created that alienation, that distance between Japanese and American culture. If we were to gauge the level of global intercourse and understanding of multiculturalism by that movie, then there really was no hope at all for the future. Being American would remain synonymous with being white, and being Japanese would remain being a part of just 'one race.' My documentary, at least in its attempt, posits culture as being blurred, as something elastic and redefinable. It shows that there are people who do not believe the terms 'American' and 'Japanese' are mutually exclusive, because to do so would result in their own denial. So naturally, I had to give it that title. I suppose there is something to be 'found' in all of this. I think that in the process of being translated, being interpreted as something that we may find offensive, we discover not only the prejudices and assumptions of different cultures and peoples but ourselves. I felt that I have become a more understanding individual because of my experience as a multiethnic person."

Masa interviewed sixteen other multiethnic, multicultural people, mostly high school and college students who, having grown up in Japan, found their looks and English-speaking ability publicly admired, yet were often marginalized and seen as foreign. *Found in Translation* in many ways became the culmination of his personal struggle to come to terms with having grown up speaking two languages and negotiating two seemingly distinct cultural legacies within a purportedly homogeneous Japanese society.

"I have always been the exception. During primary school, teachers defended my twin brother and me when we were bullied by the Japanese kids in class because we looked different. I wasn't sophisticated enough to explain that my mother is Japanese, my father American. I simply accepted being 'special,' which is how my parents reassured me. I have since realized that the vantage point from which I have experienced my life—as someone caught between orthodox cultural viewpoints—is what led me to explore narratives of cultural and racial problems through filmmaking. I am often interested in characters—real or imagined—who are marginalized, who feel stifled by prevailing cultural and racial perceptions, who struggle with language development in their multilingual learning environments, who don't necessarily identify with mainstream cultural categories, and who either wither from neglect or strive to make their voices heard in discouraging surroundings."

At the time he made the film, Masa was attending college in western Massachusetts, some fifty years after I first came to that part of the country from Japan. The Americans Masa encountered had either little knowledge or no recollection of the war with Japan and had been exposed to few Asians. They had watched Japan rise from the ashes to become an economic power and a valued political ally. This meteoric ascent may have frightened and angered some; they were relieved by Japan's fall back to earth. They had seen "Made in Japan" become a symbol of high-quality products and they owned Sonys and drove Hondas. Some younger ones knew Pokemon and were fans of anime and manga. Some older ones ate tofu and loved sushi. They even went out singing karaoke.

Those were not the Americans I encountered when my family came from Japan to Pittsfield, Massachusetts, in 1953. It was only eight years after the war had ended, and wounds were still healing. John Wayne "Jap" war movies were abundant, but I don't know whether they promoted healing or reopened the wounds. "Made in Japan," which described my mother and us kids, was a derisive sign of cheap products of low quality. Most people in western Massachusetts, where we settled, had never seen an Asian before and stared at us as if we were animals in a zoo. Worse, some voiced their ignorance and a few lashed out at us with their vile revulsion. How could we understand as children why they hated us when they didn't even know us? I fought back by excelling at everything I did and secretly loving the Japanese national flag, not knowing what it symbolized to others.

To Masahiko Murotani Fox, western Massachusetts was more friendly but still a whole new cultural world. Having grown up in

Ann Arbor, Michigan, Kyoto, Japan, and the cosmopolitan city of Vancouver, British Columbia, he was amazed to encounter people whose image of Japan was Tom Cruise as a samurai or Zhang Ziyi as a geisha. He found life in a rural college town, with a student body not as ethnically diverse as he had imagined, in some ways frustrating and difficult, but it also gave impetus to his first film project. The film was an attempt to show his peers "where I was coming from" and a way to give voice to the multiethnic people he knew who felt pigeonholed by the assumptions made about them by others.

Speaking English

Where was Masa coming from and to whom did he want to give voice? He knew that his generation were not the stereotyped postwar tragic orphans, the so-called *ainoko* and *konketsuji*. Masa's generation of *haafu* were international, multilingual, and multicultural. Their experiences were heavily related to their native English language ability as well as their Japanese language ability. Growing up in a home in which English was spoken by his father, Masa acquired the language almost as naturally as he did Japanese. He also learned from experience that people who look like him are assumed to speak English. It is not only Masa's face but also his language abilities that distinguish him from most of the Japanese around him.

> I was riding on the train with my brother. We were in elementary school. An older kid came over and asked if we could speak English. It was awkward but we mumbled a few things. He asked us to come over and meet someone. There was this guy who kind of looked like us, mixed Japanese and he couldn't speak English. I remember how strange we thought it was. It [speaking English] was so natural to us.[1]

The stranger on the train confused them, because the twins had learned to do as their Japanese peers did in making assumptions about a person based on physical appearance—not only their language but their nationality, their culture, and their identity. The older kid's friend looked mixed like them, and the twins simply assumed that he would therefore speak English. They learned that as much as we are offended or even outraged that we might be stereotyped, we do the same to others.

In his film Masa wanted to explore the Japanese fascination with the English language and with what are regarded as "foreign faces." The mixed ancestry people he interviews share their beliefs that English has many associations for Japanese people—as a status symbol, a ticket to prosperity, freedom, and liberation from the constraints of society. It is a key to the outside world, a tool for making dreams come true; it symbolizes what is global, international, and cosmopolitan, synonymous with what is regarded as romantic and cool.

English is commonly found in music, television, and radio, where entertainers like Crystal Kay sing in native English as well as native Japanese. The popularity of mixed ancestry entertainers goes back to the *konketsuji boomu*, a phenomenon in the 1960s in which they were the rage. Many could not actually speak English, but because of the conflation of their physical features with English, they sometimes pretended to. The Golden Haafu, a popular singing group with their own television program, presented decidedly mixed looks but their English ability was mostly faked.

The characters in Masa's film tell how Japanese people are fascinated by their "foreign faces," and expect English to be their language. But when perfect Japanese comes from their mouths, some Japanese people can be reduced to almost complete bewilderment—a reaction that can be amusing or annoying, depending on the receiver's mood or attitude. If received negatively, the message is "you are exotic and strange." If received positively, the message is "you look exotic and strange but somewhat Japanese, and I can relate to you."

People expect certain faces to speak English, and defer to you if you do. "Foreign faces" take advantage of this, manipulating others, even police, by speaking English and pretending they cannot speak Japanese. I like to speak English with doctors because they have a totally different attitude than when I use Japanese, shifting from an authoritarian, brusque manner into a doctor-patient relationship in which they explain my ailments and therapeutic procedures in great detail, even asking whether I have more questions.

The assumption that a "foreign face" means the person is an English-speaking, foreign visitor seems automatic and pervasive. Boon, Masa's twin brother, tells an amusing story of how he was picked out of the crowd at a baseball game and approached for a television interview. Hoping to dissuade the reporter, he pretended he could not speak Japanese. His friend's mother expanded his story by claiming he was a visiting student from America doing a home stay with her. This story only piqued the interest of the television reporter and she excitedly broadcast the scene nationally.

> In Japan, my face, everything about me signifies English. People assume I can speak English, can't speak Japanese, I become an exotic symbol, a representation of all that's foreign, American, white, Western. People can't see me beyond these lines, at least superficially. My cousins, who have known me for a very long time, realize this about me and poke fun at the idea that people can't seem to see me beyond those terms. But I think they also realize that they too are fascinated by my connection with America, with Western society."[2]

Boon learned to try to take such experiences in stride as part of living in Japan. They can be amusing but also tiring, and after living in Japan for many years—for some people their entire lives—to be treated as a foreigner "fresh off the plane" can be an exhausting experience. Such experiences reinforce the feeling of separation from the majority and bring a sense of futility that one will never be able to blend in and just be like others.

Too Much Attention

> "As little kids we got a lot of attention because we looked different, we were twins, we were small. And I thought I couldn't go anywhere without people saying something to us, calling us names, taking pictures of us. We got so much attention I didn't like that at all. . . . Unwillingly, I have always been scrutinized by others. . . . Ironically, my sense of self developed in reaction to the critical eye of others."

The critical eye of others became focused on Masa and Boon early in life. In second grade, students at the public school locked them out of the classroom, chanting *gaijin* in Japanese to let them know that they were foreigners, not "one of us." The twins listened to the teacher lecture the class on how the twins were "just like them." Everyone, including the twins, probably wondered whether they really were.

I too felt the critical eye of others as a child in the United States. People stared shamelessly at me, looking at my sisters, at my mother, at my father, and back at me. They would point at us, stare, whisper to each other, or just talk out loud about us. The nuns in the Catholic school somehow crushed any negative talk and actions by my classmates, as I don't recall any mention at all of being Japanese in school, as though there was a taboo to speak of it. Outside of school, this was an entirely different matter, and the city was a terrifying jungle to me where unexpectedly a gang of kids could appear to tell me bluntly and sometimes viciously that I was not "one of them."

Masa's characters describe these experiences of receiving too much attention in Japan: other children running away from them on the playground, mothers forcing their children to stay away from them, kids calling them *gaijin*. As he grew older, Masa continued to feel the critical eyes of Japanese and Americans.

> I walked onto a crowded Tokyo-bound commuter train with my Japanese girlfriend, her two Japanese female friends, and their American G.I. boyfriends and found passengers glaring and showing their disapproval. From many Americans, I invariably get an "Are you an Army brat?" before I have the chance to explain why I spent much of my childhood in Japan and why I miraculously avoided acquiring a Japanese accent.[3]

The eyes of others in Japan are not always critical. They may be admiring—"you're so cute," "your eyes are so big," "your hair is so curly," "your skin is so white." The gaze can be positive or negative, but in either case, a person feels that he is not being treated normally. It can be terribly simple in Japan—your face seems to tell people you speak English and you don't speak Japanese, and people also seem to feel that it is okay to talk about you, to objectify you. Masa explains how this may breed a sense of being different and special, sometimes appreciated, but it often breeds frustration that people cannot see beyond the visual differences they perceive.

> Perhaps unlike the proverb, among all "the nails that stick out and get hammered down," there are always a few that inevitably stick out no matter how hard they are struck. Although I have wished many times that my identity and upbringing . . . [were] simpler, I have never felt that I wished I wasn't the person who I am. There's always something appealing about being the exception; it is just frustrating when you are in a situation where you don't want to stand out and you don't want the special treatment that you unavoidably get or you just want people to understand you without much explanation. This is when I wish that the world wasn't so visually-oriented and that looks took a back seat to character and personality.[4]

Riding the Trains

Masa's school experiences provided him with another story he wanted to tell. Going to Japanese school until eighth grade and then transferring to an international school gave him experiences in two radically different educational environments. Some mixed ancestry students who attend Japanese schools have difficult, even traumatic experiences, and others find school comfortable, are popular, and fit in well. But many feel self-conscious and vulnerable to the kind of bullying Masa describes. There are moments of conflict when they are surprised when a classmate suddenly calls them *haafu* or *gaijin* in a derogatory manner that is meant to hurt, when pointing out someone's difference is the ultimate way to gain an advantage in a struggle.

Mixed ancestry kids whose families could afford the cost have been drawn to expensive international schools since they first proliferated in Japan in the 1960s. These schools have been regarded as safe havens, a means to escape the harsh world of Japanese schools where prejudice and bullying are prevalent toward those who are different. Many mixed ancestry kids have gone to ordinary Japanese schools, however, and this is increasingly becoming a desired option.

Regardless of the level of adjustment and comfort in a Japanese school, by comparison, international school is an extraordinary experience for most kids, even described as "paradise" by some. It is a world in which they are suddenly "normal" because there are a lot of kids like them from different countries or with parents from two different places. "Everyone is a gaijin," even the Japanese, who grew up in other countries. Kids are removed from their solitary existence at Japanese school and their self-consciousness of difference, and they find a comforting place where they are not noticed for their racial appearance.

Kids describe these schools as a welcome space of acceptance where they feel free to be who they are and to be with other kids like them, switching back and forth in different languages. They relax in an environment where some claim that there is no making fun of anyone for being different in a racial, national, or cultural way. They feel at home with kids from so many countries, benefiting from the diversity and expanding their views of the world in a way impossible at a Japanese school with only Japanese kids.

International schools are not without their costs, first and foremost financial, as tuition alone is tens of thousands of dollars a year. Children also lose the familiarity and comfort of their neighborhood school, childhood friends, the satisfaction of making it in the mainstream, and acceptance to some degree as Japanese. The international school sets them on a track that further marginalizes them in Japanese society and makes a future outside Japan increasingly likely for college and work. Parents with the resources to afford international school must balance these considerations with the obvious benefits.

Masa's parents moved him to international school after seventh grade, and the difference was profoundly felt. "At the international school there were people like me, who looked like me, talked like me. So I traveled from Kyoto to Osaka to go there. There was a community." The trains and buses he rode with other kids to international school became a place of engaging with the stigma of his racial markings. He and others rode the trains performing ethnicity, working out their identity, empowering themselves. It became an integral part of their social life, their place to hang out together, with some kids riding the trains as much as four hours a day.

The following passage is from an essay by Masa on this daily drama:

> As a traveling group, the international school students often resorted to only speaking English in front of Japanese spectators to flaunt our talents and abilities, or to prevent any deciphering from bystanders because we talked and discussed openly about the very people who curiously sat listening to us. Sometimes we would speak abruptly in Japanese to shock those who didn't think we could, but mostly we spoke a comfortable mix of the two, consciously claiming our uniqueness and rightly confusing the hell out of everyone who listened. . . . For what we did, it was a constant game of variables and red herrings, ultimately to circumvent being pinned down, especially by absurdly reductionist views and labels that were part of the vernacular of our unusual existence. We readily made fun of people who thought we were different, yet we would often exaggerate our differences. We made those who presumed we didn't know the culture and language realize their presumptions . . . by speaking the regional dialect, yet we sometimes pretended not to understand the language at all, making awkward gestures and seeming oblivious to our surroundings.
>
> In one sense, our actions were despicably rude, but in another, this helped reaffirm our identity as those who didn't fit in the mainstream in any descriptive code or label. It undoubtedly liberated us, for we could never linguistically—and many of us physically—be regarded as a "normal" Japanese, or a "normal" gaijin or foreigner for that matter. If Japanese people didn't think we were Japanese, could we just passively accept that we weren't? Trains, thus, became a stage for our public ostentation to proclaim that we were "special," that we were "different" and "indecipherable," that we inherently had special rights, talents, and privileges that those who sat facing us didn't. I often wish I could return to those times and relish the sense of empowerment we acquired by being in and creating those situations.[5]

Their exuberant and daring experiences riding together were in sharp contrast to when they rode the trains alone and became vulnerable as a lone person who is different.

> But the joys didn't necessarily come every time we stepped onto the train. Feeling empowered as a group is one thing, but at the end of

the day, being by yourself can be quite another. The attention, of course, is still on you, but you don't have as much recourse as you do in a group. Instead, one becomes hyper-sensitive and self-conscious without being able to brush that off. If one does not stare back and instead puts his head down to shrug off the attention, which many of us did, people don't necessarily feel threatened by your single presence—you become the inviting focal point of everybody's gaze. I tended not to like this sort of attention and was compelled to escape it. Sometimes you just wish you melded into the masses.[6]

Leaving the Bubble

Masa also wanted to tell another side to the story. While the international schools are idealized, the reality is that there are almost no role models of bilingual, bicultural adult teachers, staff, or administrators, and the bilingual, bicultural abilities of the students are actually ignored and even discouraged in practice. Masa charges that the schools do not serve their bicultural students well, that Japanese language and culture are not valued at the same level as English and American culture, and that in most of the schools the curriculum is U.S.-based and prepares students only for American colleges.

A different reality sets in as soon as one leaves the gates of the school or departs at a train station with one's traveling mates. It also hits hard at graduation. Most graduates head for U.S. colleges, since their English-based education has put them on that track. In their own minds, they may be "returning" to a country in which they have never lived. While many claim that they have the best of both worlds and can flexibly fit in anywhere, some acknowledge that the international school students have their own culture and can only fit in with those peers.

They may find some comfort in the United States but they also find dissonance and a mixture of relief and boredom. Some say they enjoy their invisibility, but others say they miss the special treatment, wondering why no one is looking at them. Race may disappear or it may continue to be a major concern, but with a twist: to Japanese they were white American; to Americans they are Japanese. They felt "different" growing up in Japan and thought they would escape this in the United States, but then felt different once again. People may tell them that they are "Asian American," but they have difficulty connecting with those of Asian ancestry who grew up in the United States. They may feel that they just don't know how to act American, recognizing, sometimes painfully, that they have to be more assertive, which feels aggressive and impolite. To them, Americans are impatient, rude, and self-centered—talking loudly, and getting rewarded for it.

The dramatic shift in how others see them may be jarring and unsettling. Being perceived as Japanese is a new and strange experience for them. They may become a symbol of Japan to Americans who know nothing about the culture, meeting ignorance about Japan and enduring racial jokes about Hiroshima. Boon and Masa encountered this in New England, where they came for high school and college, when people viewed them as Japanese, as Asian, and had a hard time accepting them as American. Ironically, the Japanese flag became a symbol associated with them, something they could never have imagined in Japan. Perceived as Japanese and made to feel Japanese in the United States, they tried to take on that identity. Depending on where they were, people attempted to assign or deny various other identities. Masa explains:

> "To my college friends, my brother and I were the 'Japanese twins,' yet in New York, where I resided for two years, I was Turkish, Filipino, Persian, Hawaiian, Dominican, Mexican, and a myriad of other ethnicities. Even in Hawaii, where I tend to blend in, a 'local' Japanese-American man took issue with my name, 'Masa,' even after I explained to him that I was Japanese. 'Well, so am I,' he retorted. Only when I explained that I had been born and raised in Japan and spoke the language fluently—skipping, of course, the intricacies of my transience—did he deem my name 'appropriate.'"

If students from international schools expect U.S. college life to be like their experience at school, they are surprised to find that nobody seems to understand how they feel. Discovering that they are "not American" may leave them feeling that there is nowhere left to go. Some kids return to Japan. I wonder whether they are building bridges or falling through the cracks. They may have the potential to play a role in bridging, blending, and helping others to overcome barriers, but finding situations where they have this opportunity is not easy. The danger is that they become partially proficient in different languages and culture, but the reality of the working world is that you have to be completely proficient in at least one language and culture. I became a professor at Tokyo University partly through my bilingual abilities, but my work required me to be fully fluent in one language, in my case, English. Intermediate skills in both languages would not have been enough.

This dilemma has prompted some parents—who may be able to afford the tuition of international school—to send their children to Japanese schools. Some do this with a belief that it is in the child's best interest to be completely immersed in one language and one culture. *Found in Translation* shows the story of Jeff Bergland, a father who wanted his children to avoid the problems that he had as an American in Japan and that his wife had as a Japanese in the United States. Their solution was to raise their children in one country, one culture, and in one language. Although he is a native English speaker, he spoke Japanese to his son. His son describes himself as "a Japanese who can't speak English." This designation deprives the person of the social capital gained by being perceived as an international *haafu* who speaks English. It places a person instead in the same category previously occupied only by those without the resources to be bilingual, such as the so-called *shima haafu* in Okinawa, children raised usually by single mothers without the presence and resources of the American father. But now the distinction is not so sharp and more mixed ancestry people are appearing with Japanese as a native language, varying degrees of English, and other languages as second or third languages. Isao Fujioka, a graduate student at Tokyo University, is one such person, who grew up in Kansai as a native speaker of Japanese with English a distant second language, even though his native English-speaking father from Ireland was in the home. He later empowered himself by learning English and attending graduate school in the United States.

Masa feels that other people have prescribed one way of being mixed by glorifying the benefits, a view he seeks to balance by showing that there are other equally valid and authentic ways of being mixed. In his film, people question whether they, or anyone else for that matter, are really "double," and they talk about the positive aspects of a bilingual mixed experience while revealing the disadvantages of feeling incomplete in either culture.

They also discuss labels. Like the debate in the U.S. about the term *hapa*, the use of labels in Japan has been controversial. The Japanese media has bowed to pressure from English-speaking parents who claim that *haafu* is derogatory, and the term has been placed on the list of discriminatory language to avoid. But in a strange logic, because the politically correct *daburu* is not a recognizable term, the previously rejected *konketsu* is the suggested replacement.

On the street, people continue to use *haafu* because it is recognized by others. But many say they prefer to avoid being labeled by any term, claiming that labels are for people who don't know them and need some word to categorize. They see any term as incomplete, setting boundaries, limiting them to a certain identity. Even *haafu* indicates that they are *haafu* before they are anything else. The following are voices from *Found in Translation*.

> I don't really care about *haafu*; to me, it's neither positive nor negative, it doesn't affect me; I feel I'm beyond those words. But I'm not double; I'm not completely whole in either world. I feel like those terms are for others who don't know us, who need a term to identify us and reduce us to something they can understand; they are reductionistic.[7]

Some just want to be considered Japanese.

> Especially because I'm living here, I would like to be accepted more as a Japanese person who has foreign blood mixed in, living here just like them.[8]

Telling "Our" Story in Twenty-First-Century Japan

Masa started making films because he felt that "our" story needed to be told, but as he met more people with different stories he realized how he was connected to them, and he drew his circle larger to contain their stories too. He went to Hawaii and found stories there. Ogasawara (the Bonin Islands), another cultural crossroads, called to him and he went there and gathered more stories. He put his story in perspective, expanding his consciousness and asking more questions.

"Many of the interests I developed and the projects I undertook were informed and motivated by my own experience. . . . But when I learned about mixed race children growing up in Okinawa I found a different set of paradigms to be in operation. Many of these people are from single-parent families, grow up without adequate access to an English education, and encounter a more heinous form of racism, much of which derives from the stigma attached to the strong military presence there, one that is based on the stereotypical image of the Japanese mother as promiscuous and the child as illegitimate.

"This prompted an immediate reconfiguring of my identity as a bicultural, biracial person, which I thought was more or less experientially uniform, and called for my relatively positive experience to be situated within the context of class, language ability, and gender in Japan. What if I had grown up in a place like Okinawa? What if I did not have a father? What if I had not learned English at home and could not speak it? What if I was a girl? What if my foreign parent had been my mother and not my father? In the comfort of a bilingual existence, not only did I take my linguistic abilities for granted, I was also ignorant of the vastly different identities developed within the wide range of multiethnic experiences."

I became interested in Masa because I recognized that he was a young person determined to tell "our" story. This is something I have done on and off over much of my adult life, often with a sense of being the only one doing it. But when Masa contacted me to ask whether he could interview me for his film, I was in an "off" period. I thought I was through with the topic and could move on to other things. I had a feeling that nothing will change, at least not in my lifetime—Japanese people will never understand who I am, who we are. I was tired of dealing with their reactions to my face on a daily basis. I suffered ethnic fatigue, doubting Boon's idealistic vision:

Overt racism is less, but different forms of racism come out in certain situations. People make judgments about the way you look. Japanese

can't get over it, accept someone as Japanese, if they don't look like
Japanese. . . . It might be idealistic, but people are mixing and cultures are blending and we are starting to question what race means
and I think you just have to see people beyond those lines.[9]

But today, I know that I am not alone, and I am encouraged by the
many others working in diverse ways. Masa is one of a number of rising filmmakers, artists, photographers, musicians, scholars, and jour-
nalists determined to tell "our" story. In 2008 Ogata Mariko contacted
me through the social network Mixi and said that she and a group of
others would love to meet with me. They had all read my book and
were thrilled that I was coming to their city. The following year I connected with the Hafu Project, started by Marcia Yumi Lise and Natalie
Maya Willer, which profiles *haafus* with photographs and interviews
that shed light on the experience of living between two cultures. They
have shown the Hafu Project in London and Tokyo and at the 2011
Hapa Japan conference in Berkeley. Filmmakers Megumi Nishikura
and Lara Perez Takagi are also exploring the question of what it means
to be mixed Japanese in twenty-first-century Japan through a documentary film, *Hafu*. Ed Sumoto, a subject of their film, is active in
Mixed Roots, a global social network, and hosts a radio show featuring mixed race themes on which I was a guest in summer 2010. Mixed
Roots hosts Shake Forward—mixed race artists promoting social dialogue with music—and also organizes youth workshops and exhibi-
tions as well as essay and art contests. In summer 2011, Ed organized
a modest "international" conference on mixed race issues. One of the
presenters, Hyoue Okamura, maintains a website and participates in
the newly formed Haafu Research Group, led by people who are not
themselves *haafu*—an indication that the theme has broader appeal as
a symbol of the emerging multiethnic nation.

These individuals move beyond complaint and celebration; they
empower themselves and others, creating greater understanding of
who "we" are. While I am all for establishing a *haafu* identity, I resist
being placed too firmly within that category as one separate and distinct from Japanese. I also see a route to empowerment through being
Japanese. One way to feel more Japanese and be accepted as Japanese

is to become Japanese, and let people know that you are Japanese. By "Japanese" I do not mean ethnicity, I mean nationality. Though I was born in Japan I was not able to acquire Japanese nationality because my father was not Japanese, but the nationality law now enables anyone with a Japanese mother to get nationality. After living in Japan for many years I decided I would naturalize. Now I can say much more easily and with self-confidence that I am Japanese. The passport is a legal document, something tangible, a symbol of belonging. My passport helps at airports when I am hassled by police looking for terrorists. I feel empowered with my Japanese passport, with more self-assurance and an expectation of acceptance by others that I am Japanese. I do not complain about "you Japanese." I include myself.

In his film Masa asked me to help tell the story as a scholar. The part that I can tell is that the problem is not within us, it is in the system, far beyond us, in myths and ideologies of a homogeneous, mono-ethnic nation that have characterized images of post–World War II Japan. We are placed outside the boundaries of the Japanese—"we" are "mixed" and "they" are "pure." But I want to say that we may be impure and so are they and so are we all. The problem is in the consciousness of duality. I want to say strongly and clearly, "We are Japanese! Don't separate us! Don't call us *gaijin*! Don't call us *haafu* to distinguish us from you! We are Japanese too! There are many of us who look different but are the same. There are many who look the same who are different. I am not asking just to be tolerated or accepted. I am simply telling you who I am."

I want to question the categorization that creates majorities and minorities, the way in which words are developed to carve the world into "them" and "us." This requires redefining the words we use to label, distinguish, and put people into categories. The Japanese language has not kept pace with social realities. I want to expand the borders of the nation by re-imagining who is Japanese. We have a role to play in this development far beyond our numbers. Sometimes those in the margins can help those in the mainstream to see more clearly through the fog that clouds their brains. In Masa's latest film, he challenges concepts of race and culture even further through the story of Michael, a man with no ethnic ties to Japan though he was born and raised in Kyoto. Masa shows the irony and frustration of a man who many Japanese can only see as a foreigner, who is confined to the role of cultural curiosity. He is looked to as a commentator and authority on American life, a country he does not call home.

Masa's forays into research and film have shown him that issues of race, culture, and identity are what drive him to understand the problems of the modern world and motivate him to help forge social change.

> "I believe that the study of multiculturalism, of multiethnic, multicultural people, their identities and communities, gives us greater insight into the idea of culture and its constitution, its parameters, and its inherent contradictions. This liminal space which multiethnic people inhabit allows us to see meanings and imaginings of other more dominant spaces where self-evaluation is often absent but needed."

In telling our story, Masa has transformed himself by moving beyond the confines of his own experience and others' experiences close to his, challenging himself to connect with lives far different from his as well. In his work Masa tries to increase awareness and challenge the status quo, exploring his identity and engaging with others, trying to comprehend his own experience and the large spectrum of multiethnic experiences and what they tell us about our own and others' cultural convictions. From his position in cultural borderlands he examines these issues and reveals and deconstructs prevailing racial and cultural beliefs, breaking down the artificial divisions between "us" and "them."

Epilogue

When I first began this study some thirty years ago, it seemed like an intensely self-centered, individualistic journey of an unusual identity. People would smile when I explained what I was studying, as if to say, of course, you are just trying to solve your own identity problem by studying strange people like yourself. My work seemed of little value beyond the level of personal and minority group identity, irrelevant to the larger issues.

I have come to see that this view was limited by my own understanding and that of others. I realize that we write about what we need to know and write to find out about ourselves. But I did not realize how much the personal is political and the political is personal. As I reflected on my own life I could see glimpses of these connections but it was through listening to the stories of others that my understanding grew.

There is a paradox in these stories of how personal development ripples out into community development. The individual's attempts to make meaning connect a person to resources beyond the self, with a sense of commonality and community with others. Connections with all parts of the self lead to connections with others.

In these stories I have explored how a few people have struggled with living with the particular circumstances of a mixed heritage. We are commonly forced to choose, to come up with extreme solutions, either/or answers, and adopt a dichotomous vision of the world. These pressures vary by context—where we are positioned geographically, in what developmental stage of life, and in what historical moment.

When I first studied this field in the 1980s I was obsessed with declaring difference. It was a time when I joined with people who had been marginalized; we asserted our otherness and celebrated our unity. This meant reveling in the differences, drawing lines, and setting standards for community membership. I divided the world into oppressors and oppressed, and my self-chosen identity as an oppressed minority had little room for the oppressor, even my white father or his genes in me. At times these pressures were powerful and seductive in their simplicity, providing a safe haven where I could rest and lick my wounds—a place of respite with my chosen group. Despite these contextual pressures toward dichotomies, separation, and conflict, there was also a corrective trend inside me, telling me it wasn't right, urging me on toward a new consciousness, a voice telling me I could not stay there, closing my gates to those I called outsiders. I could see that dichotomies were dangerous, that dehumanization depends on a clear Us/Them binary. I began to feel like I was stagnating, suffocating, in denial, killing part of myself. I knew I needed to venture out to seek new connections; this was frightening because I was vulnerable and risked being wounded once again. But I sensed I needed to open the gate to the stranger who is not only out there but also within me. I needed to embrace my own otherness in liminal space.

Early in my studies I encountered someone who provided a view of this dynamic process as transitioning toward meaning, balance, wholeness, and connectedness. The ideas of Richard Katz on synergy and healing became a foundation for understanding this process that I was observing in myself and others, in which there is a profound change in awareness and worldview, a transformation that brings with it new ways of experiencing the self embedded in and expressive of community. This process involves development of a synergistic view in which we value the coming together of cultures, their interrelations, and the creation of an often unexpected, new and greater whole from the disparate, seemingly conflicting parts. In this synergistic pattern, phenomena exist in harmony with each other, maximizing each other's potential; we experience how apparently dissonant combinations can produce a more effective total resource than either one can when functioning separately. We see ourselves limiting our identity when we try to fit it into the norms of any one group; we expand our identity when we try to express it more fully in its complex and rich form. This movement brings us into alignment with others while we maintain our integrity as individuals who are also part of communities. Yet the contexts that push and pull us toward a dichotomous either/or worldview and way of being are constantly in play.

The individuals in these stories resist forcing themselves into existing identity paradigms and define their hybrid identities by the salient features in their lives. They are inspired to share their personal journeys to increase public awareness, educating within and outside their communities. Giving voice to their concerns, they form social and political organizations to strengthen identities, build social bonds and support networks, and establish legitimacy within communities. Their activities are a way of creating a third space, in which they find their own voice and help others to find theirs, advocate on their own behalf, for their own cause, and identify as "both," rather than being forced to choose between identities and cultural groups.

In this process they move beyond the personal by placing their lives in a broader social context, believing that they have been given the opportunity to unite different worlds. They see our struggle as transcendence, requiring capabilities to overcome boundaries and limitations imposed by self, others, or systems. In this transformation they experience vulnerability in such a way that they move beyond themselves and their own personal needs. They connect not only with all parts of themselves but also with others and a realm beyond themselves in communal efforts. They become cultural healers, with a felt responsibility to work in ways that bring people together, despite their differences, fully realizing their common humanity.

Lessons from Three Conferences

Tokyo, February 2010

In February 2010 I was invited to give a keynote talk in Tokyo for a symposium, "Shifting Borders and Mixing Peoples: Reconsidering Who Is Japanese." I wondered why I had been selected. I have never tried to tell big stories, just the story of my people, our story. I even asked them, "Why me?" They explained that several professors had read my work on Amerasians and felt that it has meaning far beyond that small group. They wanted me to tell them what that story might mean for all of us—what the margins mean for the mainstream.

My talk was titled "Border Crossing Identities: Overcoming the Barriers to 'Us vs. Them' Consciousness," and I addressed how the influx of newcomers was challenging the society to be multicultural by raising the question, "Can foreigners become Japanese?" I argued for expanding the boundaries of the nation by not distinguishing new citizens as a separate and marginalized population but integrating them into mainstream society. I questioned the popular concept of *kyosei*—living together harmoniously with those who are different, which is still based on an Us versus Them dichotomy. I advocated expanding and making more inclusive the idea of "Japanese"—as multicultural citizens of Japan, rather than insiders accepting outsiders with the Us versus Them distinction remaining. I told the audience that for this to happen, the definition of Japanese has to move from ethnic-based to citizenship-based.

I used myself as an example, claiming that someone who looks like me, talks like me, someone who has lived abroad much of his life and is culturally different is still Japanese. I maintain that I am Japanese; because I am a citizen, therefore I am Japanese, as are all others who are Japanese citizens. I accept that I am an "impure Japanese" and assert that all Japanese are similarly impure. Following the symposium, a group of young people gathered around me and told me that they believe in my message. I realized that my seemingly narrow topic has relevance far beyond the relatively small group of people about whom I write.

The next day I met with Matsui Michio, an extraordinary journalist and educator, who introduced me to editors at Shueisha, the publishing giant that printed my first book, *Amerasian Children*. Sections of that book have been reprinted in social studies textbooks used nationwide in Japan in junior high schools to introduce the subject of Japan as a multicultural society. This time Matsui wanted me to go beyond that book's scope and write for a general audience about the global skills Japanese need to survive in the twenty-first century; he assured me I have an important message and a ready audience. I headed to the airport invigorated by the conference and my meeting with Matsui, hopeful that a new day is dawning in Japan.

I was quickly brought back down to earth. Just as I was leaving the airline counter, I was stopped by a person in plain clothes who claimed to be a police officer. He addressed me in English, flashing a badge: "Excuse me, I am the police and would like to ask you a few questions."

I bristled at this intrusion and told him, *Eigo ga wakaranai* (I don't understand English), and kept walking.

He hurried after me, switching to Japanese: *Sumimasen, keisatsu desu ga, chotto shitsumon ga arimasu.*

I snapped back, *Nihongo mo wakaranai* (I don't understand Japanese either).

His expression changed and he smiled, asking, *Ah, Nihonjin desu ka?* (Oh, are you Japanese?).

I pulled my passport from my shirt pocket, flashed it in his face, and said, *Hai, Nihonjin desu yo!* (Yes, I am Japanese!).

He apologized for bothering me, saying *Sumimasen ga, ayashii gaikokujin o sagashiteiru no de* (Sorry, but we are looking for a suspicious foreigner).

I challenged him, *Hontou ni keisatsu desu ka?* (Are you really the police?).

He assured me he was, showing me his badge again.

I suddenly became more anxious than angry but still asked, *Dou shite boku ni kiite irun desu ka?* (Why are you hassling *me*?).

Of course, I knew that the answer was in my face. The borders may be shifting and people may be mixing, but racial profiling remains. It will be a while before faces like mine are regarded as Japanese. A passport can empower but not solve all the problems of new citizens. I read in the newspaper that the Sumo Association is concerned that foreign wrestlers are becoming Japanese through naturalization. In the past the association has questioned whether it was possible for a foreigner to achieve the highest rank of *yokozuna*, when only Japanese possess the essential quality of *hin*. Now they will discriminate between native and naturalized Japanese, convinced that only natives can be true Japanese. The importance and difficulty of my work is only more apparent.

Chicago, November 2010

In November 2010 I attended the first Critical Mixed Race Studies conference in Chicago, where I participated in the session "Creating and Performing Amerasians" with Eriko Ikehara, Cathy Schlund-Vials, and Cindy Howe. I spoke about my storytelling, "The Celtic Samurai," which depicts my family's transnational journey. After it was over we went to hear our friends Mitzi Uehara Carter and Yumi Wilson. Halfway through her presentation, Yumi mentioned matter-of-factly that her mother had been a prostitute. I was surprised and wondered how others in the audience reacted. Yumi had told me this before, when she asked for my help in finding her mother's family in Japan. She was reunited with the one uncle who still loved her late mother and wanted to meet Yumi. He was blind, she was mostly mute in his language; their encounter was one of the most beautiful moments in Yumi's life.

I was surprised that she told this audience about that aspect of her mother's life; the moment passed and Yumi finished her presentation, drawing no questions about her mother. But I was stuck on what Yumi had said because most of us take the position of objecting to war bride stereotypes by telling our audience that *my* mother was different. I talk about how my mother was highly educated and came from a *hatamoto* family who were direct retainers to the shogun, in other words, an elite samurai family background. This is my way of fighting the stereotype. While it does so by providing contradictory and alternative images and stories, it does not challenge the basic moralistic and dualistic thinking that sees "good women" and "bad women." What Yumi said, even without explanation, challenges our beliefs in the whole system that creates prostitution and the value judgments we make in our "blaming the victim" mentality. The self-narratives that we use to bolster our own self-esteem may be based in such flawed thinking.

Yumi's simple statement shook me deeply and had me question what I was doing, what we were doing. Why were we there telling our stories? Why are we doing research, what am I doing in my "Celtic Samurai," in writing this book, how did we select the stories to tell? What did we censor and what did we reveal? What was individual about our experiences and what was determined by systems of men with power coming together with women with needs? What is unique and what is contextual, embedded in systems of European colonialism and American imperialism and hegemony? Who are our mothers, the Asian women who marry American men; who are our fathers, the American men who marry Asian women; who are we, their children; and who are the people of mixed ethnicities in other configurations? Are we victims? Do we have agency?

I am more determined than ever to tell "our" story by continuing to ask these questions. Who are "we," and are we embracing the complexity of our experiences? We know that none of us really inherits "the best of both worlds." We receive the best and we receive the worst. We attempt to find connections with all of our parts. We struggle for balance, strive for wholeness, and search for meaning in what we've been given.

Berkeley, April 2011

The Hapa Japan conference was a remarkable event, with many of us delighted to be there but wondering whether it was a beginning or an ending. I was honored as one of the pioneers who had come together with a new generation of scholars and artists and other interested persons, but beyond the euphoria we discovered that many of us had doubts about the event. Was it just a sentimental reunion, with a few relics and appreciative younger scholars gathered, or was there really something around which we could organize and move forward? But over the course of the three days we found that many of us were invigorated and determined to revive our work and continue. There was nostalgia and celebration but also new energy to keep this area of study alive. The "Hapa Japan" theme, bringing together the Hawaiian term *hapa* with Japan, blending two worlds, emphasized how the transnational focus is the way of the future. The people who assembled there, some from Japan, a few from other countries, also addressed the coming together of Japanese and American, and, for me, legitimized the attention I have given for many years to a broad view of the issues that go beyond national borders. Future events are being planned on both sides of the Pacific, each inclusively Japanese and American.

My personal contribution was to consult with the organizer, Duncan Williams, and suggest the inclusion of diverse people and perspectives, a view that he enthusiastically shared. As I considered the various people who would make the conference successful, I realized the broad extent of the network I have created and of my involvement in these issues over many years. This network has been especially enhanced by alternating long periods of research and residence in both Japan and the United States.

I also offered to do a storytelling rather than a traditional academic paper as a way of crossing borders between academia and the public. "The Celtic Samurai" is an expression of how the personal is political and how the connections we find with ourselves can bring forth connections with others. The conference gave me a clearer sense of the role I have played and can play as I move into a stage of life in which I will seek to contribute through my own work and mentoring the work of others. Although I have often tried to move away from this focus, I keep coming back to it, or it keeps coming back to me, connecting me to a vital source of energy discovered in my youth and described so well by William James.

> A man's character is discernible in the mental or moral attitude in which, when it first came upon him, he felt himself most deeply and intensely active and alive. At such moments there is a voice inside which speaks and says, "this is the real me!" . . . I feel a sort of deep enthusiastic bliss, of bitter willingness to do and suffer anything . . . and which, although it is a mere mood of emotion to which I can give no form in words, authenticates itself to me as the deepest principle of all active determination which I possess.[1]

Final Reflections

When I was a young man troubled by the meaning of life, I decided that if there is a purpose to my existence perhaps it is related to my birth to a Japanese mother and American father, following a tragic war. They were two people who came from different countries—countries that divided the world into Us and Them and killed each other until one stopped fighting.

As I grew up I saw that the world was divided into sexes, nations, races, and religions. I realized people always wanted to see the world in Black and White, East and West, Japanese and American. Japanese saw me as American. Americans saw me as Japanese. But I could not see what they were seeing. And I could not feel their fear or hatred of each other. If I hated Japanese, didn't I hate my own mother? Didn't I hate myself? If I hated Americans, didn't I hate my own father? Didn't I hate myself?

Whenever I tried to simplify the world by dividing people into Us and Them I saw myself in the Other. I saw the Other in myself.

I began to see this as my fate and purpose—to live in borderlands of nations and races. I decided that my identity would cross borders. I would free myself from loyalty and subordination to any ideologies, cultures, systems, worlds, nations. Instead, I would claim belonging to many countries. I would fight to belong and fit in everywhere. I would fight for inclusion, for all, aligning myself with those excluded. I would belong only to groups that would have anyone as a member. These would be my ideals.

I am no longer a young man, and questions of identity do not occupy my thoughts. But I still find meaning in living in the borderlands—marginal, hybrid, liminal spaces, between and among worlds. The United States is my home and Japan is my home, but I also feel that homelessness is my home—I am at home with a lack of home or belonging. I often feel out of place. I enjoy the freedom and accept the loneliness of this position.

I am Japanese and American, but I know that most Japanese do not consider me Japanese and many Americans do not see me as a real American. In either country the dominants say that they are the real Japanese and the real Americans and all others are not. They discriminate and exclude; they try to force the "minorities" to be like them. They force me to reflect on my identity, to gain self-respect and dignity and to fight against their oppression. I assert my identity and declare my belonging. I claim my rights and bear my responsibilities as a citizen, in both countries.

The boundaries between people disturb me. When we see the world as Us versus Them, drawing firm lines of nations, races, genders, or religions, we construct barriers that we are willing to fight and kill to defend. I try to make these boundaries more pliant, permeable, flexible. I am a Japanese who is also American; I am Westerner and Easterner; I am a man who takes care of kids; I am a Catholic who is Buddhist. I identify with all these groups, not confining myself to any.

I live with these tensions, these apparent contradictions. I claim many identities yet refuse to be limited by any of them. I recognize the many differences among people yet insist on seeing the commonalities, for they can be the source of empathy, compassion, and transformation. It is when we feel the connections with others that we experience joy in overcoming our existential isolation.

I struggle every day to keep from falling into the abyss of separating people too strongly, of believing that We are more human than Them. For this is an illusion, for some people a delusion, that threatens our survival and enables Us to kill Them, to see the world in violent binaries—human-inhuman divides.

I try to see the Other in myself and myself in the Other. I try to be human and regard others as human. Living in multicultural communities with the complexities of our times demands that we develop a perspective, a consciousness, a worldview, and identities that take into account the whole planet, acknowledging the interconnectedness of all beings.

Notes

Chapter 1

1. Norma Field, *In the Realm of a Dying Emperor: A Portrait of Japan at Century's End* (New York: Pantheon, 1991), 37.
2. Field, *Realm of a Dying Emperor*, 37–38.
3. Ibid., 39.
4. Norma Field, *From My Grandmother's Bedside: Sketches of Postwar Tokyo* (Berkeley: University of California Press, 1997), 145.
5. Ibid., 7.
6. Field, *Realm of a Dying Emperor*, 265.
7. Ibid., 265.
8. Field, *Grandmother's Bedside*, 121.
9. Stephen Murphy-Shigematsu, "Multiethnic Japan and the Monoethnic Myth," *MELUS* 18, no. 4 (1993): 63–80.
10. Field, *Grandmother's Bedside*, 12.
11. Stephen Murphy-Shigematsu, *Voices of Amerasians: Ethnicity, Identity, and Empowerment in Interracial Japanese Americans* (PhD diss., Harvard University, 1986), 88.
12. Stephen Murphy-Shigematsu, "Obaachan, What Do *You* Want to Do?" in *Wondrous Child: The Joys and Challenges of Grandparenting*, ed. Lindy Hough (Berkeley, CA: North Atlantic Books, 2012), 255–262.
13. Edward Said, *Out of Place: A Memoir* (New York: Knopf, 2000).

Chapter 2

1. Claudine Chiawei O'Hearn, introduction to *Half and Half: Writers on Growing Up Biracial and Bicultural*, ed. Claudine Chiawei O'Hearn (New York: Pantheon, 1998), ix–x.

2. May Lee Chai, *Hapa Girl: A Memoir* (Philadelphia: Temple University Press, 2007), 206.

3. Ibid., 80.

4. Lowry C. W. Pei, "Memories of Being an American Kid," in *Bridge* 7, no. 1 (Spring 1979): 11.

5. Sui Sin Far, "Leaves from the Mental Portfolio of an Eurasian," in *Turning Shadows into Light*, ed. Mayumi Tsutakawa and Alan Chong Lau (Seattle: Young Pine Press, 1982), 124.

6. O'Hearn, xii.

7. Peter Nien-chu Kiang, "Wanting to Go On: Healing and Transformation at an Urban Public University," in *Immigrant Voices: In Search of Educational Equity*, ed. Enrique (Henry) Trueba and Lilia I. Bartolome (Lanham, MD: Rowman & Littlefield, 2000), 158.

8. Ibid., 160.

9. Ibid., 162.

10. Ibid., 164.

Chapter 3

1. Lane Ryo Hirabayashi, "On Being Hapa," *Hokubei Mainichi* (February 7, 1986): 1.

2. George Kitahara Kich, *Eurasians: Ethnic/Racial Identity Development in Biracial Japanese/White Adults* (PhD diss., Wright Institute, 1982).

3. Stephen Murphy-Shigematsu, "Addressing Issues of Biracial/Bicultural Asian Americans," in *Reflections on Shattered Windows: Promises and Prospects for Asian American Studies*, ed. Gary Okihiro et al. (Pullman: Washington State University Press, 1988), 111–116.

4. Lane Ryo Hirabayashi, "The Best of Both Worlds? Reflections on the Bi-cultural Experience," *Echoes from Gold Mountain: An Asian American Journal* (1982): 76–78.

5. Lane Ryo Hirabayashi, "Understanding the 'Happa' Experience," *Pacific Citizen* (April 20, 1984): 1.

6. Rocky Kiyoshi Mitarai, "Hate Crime in Japantown," in Pearl Fuyo Gaskins, *What Are You? Voices of Mixed-Race Young People* (New York: Henry Holt, 1999), 148.

7. Ibid., 149.

8. Ibid., 147–148.

9. Ibid., 149.

10. Ibid., 146.

11. Hirabayashi, "Understanding the 'Happa' Experience," 1.

12. Mitarai, "Hate Crime," 150.

13. Lane Ryo Hirabayashi, "Is the Japanese American Community Disappearing?" *Pacific Citizen* (December 17, 1993), B15–16.

14. Rebecca Chiyoko King-O'Riain, *Pure Beauty: Judging Race in Japanese American Beauty Pageants* (Minneapolis: University of Minnesota Press, 2006).

15. Stewart David Ikeda, "Adoption, Hapas, and Asian-American Heritage: On the Future of the 'Traditional Non-traditional' Japanese-American Family" (Asian-American Village, 2010), http://www.imdiversity.com/villages /asian/family _lifestyle_traditions/ikeda_adoption_hapas_heritage.asp.

16. Ibid.

17. Lane Ryo Hirabayashi with Kenichiro Shimada, photographs by Hikaru Carl Iwasaki, *Japanese American Resettlement through the Lens: Hikaru Carl Iwasaki and the WRA's Photographic Section, 1943–1945* (Boulder: University Press of Colorado, 2009).

Chapter 4

1. Stephen Murphy-Shigematsu, *Amerajian no kodomotachi: Shirarezaru mainoriti mondai* [Amerasian Children: An Unknown Minority Problem], trans. Sumiko Sakai (Tokyo: Shueisha Shinsho, 2002).

2. Oshiro Yasutaka, "Kokusaiji no kakaeru mondai" [The Problems of the International Children], in *Okinawa no bunka to seishineisei* [Okinawa Culture and Mental Health], ed. Yuji Sasaki (Tokyo: Kobundo, 1984), 135–146.

3. Uezato Kiyomi, *Amerajian: Mou hitotsu no Okinawa* [Amerasians: Another Okinawa] (Kyoto: Kamogawa Shuppan, 1998).

4. Stephen Murphy-Shigematsu, "Okinawa no nichibei haafu ni tai suru sutereotaipu" [Stereotypes of Okinawa's Amerasians], in *Okinawa ni hito to kokoro* [The People and Spirit of Okinawa], Okinawa Psychological Association (Fukuoka: Kyushu University Press, 1994), 53–57.

Chapter 5

1. George Kitahara Kich, "In the Margins of Sex and Race: Difference, Marginality, and Flexibility," in *The Multiracial Experience: Racial Borders as the New Frontier*, ed. M. P. P. Root (Thousand Oaks, CA: Sage, 1996), 263–276.

2. Beverly Yuen Thompson, "Fence Sitters, Switch Hitters, and Bi-Bi Girls: An Exploration of Hapa and Bisexual Identities," *Frontiers: A Journal of Women's Studies* 21:1, 2 (2000): 179.

3. Wei Ming Dariotis, "On Becoming a Bi Bi Grrrl," in *Restoried Selves: Autobiographies of Queer Asian / Pacific American Activists*, ed. Kevin K. Kumashiro (New York: Haworth Press, 2003), 38.

4. Dariotis, "On Becoming," 38.

5. Wei Ming Dariotis, "On Growing Up Queer and Hapa," in *Multiracial Child Resource Book: Living Complex Identities*, ed. M. P. P. Root and Matt Kelley (Seattle: Mavin Foundation, 2003), 103.

6. Dariotis, "On Becoming," 38.

7. Ibid., 39.

8. Karen Maeda Allman, "(Un)Natural Boundaries: Mixed Race, Gender, and Sexuality," in *The Multiracial Experience*, ed. Root, 277–278.

9. Claire Huang Kinsley, "What Do I Look Like?" in *Miscegenation Blues: Voices of Mixed Race Women*, ed. Carol Camper (Toronto, ON: Sister Vision Press, 1994), 87.

10. Dariotis, "On Becoming," 40.

11. Dariotis, "On Growing Up," 104.

12. Wei Ming Dariotis, "Hapas: A Community Based on Shared Difference," in *The New Face of Asian Pacific America: Numbers, Diversity, and Change in the 21st Century*, ed. Eric Lai and Dennis Arguelles (San Francisco: Asian Week, and Los Angeles: UCLA Asian American Studies Center Press, 2003), 118.

13. Wei Ming Dariotis, "Hapa: The Word of Power," *Hyphen Magazine* (December 3, 2007): http://www.hyphenmagazine.com.

14. Ibid.

15. Paul Spickard, afterword in Kip Fulbeck, *Part Asian, 100% Hapa* (San Francisco: Chronicle Books, 2006), 261–262.

16. Alec Yoshio MacDonald, "Check the Label," *Nichibei Times* (July 9–15, 2009): 7.

Chapter 6

1. Rudy P. Guevarra, "Clueless," in *Crossing Lines: Race and Mixed Race across the Geohistorical Divide*, ed. Marc Coronado, Rudy P. Guevarra, Jeffrey A. S. Moniz, and Laura Furlan (Lanham, MD: Rowman & Littlefield, 2005), 15–17.

2. Evelyn Hu-DeHart, "Asian Latinos," in *Oxford Encyclopedia of Latinos and Latinas* (New York: Oxford University Press), 123.

3. Gloria E. Anzaldua, "(Un)natural bridges, (Un)safe spaces," preface to *This Bridge We Call Home*, ed. Gloria E. Anzaldua and Analouise Keating (New York: Routledge, 2002), 4.

Chapter 7

1. Mitzi Uehara Carter, "I'm Fixin' to Go to Store," *Grits and Sushi: My Musings on Okinawa, Race, Family, Militarization, Blackness, and the South* (December 1, 2010): http://gritsandsushi.com/.

2. Mitzi Uehara Carter, "My So-Called Identity," in *What Are You? Voices of Mixed-Race Young People*, ed. Pearl Fuyo Gaskins (New York: Henry Holt, 1999), 204. Quoted passages are drawn from Carter's essay "On Being Blackanese," published by the online journal *Interracial Voice* in April 1996; the essay first appeared in *The Raging Buddha* e-zine when the author was a senior ar Duke University.

3. Ibid., 203.

4. Carter, "Imagining Okinawa," *Grits and Sushi* (September 30, 2010).

5. Carter, "My So-Called Identity," 205.

6. Ibid., 202.

7. Ibid., 203.

8. Carter, "About," *Grits and Sushi*.

9. Ibid.

10. Tatsu Yamato, "Roots: Random Thoughts on Random Hair," in *What Are You?*, ed. Gaskins, 168–169.

11. Mitzi Uehara Carter and Aina Hunter, "A Critical View of Academic Perspectives of Blackness in Japan," in *Multiculturalism in the New Japan: Crossing the Boundaries Within,* ed. Nelson Graburn, John Ertl, and R. Kenji Tierney (Oxford and New York: Berghahn, 2008), 194.

12. Ibid., 195.

13. Ibid.

14. Ibid., 196.

15. Ibid., 194.

16. Carter, "Imagining Okinawa," *Grits and Sushi*.

17. Carter, "Warm Reception," *Grits and Sushi* (January 18, 2011).

Chapter 8

1. Marshall Bennett, "Life in Translation: *Winter Sonata* as an Allegory of One Adoptee's Search and Discovery," *Korean Quarterly* 7, no. 4 (Summer 2004): 3.

2. Ibid.

3. Marshall Bennett, "Colors," *Korean Quarterly* 11, no. 3 (Spring 2011): 4–5.

4. Marshall Bennett, "Kimchee Reflections and the Sonata Daydream," *Fukuoka State Teacher's Journal* 3 (Spring 2004): 5–8.

5. Joyce Fujioka, "An Adopted Way of Life," *AsianWeek* (November 26–December 2, 1998), http://asianweek.com/112698/coverstory.html.

6. Jane Jeong Trenka, *The Language of Blood* (Minneapolis: Graywolf Press, 2005), 121.

7. Katy Robinson, quoted in Fujioka, "An Adopted Way of Life."

8. April Elkjer, "Transracial Adoption Crosses the Color Line," *Nichi Bei Times* (July 20, 2009), 12.

9. Marshall Bennett, "Wisps," *Korean Quarterly* 7, no. 3 (Spring 2003): 2–4.

Chapter 9

1. Sarah Sakhaee Kashani, "Colonial Migration to the 'Manchester of the Orient': The Origins of the Korean Community in Osaka, Japan, 1920–1945," in *Japan's Diversity Dilemmas*, ed. Soo im Lee, Stephen Murphy-Shigematsu, and Harumi Befu (Lincoln, NE: iUniverse, 2006) 169–190.

2. William Wetherall, "Chong v Tokyo, 2005: Not Allowing Aliens to Hold Civil Service Posts Is Not Unconstitutional," http://members.jcom.home.ne.jp/yosha/yr/citizenship/Chong_v_Tokyo_2005.html.

3. William Wetherall, "Tei Taikin on Nationalism and Koreans in Japan: The Wrongs of 'Zainichi' Victimhood and the Rights of Naturalization," http://members.jcom.home.ne.jp/yosha/yr/bibliographies/Bibliography_minorities_Tei_Taikin.html.

Chapter 10

1. Akemi Johnson, "Do You Speak . . . ? Multicultural Awareness in Okinawa," *Nichibei Times* (July 11, 2009): 11.

2. Akemi Johnson, "On Fractions," *Creative Non Fiction* (December 2004).

3. Johnson, "Do You Speak . . . ?" 11.

4. Akemi Johnson, "To the U.S. and Back: Fostering a Positive Japanese American Identity over Generations," *Immigration Studies* (Naha: International Institute for Okinawan Studies, University of the Ryukyus, March 2010), 6:125.

5. Johnson, "Do You Speak . . . ?" 11.

6. Johnson, "On Fractions."

7. Pearl Fuyo Gaskins, ed., *What Are You? Voices of Mixed-Race Young People* (New York: Henry Holt, 1999).

8. Johnson, "On Fractions."

9. Ibid.

10. Johnson, "To the U.S. and Back," 124.

11. Johnson, "On Fractions."

12. Ibid.

13. Ibid.

14. Ibid.

15. Johnson, "Do You Speak . . . ?" 11.

16. Johnson, "To the U.S. and Back," 124.

17. Johnson, "On Fractions."

18. Johnson, "Do You Speak . . . ?" 11.

19. Johnson, "To the U.S. and Back," 125.

Chapter 11

1. *Found in Translation*, DVD, directed by Masahiko Murotani Fox (Japan and USA.: TwinFox Production, 2005).

2. Ibid.

3. Masahiko Murotani Fox, "Trains" (unpublished essay, 2004).

4. Ibid.

5. Ibid.

6. Ibid.

7. *Found in Translation.*

8. Ibid.

9. Ibid.

Epilogue

1. Henry James, *The Letters of William James* (Boston: Atlantic Monthly Press, 1920), 199.

Recommended Readings

Works cited in the notes are not listed here.

Chapter 1

Dower, John W. *Embracing Defeat: Japan in the Wake of World War II*. New York: Norton, 2000.

Fish, Robert A. "Mixed-Blood Japanese: A Reconsideration of Race and Purity in Japan." In *Japan's Minorities: The Illusion of Homogeneity*. Edited by Michael Weiner. 2nd ed. New York: Routledge, 2009. 40–58.

Michener, James A. *Sayonara*. New York: Bantam Books, 1954.

Murphy-Shigematsu, Stephen. *Amerajian no Kodomotachi: Shirarezaru Mainoriti Mondai* [Amerasian Children: An Unknown Minority Problem]. Translated by Sumiko Sakai. Tokyo: Shueisha Shinsho, 2002.

———. "The Celtic Samurai." In *War Baby / Love Child: Mixed Race Asian American Art*. Edited by Wei-ming Dariotis and Laura Kina. Seattle: University of Washington Press, 2012.

———. "Where Are You From?" *Mainichi Weekly*, March 20, 2004.

Spickard, Paul. *Mixed Blood: Intermarriage and Ethnic Identity in Twentieth-Century America*. Madison: University of Wisconsin Press, 1991.

Wagatsuma, Hiroshi. "Mixed-Blood Children in Japan: An Exploratory Study." *Journal of Asian Affairs* 2, no. 2 (1976): 9–16.

Chapter 2

"How to Tell Japs from the Chinese: Angry Citizens Victimize Allies with Emotional Outburst at Enemy." *Life*, December 22, 1941, 81–82.

Kiang, Peter Nien-chu. "Asian American Resource Workshop: Art and Culture for the Community." *East Wind* 2, no. 1 (1983): 11–14.

———. "China Reflections on Three Generations." *Sampan*, February 1983, 21–26.

———. "Crouching Activists, Hidden Scholars: Reflections on Research and Development with Students and Communities in Asian American Studies." In *Engaging Contradictions: Theory, Politics, and Methods of Activist Scholarship*. Edited by Charles R. Hale. Berkeley: University of California Press, 2008. 299–318.

Chapter 3
Erikson, E. H. "The Concept of Identity in Race Relations: Notes and Queries." *Daedalus* 95, no. 1 (Winter 1966): 45–171.

Chapter 4
Allen, Matthew. *Identity and Resistance in Okinawa*. Lanham, MD: Rowman and Littlefield, 2002.

Hein, Laura, and Mark Selden, eds. *Islands of Discontent: Okinawan Responses to Japanese and American Power*. Lanham, MD: Rowman and Littlefield, 2003.

Inoue, Masamichi S. *Okinawa and the U.S. Military: Identity Making in the Age of Globalization*. New York: Columbia University Press, 2007.

Matsumori, Akiko. "Ryukyuan: Past, Present and Future." In *Multilingual Japan*. Edited by John C. Maher and Kyoko Yashiro. Clevedon, UK: Multilingual Matters, 1995. 19–44.

Murphy-Shigematsu, Stephen. "Challenges for Multicultural Education in Japan." *New Horizons for Learning Online Journal* 9, no. 2 (Spring 2003). http://www.newhorizons.org.

———. *Multicultural Encounters: Case Narratives from a Counseling Practice*. New York: Teachers College Press, 2002.

———. "Narratives of Living in the Borderlands of Race and Nation in Japan." In *Transcultural Japan: At the Borderlands of Race, Gender, and Identity*. Edited by David B. Willis and Stephen Murphy-Shigematsu. London: Routledge, 2008. 282–304.

Taira, Koji. "Troubled National Identity: The Ryukyuans/Okinawans." In *Japan's Minorities: The Illusion of Homogeneity*. Edited by Michael Weiner. London: Routledge, 1997. 140–177.

Tanaka Hiroshi. *Zainichi Gaikokujin* [Foreign Residents in Japan]. Tokyo: Iwanami Shinsho, 1991.

Ueunten, Wesley. "Okinawan Diasporic Identities: Between Being a Buffer and a Bridge." In *Transcultural Japan: At the Borderlands of Race, Gender, and Identity*. Edited by D. B. Willis and S. Murphy-Shigematsu. London: Routledge, 2008. 159–178.

Chapter 5

Fulbeck, Kip. *Part Asian, 100% Hapa*. San Francisco: Chronicle Books, 2006.

Gamble, Adrian E. *Hapas: Emerging Community, Emerging Identity, and the Social Construction of Race*. Honors Thesis, Program in Comparative Studies in Race and Ethnicity, Stanford University, 2004.

Kich, George Kitahara. "The Developmental Process of Asserting a Biracial, Bicultural Identity." In *Racially Mixed People in America*. Edited by Maria P. P. Root. Newbury Park, CA: Sage, 1992. 304–317.

Williams-Leon, Teresa. "The Convergence of Passing Zones: Multiracial Gays, Lesbians, and Bisexuals of Asian Descent." In *The Sum of Our Parts: Mixed Heritage Asian Americans*. Edited by Teresa Williams-Leon and Cynthia L. Nakashima. Philadelphia: Temple University Press, 2001. 145–162.

Chapter 6

Anzaldua, Gloria E. *Borderlands / La Frontera: The New Mestiza*. 3rd ed. San Francisco: Aunt Lute Books, 2007.

Chung, Sheila R. "Raising Asian-Latinos." In *Multiracial Child Resource Book: Living Complex Identities*. Edited by Maria P. P. Root and Matt Kelley. Seattle: Mavin Foundation, 2003. 178–185.

Coronado, Marc, Rudy P. Guevarra, Jeffrey A. S. Moniz, and Laura Furlan Szanto, eds. *Crossing Lines: Race and Mixed Race across the Geohistorical Divide*. Lanham, MD: Rowman and Littlefield, 2005.

Guevarra, Rudy P., Jr. *Becoming Mexipino: Multiethnic Identities and Communities in San Diego*. New Brunswick, NJ: Rutgers University Press, 2012.

Hall, Christine Iijima, and Trude I. Cooke Turner. "The Diversity of Biracial Individuals: Asian-White and Asian-Minority Biracial Identity." In *The Sum of Our Parts: Mixed Heritage Asian Americans*. Edited by Teresa Williams-Leon and Cynthia L. Nakashima. Philadelphia: Temple University Press, 2001. 81–92.

Hu-DeHart, Evelyn. "Latin America in Asia-Pacific Perspective." In *Asian Diasporas: New Formations, New Conceptions*. Edited by Rhacel S. Parreñas and Lok C. D. Siu. Stanford, CA: Stanford University Press, 2007. 29–62.

Ishi, Angelo Akimitsu. "Between Privilege and Prejudice: Japanese-Brazilians in 'The Land of Yen and the Ancestors.'" In *Transcultural Japan: At the Borderlands of Race, Gender, and Identity.* Edited by David Blake Willis and Stephen Murphy-Shigematsu. London: Routledge, 2008. 113–134.

Chapter 7

Carter, Mitzi Uehara. "I Felt a Whole Lot Stronger." In *What Are You? Voices of Mixed-Race Young People.* Edited by Pearl Fuyo Gaskins. New York: Henry Holt, 1999. 197–199.

Kilson, Marion, and Florence Ladd. *Is That Your Child? Mothers Talk about Rearing Biracial Children.* Lanham, MD: Lexington Books, 2008.

Rockquemore, Kerry Ann, and Tracey A. Laszloffy. *Raising Biracial Children.* AltaMira Press / Rowman and Littlefield, 2005.

Root, Maria P. P., and Matt Kelley, eds. *Multiracial Child Resource Book: Living Complex Identities.* Seattle: Mavin Foundation, 2003.

Wagatsuma, Hiroshi. "Mixed-Blood Children in Japan: An Exploratory Study." *Journal of Asian Affairs* 2, no. 2 (1976): 9–16.

Chapter 8

Hübinette, Tobias. "Asian Bodies Out of Control: Examining the Adopted Korean Existence." In *Asian Diasporas: New Formations, New Conceptions.* Edited by Rhacel S. Parreñas and Lok C. D. Siu. Stanford, CA: Stanford University Press, 2007. 177–200.

———."From Orphan Trains to Babylifts: Colonial Trafficking, Empire Building, and Social Engineering." In *Outsiders Within: Writing on Transracial Adoption.* Edited by Jane Jeong Trenka, Julia Chinyere Oparah, and Sun Yung Shin. Cambridge, MA: South End Press, 2006. 139–150.

Chapter 9

Chong Yong Hye. "Aidentiti o Koete" [Beyond Identity]. In *Sabetsu to Kyosei no Shakaigaku* [Sociology of Prejudice and Coexistence]. Edited by Inoue Shun et al. Tokyo: Iwanami Shoten, 1996. 1–33.

Lee, Soo im, Stephen Murphy-Shigematsu, and Harumi Befu, eds. *Japan's Diversity Dilemmas: Ethnicity, Citizenship, and Education.* Lincoln, NE: iUniverse, 2006.

Lee Soo im and Tanaka Hiroshi. *Gurobaru Jidai no Nihon Shakai to Kokuseki* [Japanese Society and Citizenship in the Global Age]. Tokyo: Akashi Shoten, 2007.

McNeill, David. "'I Want to Make Japan a Better Place to Live': Korean Nurse Blocked from Promotion by Tokyo Vows to Fight On." *Japan Times,* Feb. 1, 2005.

Murphy-Shigematsu, Stephen. "Dilemmas of Human Relations of Korean International Students in Japan." In *Japan's Diversity Dilemmas: Ethnicity, Citizenship and Education.* Edited by Soo im Lee, Stephen Murphy-Shigematsu, and Harumi Befu. Lincoln, NE: iUniverse, 2006. 213–232.

———. "Diverse Forms of Minority National Identities in Japan." In *Japan's Diversity Dilemmas.* Edited by Soo im Lee, Stephen Murphy-Shigematsu, and Harumi Befu. Lincoln, NE: iUniverse, 2006. 75–99.

———. "Ethnic Diversity, Citizenship, and Education in Japan." In *Diversity and Citizenship Education: Global Perspectives.* Edited by James A. Banks. San Francisco: Jossey-Bass/Wiley, 2004. 303–332.

———. "Ethnic Diversity, Identity and Citizenship in Japan." *Harvard Asia Quarterly* 8, no. 1 (Winter 2004): 51–57.

Tei Taikin (Chung Daekyun). *Zainichi Kankokujin no shuen* [The End of Koreans in Japan]. Tokyo: Bungei Shunju, 2001.

———. *Zainichi: Kyosei renko no shinwa* [Japan Resident Koreans: Myths of Forced Movements].Tokyo: Bungei Shunju, 2004.

———. *Zainichi no taerarenai karusa* [The Unbearable Lightness of Being Korean in Japan]. Tokyo: Chuo Koron Shinsha, 2006.

Wetherall, William. "Nationality in Japan." In *Japan's Diversity Dilemmas: Ethnicity, Citizenship and Education.* Edited by Soo im Lee, Stephen Murphy-Shigematsu, and Harumi Befu. Lincoln, NE: iUniverse, 2006. 11–46.

Chapter 10

Johnson, Akemi. "Island Haafu, Tokyo Haafu: Learning English at the AmerAsian School in Okinawa." Honors Thesis, Department of East Asian Studies, Brown University, 2004.

Mass, Amy I. "Interracial Japanese Americans: The Best of Both Worlds or the End of the Japanese American Community?" In *Racially Mixed People in America.* Edited by Maria P. P. Root. Newbury Park, CA: Sage Publications, 1992. 265–279.

Murphy-Shigematsu, Stephen. "Multiethnic Lives and Monoethnic Myths: American-Japanese Amerasians in Japan." In *The Sum of Our Parts: Mixed Heritage Asian Americans.* Edited by Teresa Williams-Leon and Cynthia L. Nakashima. Philadelphia: Temple University Press, 2001. 207–216.

Nakashima, Daniel A. "A Rose by Any Other Name: Names, Multiracial/Multiethnic People, and the Politics of Identity." In *The Sum of Our Parts: Mixed Heritage Asian Americans.* Edited by Teresa Williams-Leon and Cynthia L. Nakashima. Philadelphia: Temple University Press, 2001. 111–119.

Root, Maria P. P. "Factors Influencing the Variation in Racial and Ethnic Identity of Mixed-Heritage Persons of Asian Ancestry." In *The Sum of Our Parts: Mixed Heritage Asian Americans.* Edited by Teresa Williams-Leon and Cynthia L. Nakashima. Philadelphia: Temple University Press, 2001. 61–70.

Spickard, Paul. "What Must I Be? Asian Americans and the Question of Multiethnic Identity." *Amerasia Journal* 23, no. 1 (1997): 43–60.

Suyemoto, Karen. "Racial/Ethnic Identities and Related Attributed Experiences of Multiracial Japanese Americans." *Journal of Multicultural Counseling and Development* 32 (2004): 206–221.

Suyemoto, Karen, and John Tawa. "Multiracial Asian Americans." In *Asian American Psychology: Current Perspectives.* Edited by Nita Tewari and Alvin N. Alvarez. New York: Psychology Press, 2009. 381–398.

Chapter 11

Kamada, Laurel D. *Hybrid Identities and Adolescent Girls: Being "Half" in Japan.* Bristol, UK: Multilingual Matters, 2010.

Murphy-Shigematsu, Stephen. "Mixed Identities." *Nishimachi Internationalist* 32, no. 2 (Spring/Summer 2004). 2–3.

————. "Multiethnic Identities in Japan." In *Japan and Global Migration: Foreign Workers and the Advent of a Multicultural Society.* Edited by Michael Douglass and Glenda S. Roberts. Honolulu: University of Hawaii Press, 2003. 196–216.

Murphy-Shigematsu, Stephen, and David Blake Willis. "Transcultural Society." In *The Demographic Challenge: A Handbook about Japan.* Edited by Florian Coulmas, Harald Conrad, Annette Schad-Seifert, and Gabriele Vogt. Leiden: Brill, 2008. 293–315.

Nitta Fumiteru. *Kokusai Kekkon to Kodomotachi* [International Marriage and Children]. Translated by Fujimoto Tadashi. Tokyo: Akashi Shoten, 1992.

Willis, David Blake, and Stephen Murphy-Shigematsu. "Ethnoscapes and the Other in 21st-Century Japan." In *Transcultural Japan.* Edited by David Blake Willis and Stephen Murphy-Shigematsu. London: Routledge, 2008. 305–324.

————. "Transcultural Japan: Metamorphosis in the Cultural Borderlands and Beyond." In *Transcultural Japan.* Edited by David Blake Willis and Stephen Murphy-Shigematsu. London: Routledge, 2008. 3–44.

About the Author

Stephen Murphy-Shigematsu was born in Tokyo to a Japanese mother and Irish-American father and raised in Massachusetts. He received a doctorate in counseling and consulting psychology from Harvard University, was a Fulbright scholar in Japan, and professor at the University of Tokyo. He is currently consulting professor in the School of Medicine and affiliated faculty in Comparative Studies in Race and Ethnicity at Stanford University, and faculty at Fielding Graduate University. His writing includes the *Multicultural Family* blog, essays, journal articles, and books, including *Multicultural Encounters: Case Narratives from a Counseling Practice* (2002) and *Amerasian Children: An Unknown Minority Problem* (2002, in Japanese).

WITHDRAWN

CPSIA information can be obtained
at www.ICGtesting.com
Printed in the USA
LVHW091025231219
641389LV00006B/208/P

9 780804 775182